Handbook on Teaching Undergraduate Science Courses

A Survival Training Manual

Gordon E. Uno
University of Oklahoma

BROOKS/COLE

TM

THOMSON LEARNING

Brooks.Cole
511 Forest Lodge Road
Pacific Grove, CA 93950
USA

For information about our products, contact us:
Thomson Learning Academic Resource Center
1-800-423-0563
http://www.brookscole.com

International Headquarters
Thomson Learning
International Division
290 Harbor Drive, 2nd Floor
Stamford, CT 06902-7477
USA

UK/Europe/Middle East/South Africa
Thomson Learning
Berkshire House
168-173 High Holborn
London WCIV 7AA

Asia
Thomson Learning
60 Albert Street, #15-01
Albert Complex
Singapore 189969

Canada
Nelson Thomson Learning
1120 Birchmount Road
Toronto, Ontario MIK 5G4
Canada
United Kingdom

0-030-25926-6

The Adaptable Courseware Program consists of products and additions to existing Brooks/Cole products that are produced from camera-ready copy. Peer review, class testing, and accuracy are primarily the responsibility of the author(s).

TABLE OF CONTENTS

CHAPTER I. THE FIRST YEAR IS ABOUT YOUR SURVIVAL

The title of this chapter suggests that the first year of your new faculty position will be very busy. Expect it to be hectic. But don't panic, because there are people and information available to help you develop your course(s) and teach better. I hope this handbook provides you with many ideas about how to improve your course and your instructional skills. The focus of the handbook is not about how to get tenure, although by being a better teacher your chances for tenure are improved.

What this handbook does contain is my personal, eclectic collection of ideas, suggestions, and examples of what one might include in a student-oriented, dynamic, interesting course in biology, and how one might teach such a class. This book also includes some background information about how students learn and other pedagogical issues. The handbook has been developed with the idea that many people in your position prefer readily accessible information without having to wade through the philosophical background and educational research that support the information contained herein. Each chapter, however, includes references to which you should refer to obtain more detailed information. This handbook is based on many people's years of experience in the classroom-- people who have succeeded through trial-and-error, innovation, and reflection on teaching. The suggestions are intended to provide you with a stimulus--a potpourri of ideas from which you might choose a few to try out in your new class. Remember, all ideas may not work for everyone, however, you should give new ideas a couple of chances to succeed in class before you scrap them, revising and fine-tuning your teaching practices along the way.

None of the information in this handbook will be helpful until you modify it to fit your own teaching style and actually try the method in class. As one graduate student said after completing a course in teaching-- "knowing about these things does not make one a better teacher. After all, one does not need to know how a car engine works to drive." One hopes that this person has a car that never breaks down and a class without problems. Unfortunately for us, however, there are few teaching garages to which we can take our courses where someone else fixes them.

You should skim through the entire handbook to get an idea of what it contains, and then read appropriate sections as you begin to prepare your course(s). It may seem that there is an overwhelming amount of information to absorb and use, however, it is not intended that you read this handbook from cover to cover. You may want to begin with Chapter 12 about how to organize your course and then branch out from there. Or, you may want to refer only to those chapters pertaining to specific problems that currently confront you and to use other sections as a catalyst for revising your class.

I suggest that you focus first on what you want your students to know, value, and be able to do by the end of your course, and then build your course around those objectives. If you have already taught a course, you may want to make selected changes in your class and the way you teach rather than trying to revise everything at once. You might add two or three new labs and discussion topics or try a different approach to teaching every semester until you are completely satisfied with your course. But if you decide to do something new, start at the *beginning* of the course. Don't spring the innovative style on the students in the middle of the semester. If you have lectured to students for four weeks and then suddenly ask them to become involved in a discussion on enzymes, be prepared for a lot of silence or protesting from students. Start your course in the innovative way you would like to teach.

You probably have taken a TA-training course in graduate school, however, that experience, and TAing in general, will not have prepared you for your faculty position. The biggest differences are the amount of time that you will have to spend in getting your own class organized, the responsibilities that result from you being completely in charge of your own course, and the pressures (stress) related to the responsibilities that you have. You should try out your old methods and new ideas and see which you need to modify to suit your students, class, and personality. But whether you have been teaching for 20 years or have just started, always think about how you can make your course better **for your students** and how you can help them learn about, participate in, and appreciate science and biology.

GENERAL TEACHING PHILOSOPHY

First, you need to know what works and what doesn't so that you can emphasize beneficial activities and avoid the pitfalls that plague novice instructors. Remember, you should not fill up your class time just by talking. In fact, lecturing is the least desirable method of teaching. The following is a generalization of how most people learn. **We learn:**

> **10% of what we read**
> **20% of what we hear**
> **30% of what we see**
> **50% of what we see and hear**
> **60% of what we write**
> **70% of what is discussed**
> **80% of what we experience, and**
> **95% of what we teach.**

The figures above suggest that you will learn much more about the subject you teach than will any of your students. Recall how much you learned as you prepared a seminar for your department. If you ask your students simply to read assignments in the text and to listen to you lecture and watch films, then they won't be learning much or remembering much of what they read, hear, or see. So, how can we get our students to learn as much as possible about the subject we are teaching? We must get them involved with the subject, engage them in hands-on and minds-on activities, and get them to learn from each other. Again, think about your own experiences--will you ever forget how you conducted the experiments you designed for your dissertation work? Probably not because you were actively engaged in the investigation. You must also provide students with opportunities to discuss their ideas, to reveal their misconceptions, and to clarify their understanding. The key to successful science education is getting students to experience science as a process and to discuss the information about which they are thinking.

REASONS NON-SCIENCE MAJORS DO POORLY IN INTRODUCTORY BIOLOGY COURSES

Based on teaching 6,000 undergraduates, I have found that students often do poorly in introductory biology classes because of:

1. a lack of a solid science background;
2. an inability to think critically;
3. a negative or indifferent attitude toward science; and
4. a lack of self-discipline and study skills. (Uno, 1988)

Your students might not possess any of these problems, however, you should realize that they are not like you. Few students learn about science the way you do, are as interested in science as you, or have the background that you have (or expect them to have). The key then is not to teach the course as if you are talking to yourself or your colleagues. You must identify what problems your students possess, and then adapt your methods of instruction to meet their needs, experiences, and interests. You should think about how you will promote self-discipline and learning skills in your students, how to broaden student perceptions of and improve student attitudes toward biology, how to improve your students' thinking skills, and how to organize your course so that students leave with a solid background in the major biological concepts. Rule of thumb: don't assume your students already understand or are familiar with any topic or term. Introduce each topic with basic information or define each term, check to see if most students understand, and, if so, move along quickly to the next level.

CHARACTERISTICS OF EFFECTIVE TEACHERS

The following is a list of characteristics that students identify with good teachers. How many of them do you possess? How many of them could you cultivate in yourself if you tried?

1. Alert, appears enthusiastic.
2. Appears interested in students and activities.
3. Cheerful, optimistic.
4. Self-controlled, not easily upset.
5. Has a sense of humor.
6. Recognizes and admits own mistakes.
7. Is fair, impartial, objective, and patient.
8   Is knowledgeable.
9. Shows understanding in working with students and is sensitive to students' personal and educational problems.
10. Is friendly and courteous to students.
11. Commends effort and praises work well done.
12. Encourages students to do their best.
13. Organizes classroom procedures well, but is flexible within over-all plan.
14. Stimulates pupils through interesting and original materials and techniques.
15. Conducts practical demonstrations and gives clear explanations and directions.
16. Encourages students to work through their own problems and evaluate their accomplishments.
17. Disciplines in quiet, dignified, and positive manner.
18. Gives help willingly.
19. Foresees and attempts to resolve potential difficulties.
20. Is an effective questioner and listener, encouraging widespread response from students.

INSTRUCTIONAL RESPONSIBILITIES

Consider the following responsibilities of an instructor to his/her students. Instructors should:

1. Define a body of content that meets curricular needs within the Department, but that is also attractive to students outside your Department. (Ask faculty and students what they would like to see included in the course, and to review goals, objectives, and course materials that have been assembled for the course.)

2. Describe for students in clear and concise terms what they are expected to learn and do throughout the course. (Share with students the instructional objectives you have developed for the course and for them.)

3. Use course activities (e.g. lectures, labs, student assignments) that encourage active learning and that enable students to meet course objectives. (Continually refer to objectives when developing and conducting activities, and ask students for feedback on the effectiveness of activities.)

4. Help students determine their progress in meeting course objectives by continually monitoring student understanding. (Do this informally by giving quizzes or asking students for self-assessments of their progress, and formally, through exams and other graded activities.)

5. Develop and implement evaluation procedures that measure the extent to which students have mastered the course objectives. (Use a variety of evaluation procedures, and match test items to the course objectives.)

6. Provide a supportive environment in which all students have the opportunity to succeed. (Maintain a class atmosphere that is open and informal, and provide ample opportunity for out-of-class contact).

7. Demand excellence from students, and communicate these high expectations to them--if you don't, you're shortchanging them. (Set high, but attainable, standards for classroom performance.)

8. Prepare your students to learn by helping them see the difference between memorizing and understanding information, and emphasize the importance of time and effort spent on learning. (Help your students develop their decision-making and critical thinking skills.)

9. Encourage student-faculty contact in the classroom and encourage cooperation among students. (Respect diverse talents and ways of learning and accommodate diversity in your class by teaching the same subject in different ways.)

10. Present information clearly and effectively, and make it meaningful and relevant to your students. (Bring in articles from newspapers and magazines related to your topic of the day.) (Adapted from Davidson and Ambrose, 1994; Jensen, 1994)

Goals for a Biology Program

Education in biology should sustain students' interest in the natural world, help students explore new areas of interest, improve their explanations of biological concepts, help them understand and use inquiry and technology, and help them make informed personal and social decisions. Students should learn and understand how to use biological information and the process of scientific investigation in their daily lives. The following paragraphs outline six goals for biology and science education.

1. Biology programs should **develop fundamental scientific, technologic, and health knowledge** in their students. Emphasize the development of fundamental biological knowledge organized by major unifying principles in biology (see Chap. 8).

2. Biology education should **develop an understanding of, and ability to use, the processes and methods of scientific inquiry.** Although descriptions of this goal have changed during the last 200 years, the goal remains essentially the same. All programs and materials in biology education should include this goal.

3. Biology education should **prepare citizens to make responsible decisions about social issues that relate to science, technology, the environment, and health.** Because science and technology are integral to our society, a contemporary biology curriculum should include a social component.

4. Biology education should attempt to **meet students' personal needs.** Aspects of science education such as critical thinking and reasoning, problem solving, scientific attitudes, and values lend themselves to the personal development of students at the college level.

5. Biology education should **inform students about careers in science.** Biological research and technological development continue through the direct work of scientists and engineers and through the indirect support of society.

6. The **content of any biology program** should:
   - be introduced with recognition of students' prior understanding of biology, and future potential,
   - have personal and social meaning to students and should enhance their ethical decision making,
   - extend and elaborate the students' understanding and appreciation of science,
   - be taught in a variety of ways that demonstrates the processes, skills, and values of biology,
   - challenge all students at some basic level and promote all dimensions of biological literacy and open-ended learning, and
   - be assessed in appropriate contexts. (adapted from BSCS, 1994)

CONSIDERATIONS AS YOU DESIGN YOUR COURSE

As you begin to prepare your course, you need to:
1. determine what you want your students to know, value, and be able to do by the course's end;
2. identify your course objectives based on this determination;
3. decide on laboratories, activities, and demonstrations that will help your students meet those objectives;
4. consider how you will assess student performance and how you will know whether students have met your objectives;
5. select your textbook(s) and laboratory manual, and order books, materials, and supplies;
6. organize the activities of your teaching assistants;
7. prepare lectures and questions for discussion and find supplementary audiovisual materials; and
8. write your course syllabus. (adapted from Davis, 1992)

Always keep in mind what you want your students to know, value, and be able to do after they have completed your course (see chapters 6, 7, and 8). Organize your course to help students reach these objectives, focusing on how you will know if the students have done so. Also, consider how you will help your students *learn* biology—be less concerned with what information to "teach" to your students and more concerned with how your students "think." As you plan, consider how you teach as well as what you teach. The following page shows the components of an exemplary biology program (CELS, 1993). Compare your course to this list.

COMPONENTS OF AN EXEMPLARY BIOLOGY PROGRAM

Student Perspectives
> Promotes student excitement about biology
> Improves student comfort level with science, empowers the learner
> Fosters understanding of the nature of science

Content
> Teaches relevance of biology to the real world
> Makes process and content co-equal
> Fosters information literacy, including tools for lifelong learning
> Includes breadth and depth of information
> Sacrifices breadth for depth of big ideas
> Teaches unifying themes or concepts, and basic biological principles

Process
> Includes investigative laboratories or investigative experiences
> Includes use of biological techniques
> Includes use of quantitative skills
> Includes field exercises
> Includes writing/communication/literature search techniques
> Includes use of computers

Pedagogy
> Accommodates a variety of learning and teaching strategies
> Fosters critical thinking and problem solving
> Includes collaborative, small-group learning
> Includes active participation
> Uses a variety of assessment strategies
> Uses assessment based on course objectives
> Reduces the importance of grades to encourage real inquiry

Program Administrators
> Includes faculty and teaching assistant development
> Planning includes goals and objectives, outcomes, and assessments
> Includes mechanisms to reward faculty
> Has adequate budget, facilities, and administrative support
> Has an advocate
> Includes mechanisms for outreach to disseminate program

Coalition for Education in the Life Sciences (CELS, 1993)

At the end of most chapters, you will have an opportunity to reflect upon and evaluate your own teaching. After reading this chapter, how do you and your class compare to some of the ideals espoused here? Which ideas do you like, and how will you incorporate them into your class? How will you promote student learning and help your students experience science as an active process? Use this space to keep notes and to develop your ideas and overall plan.

CHAPTER II. WHAT YOUR LIFE WILL BE LIKE DURING THE FIRST YEARS

CASE STUDIES OF NEW FACULTY MEMBERS ABOUT THEIR FIRST YEARS OF TEACHING

Rob Reinsvold, University of Northern Colorado
1. How would you describe your first year(s) of teaching?

My first years of teaching were stimulating, demanding, fulfilling, fatiguing, and satisfying. It took more time and effort than I expected but I can honestly say I enjoyed it. Although I know I have improved, there is still so much I need to learn about how to teach.

My first exposures to teaching came as a graduate teaching assistant at Colorado State University and an instructor at Purdue University. My first "real" teaching position where I was in complete control of the operations of my courses was at Kalamazoo College. I taught courses in ecology, botany, environmental science, and ethnobotany. I enjoyed the interaction with colleagues from other disciplines and the integration of knowledge across the campus. During that year I realized that teaching required constant learning, not just of the subject matter but also about how best to help students learn that knowledge.

For the last five years I have taught at the University of Northern Colorado in the Department of Biological Sciences. Enrollment of this campus falls between Purdue and Kalamazoo College with about 10,000 students. As before, I teach a variety of topics to a variety of students. I learned I needed to develop a rich repertoire of teaching strategies to address the challenges of each new course or type of student.

One major part of the mission of the University of Northern Colorado is teacher preparation. To me, teaching the teachers of tomorrow encourages me to constantly reflect on my own delivery. The challenges are different in some aspects and yet similar in others. I continue to learn. I strive to improve. And gradually, I think my teaching is becoming easier as I become more experienced. I do enjoy it!

2. What is the best thing about teaching?

The best thing about teaching is interacting with students helping them discover knowledge on their own. I know I've accomplished something worthwhile when I can stimulate a student to develop and use his/her natural curiosity. Motivating students is a challenge I relish. I always enjoyed learning even though I didn't always find it easy. Since effective teaching requires being up-to-date, and informed, teaching is the closest thing to learning itself.

3. What is the worst thing about teaching?

To me the worst thing about teaching is the required baggage of the educational system such as preparing and evaluating exams, and assigning final grades. I feel it is unfortunate that many students are more interested in a letter grade than in learning. I am discouraged also by student dishonesty and irresponsibility. Cheating and plagiarism are probably byproducts of the emphases on grades. As teachers, though, we have to deal with these behaviors, along with excuses, laziness, procrastination, and poor attention to quality. These items don't have to be obstacles; instead they can be viewed as more challenges. Nonetheless, they often frustrate me.

4. What were the most surprising aspects about teaching on your own?

I was naive; I assumed students were taking my classes because they had a sincere interest in the subject matter and a willingness to do what it took to get the most out of them. Although I knew rationally that not all students were like I was when I was a student, I initially operated as if they were. Like most PhDs, I had survived and succeeded in the educational system as it was and tended to teach the way I was taught. Although I "covered" the material, my students were not learning as much as I thought they could, so I started placing greater emphasis on methods to enhance learning rather than "covering" material.

I was also surprised by the amount of time I needed to prepare for each class, even if I knew the material. I often devoted eight hours to review, condense, and organize the content material for each one hour lecture. Now, course preparation still takes much of my time but I shifted the emphasis to thinking of how to present information so students can learn.

Processing student exams also took a lot of time. In large classes I often used multiple-choice exams so I could get them back to students promptly. Although grading was faster, preparing an effective multiple-choice exam that tested higher levels of thinking took several days. Essay exams were easy to write, yet took a long time to grade, and I had the hard task of deciding what each grade actually meant. Along with advising, committees, task forces, research, lab prep, and strategic planning, it is amazing how little time is left.

5. *What were your students like and how did you deal with their problems?*

Kalamazoo College attracted high achievers. Often they were at the top of their class in high school. In college, though, their peers were more compatible and sometimes even better. For many freshmen, this was a humbling experience. They were used to receiving nothing but A's and were shocked when they received B's or C's. The grade was more important than the product. Conflicts were inevitable. They knew I was a fresh PhD and didn't hesitate to challenge my judgments. I had high expectations and held the students to a high standard. When they complained, I naturally got defensive. Unfortunately this was viewed as insensitivity. In one class, things almost got out of hand. I thought I was losing their respect and my credibility. The course was in environmental science and fulfilled an option in their general education so a majority of the students were not science majors. I now understand one problem was the amount of mathematics I incorporated into the course. At the time I was frustrated and started doubting my own decisions. Fortunately I sought help from my colleagues. They supported my expectations as reasonable and within a realistic level of difficulty. A colleague from history suggested I ask students to give feedback on a midterm evaluation. This helped. It gave me constructive input on how to improve the course while there was still time left in the quarter to make a difference, it also help defuse the anger of the few complaining students. As it turned out, most students felt that although I expected a lot, my expectations were fair.

At the University of Northern Colorado, we have a diversity of students. Many students are the first generation in their families to enter college. These students often need help relating to the total college environment. The demands of school, social life, and work are hard for them to separate. Their study skills are generally weak. Also, they often do not see the relevancy of the subject matter. For increasing their study skills, I have strongly supported another program called Supplemental Instruction. It is not tutoring or additional lectures. Instead, an advanced student sits in my class and takes notes on the material. Then, he organizes several voluntary sessions for students to explore other ways to understand and learn the material. They explore several techniques such as concept mapping, cooperative learning groups, analogies, models and metaphors. It is intentionally not re-lecturing. Students often respond better to someone closer to their own age and level. In addition,

I get feedback from the supplemental instructor on areas of extra confusion or difficulty.

UNC also has a significant number of non-traditional students. Many of these students are older, returning to school after years of doing something else such as raising a family. Several are single parents. Time management is their major concern. Surprisingly I think they are better skilled at budgeting the time needed for various tasks than are traditional students.

Students also mature academically and intellectually as they progress through school. Many freshman are very concrete thinkers; to them there is one right answer for every question. Many seniors and graduate students have progressed to higher cognitive levels and realize most questions have several possible answers. A paper by Nelson (1989) describes a model for the development in critical thinking. I found that if I tried to give complex learning activities to students in the lower modes of thinking, I nearly always failed. I realized we need to know where our students are and meet them there. Then we can help bring them to where we want them to eventually arrive.

6. *How do you evaluate your students, and how do you evaluate the efficacy of your own instructional methods?*

Evaluation of students:

To determine how effectively students have accomplished goals and objectives of my courses, I use a variety of methods, including exams, reports, papers, critiques, journals, presentations, and discussions.

The type of examination depends on the size and subject of the specific course. Students want and deserve to get the results of an exam promptly. For that reason, I usually use multiple-choice questions in large classes. I am aware of the concern that multiple-choice exams may not test how a student thinks. However if skillfully written, an effective multiple-choice exam can require higher levels of thinking, but writing a "good" multiple-choice exam can take a lot of time. One limitation of this type of exam is students may use careful reasoning yet misinterpret the question because of the way it is worded. I give each student an extra sheet attached to the exam to explain their reasoning on any question, especially if they think there are no correct answers or more than one "best" answer. [This also gives me feedback on unexpected typographical errors that were inadvertently left in the exam.]

In smaller classes I prefer essay exams. I can better evaluate if the student's understanding is comprehensive and thorough. Essays put more stress on the student and often take them more time to answer. This is a problem if the exam is given during the regular 50 minute class meeting. If the course has an accompanying lab period, I give it then. This allows students more time and reduces the stress.

More recently I have adopted a modified take-home exam format: Three to four days prior to the exam day (such as over a weekend), I give students a copy of 6-8 possible essay questions. I tell them up-front that the exam will consist of all or some of those exact questions. They are encouraged to do whatever research they need and discuss their ideas with their classmates. Then on the day of the exam they are required to write their response without the aid of notes or other assistance. It forces the students to thoroughly research a topic and organize their thoughts in advance. To be effective, the questions must be complex enough so that students cannot merely memorize a response from fellow students. I have been quite pleased with this type of exam because it works as both a learning and evaluation activity.

Students need to know what we expect. Exams shouldn't be approached as a guessing game by students of what they think I will ask or how I will ask it. Students should have some idea what I think makes a "good" essay and what makes a "bad" essay. The semester is too short for students to write-off the first exam as a lesson in how this instructor gives exams.

Evaluation of my own effectiveness:

Our department and College require all instructors to use a student evaluation instrument at the end of the course. Eventually I get to see the tabulated results and any individual responses given voluntarily. Unfortunately, these often reach me over a semester later so their value to help me make improvements is diminished.

Because of the unavoidable delay, I sought out other methods to help me know how I'm doing and where I can improve. One of the most effective tools has been a *midterm evaluation completed by students*. The questions are open-ended and ask for specific examples. It also helps remind students of their responsibility in the learning process since I ask them to state what they are doing to contribute to their own success or failure. This instrument is useful for monitoring potential problems in the teaching of my graduate TAs as well.

Recently I started encouraging students to keep a personal journal as a way of reflecting on their own understanding of the course material (Biddle and Bean, 1987). Students won't keep a journal unless they are given credit towards their final grade, so I usually allow them to keep a journal in lieu of another writing assignment. When I read these journals I was amazed how much information they contained concerning the effectiveness of the day-to-day operations of the courses. I identified specific activities that caused more confusion than illumination. I got to see my teaching through the eyes of students. I learned new things that were never mentioned in five years of student evaluations for the same course.

I also seek the input from colleagues. This was extremely valuable during the first few years until my own confidence and comfort developed. Many of my colleagues were master teachers, and I welcomed their suggestions and assessments. However, I found there is a silent professional courtesy among most college faculty. Most will not volunteer to observe you teach or review your materials, partly due to the ideal of academic freedom. We all feel that what each of us does in his/her own class is our business and nobody else's. Finally, I constantly assess the effectiveness of each new technique or activity. I try to keep accurate notes on what went well and what were my own suggestions for improvement.

7. *Before you began teaching, what were your biggest concerns about teaching, and which came true and which did not?*

My biggest concern was knowing my subject matter completely. My specific area of expertise is mycology, but I accepted a position that did not have a need or resources to allow me to offer a course in my specialty. Now I realize I also had a broad education, and I learned how to learn. Although I still believe the instructor must know the material, I have developed the awareness that I can learn what I need to learn.

I have also accepted a change in my role in the classroom, rather than the keeper of all knowledge. I now see myself as a facilitator of student learning. The focus has shifted from me as the "teacher" to the student as the "learner." I spend more time thinking of what the students are going to learn and how best to help them do that. I lecture *less* and facilitate *more*.

8. *What were your mistakes during your first year(s) of teaching and how did you correct them?*

In the first years I felt obligated to "cover" all the necessary topics in each course...breadth first. Now I see the greater value of depth into a few topics. Also I realize now that mere transference of volumes of facts, especially in the traditional lecture format, does not lead to greater student learning. I still spend time knowing my subject matter thoroughly, yet now I spend more thought, effort, and time in creating ways to interest and motivate students.

Occasionally we all make mistakes in the content presented. I've learned to accept these mistakes, admit I made an error, and go on. The students are willing to accept some mistakes as well. In fact when I tried to cover my mistakes or cover up my ignorance, they saw right through my disguise. That's when I lost credibility.

9. *What were your best sources of information that helped you teach your classes?*

My best sources of information for both pedagogy and science were my colleagues. The coffee room was probably where I learned the most about different philosophies towards teaching and learning and solutions to common problems as an instructor, but I benefitted from numerous other sources as well. The following is a short list of the most memorable.

In science:

Briggs, John P. and F. David Peat. 1984. Looking glass universe: The emerging science of wholeness. Simon & Schuster, Inc. New York.

Kuhn, Thomas. 1976. The structure of scientific revolutions. University of Chicago Press, Chicago.

Dawkins, Richard. 1987. The blind watchmaker. W.W. Norton & Co. New York.

Leopold, Aldo. 1949. A Sand County almanac. Oxford University Press, Inc.

De Kruif, Paul. 1926. Microbe hunters. Washington Square Press, New York.

World Resources Institute, 1986, 1989, 1992. World Resources: An assessment of the resource base that supports the global economy. [*This is a series with data tables from 146 countries and a wealth of timely information–very valuable. The most recent edition is available as a CD ROM.*]

Also, I'm always scanning newspapers and magazines for timely examples to add to my courses. Comic books, TV shows, and the *National Enquirer* are also great for stimulating discussions.

In pedagogy:

Heppner, Frank. 1990. Professor Farnsworth's explanations in biology. McGraw Hill, Inc. [. *fantastic, entertaining collection of effectiv analogies and creative explanations on biologica concepts.]*

The Teaching Professor. [*A monthly publication c Magna Publications, Inc. Madison, Wisc. Eacl issue has a lot of good advice and suggestions.*]

Belenky, Mary, Blythe Clinchy, Nancy Goldberger, an Jill Tarule. 1986. Women's ways of knowing Basic Books Inc.

Paul, Richard. 1990. Critical thinking: What ever person needs to survive in a rapidly changing world. Center for Critical Thinking and Mora Critique.

BSCS. 1993. Developing biological literacy: A guide to developing secondary and post-secondar biology curricula. BSCS. [*Very helpful if you are trying to decide what to emphasize in your course.*

AAAS. 1989. Science for all Americans: Project 2061. Oxford University Press, Oxford.

National Research Council. 1990. Fulfilling the promise: Biology education in the nation's schools. National Academy Press, Wash. D.C.

Tobias, Sheila. 1990. They're not dumb, they're different. Stalking the second tier. Research Corporation, Tucson.

Tobias, Sheila. 1992. Revitalizing undergraduate science: Why some things work and most don't. Research Corporation, Tucson.

10. *What do you think are (were) your most successful teaching methods, strategies, and activities?*

Most of the time, especially in my large classes, I still use lectures as the primary means of discussing a subject. I have introduced many demonstrations or illustrations to help drive home a point or break up the monotony. A excellent source for more ideas is Heppner's book about Professor Farnsworth. One of Professor Farnsworth's early escapades is when he drives into the classroom on a big motorcycle and challenges the students to determine if his motorcycle is alive or not. I have modified this activity with a chainsaw. Earlier in my career I worked as a sawyer in Montana so I am quite accustomed to the feel of a whining chainsaw. After some small group discussion about the attributes of a living system, I put on my chaps, gloves, hard hat, goggles, and ear plugs while summarizing this list of attributes. Then I bring out the chainsaw and start it up. When asked if they think my chainsaw is alive or not, students usually say it is not alive because it doesn't eat. I point out that it does, it eats gasoline. For almost every one of the attributes on our list I can convince them that the chainsaw fits or I can cite some obvious organism that also doesn't fit that particular trait. My take home message is twofold. First, defining life is not that easy. Second, it usually cannot be defined by one single attribute and must be a combination of attributes. I use this demonstration on the first day of classes. It does capture their attention.

Another demonstration I conduct helps the students relate to the geological timescale. I take a timetable of major geological and biological events since the formation of planet Earth and condense them down to a 50 minute lecture period. I describe the scenario where the classroom is a special time machine that quickly takes us to the beginning of Earth and then races forward. At every major event I have one of my TAs blow a whistle or ring a bell. With each whistle, I stop my lecture and explain what is happening. During the first two-thirds of the class period, there are few whistles so I continue with a normal lecture. By the end of the hour I am racing through the events since they come only seconds apart. It clearly illustrates just how short humans have been on the earth.

In smaller classes I use more discussions to help facilitate learning. To be effective, students need to come prepared. If the discussion is about an article, then all the students need to have read it in order to really contribute to the conversation and understand the interpretations of the others. I require students to complete a worksheet while they read the article and bring the worksheet to class. They get no credit if they come with an empty worksheet (or one that obviously was completed 15 minutes before class).

Another successful activity in a small group is a group problem solving. Usually I pose a problem or try to get the students to pose their own. The activity involves deciding what type of information is needed to solve the problem, how valid is that information, where or how can they get the information, and what are the implications. We usually have the most fun with this activity when the problems are fictitious. Science fiction or fantasy books are filled with phenomena that seem plausible on the surface, such as a green, photosynthesizing humanoid like Swamp Thing. I use this to drive home the relationship between form and function. If an organism such as a human were capable of photosynthesis, what modifications would be required for the organism to get all of its energy and mineral needs? Often they think in very creative ways. Then we check their designs with what is known about physical constraints such as rates of photosynthesis, surface area, basal metabolic rates, etc.

All my courses use writing as a way of learning. I have found that many students, both high achievers and marginal students, lack the ability to communicate effectively, either orally or in writing. Writing takes practice, so I try to provide opportunities whenever I believe they will also learn a subject better. The assignment has to be meaningful or they don't benefit from the activity. Major research papers are divided into distinct parts such as deciding on the topic, outline, annotated bibliography, first complete draft, final draft, and oral presentation. This gives students feedback along the way rather than merely giving them one grade at the end. They have a chance to demonstrate if they have learned anything from the early feedback.

Computer software is a very powerful learning tool. One of my most successful activities uses the program SimEarth™. It is a simulation of the global system with biological, geological, and atmospheric subsystems that all interact through time. Students make predictions what may happen when they disturb the system and then test their predictions. Organisms evolve due to prevailing conditions and prior biological history.

Another method I use in a variety of my classes is concept maps. Concept maps emphasize the relationships between concepts and facts rather than teaching them as isolated bits of knowledge. The concept map is an effective tool for helping students visualize relationships and increase comprehension and recall. Maps also reflect the complexity of the student's understanding and thus are another evaluation instrument. For more information see Novak, Joseph and D. B. Gowin. 1984. Learning How to Learn. Cambridge University Press, Cambridge.

In science we are lucky; most of our classes have laboratories. These are excellent opportunities for students to investigate phenomena personally and to use hands-on activities. In Economic Botany, I have one lab at the end of the course that everyone relates to. It is a grand feast. Each student has to prepare a dish to share with the rest of the class. Before we eat, each student explains what is in the dish, where the major ingredients came from, the historical or cultural significance, and what purpose each ingredient serves in the chemistry of the final entrée. We award prizes for the best use of plants, the most nutritious, the most exotic, the most bizarre, etc. It is a great way to end a course, and I have been surprised how much research each student does concerning the plants used as food.

11. *What was the greatest help to you in preparing for your teaching position?*

The greatest help for me was having a colleague willing to listen to my ideas and give me feedback. My advice to others is to seek out that help. Find someone willing to discuss various teaching strategies with an open mind--a mentor.

12. *What else?*

What motivates students to learn? First and foremost, I think it is the grade. Second is the enthusiasm of the instructor for the course and subject matter. Finally, students will see the value in learning if they think the subject matter is relevant to their own lives or future careers. However, students don't always share your view of what will be important to them in the future. We need to help expand their horizons. Most fresh PhD's are fairly competent in their knowledge. The rest of teaching well can be developed with some time and effort. Some people believe that teaching is a gift. That is only partly true. You also need to be interested in helping students learn. I believe that part is the gift. If you don't have that you might as well choose another career.

Susan A. Gibson, South Dakota State University

These are my responses after nine months teaching at SDSU.

1. *How would you describe your first year?*

The analogy of swimming near a whirlpool is the first thing that comes to mind. I was barely staying ahead of my students. It was difficult to find the time (or energy) to consider how to change things to improve the class while the class was going. The first semester was more an exercise in survival than anything else. There was also worry that something would happen (illness, etc.) which would have thrown my classes into disarray. I didn't know where things were, how to efficiently get things done in an unfamiliar setting, or who had things that I could borrow for class and this added to the difficulty. Second semester was better. I was teaching additional classes for the first time, but had a better idea how to get things done. Also, I used the class design that had been used previously without trying to change things immediately

2. *What is the best thing about teaching?*

The best thing is finding a student who is interested. The spark when a student finally puts things together in a coherent pattern is great. Interested students also keep you on your toes with questions and interesting observations. Another neat thing about teaching is that you can pursue interesting concepts, subject material, or laboratory exercises outside your immediate research area. (You can do some things just because they are fun or interesting).

3. *What is the worst thing about teaching?*

The time investment is horrendous sometimes. It's often mentally/emotionally draining (sometimes physically as well). It's very discouraging when students don't seem to care, or their only motivation is whether they get points for doing something.

4. *What were the most surprising aspects about teaching on your own?*

The most surprising thing to me was the amount of time (detail work) it takes to organize class materials. It also took much longer than expected. There was a lot of running here and there to get pieces of information I wanted or pieces of equipment for laboratory use. Another surprising thing was how little practical knowledge students had coming into the class.

5. *What were your students like and how did you deal with their problems?*

The students were a rather wide range from those who could master the material without really trying, to those who had to work rather hard, to those who apparently assumed they couldn't do it and didn't seem to try. They had a marked tendency to wait until the night before something was due to begin to study it - this doesn't work well for classes in which the later material is built on mastery of early material. Also, they have a tendency not to do things which don't have points attached. I plan to deal with this next year by having students turn in graded questions, essays, concept maps or something each week in order to encourage them to think about the material as we go through it rather than trying to commit it all to memory 2 hours before a exam and forgetting it 3 minutes after they walk out.

Another major problem was that many students are working full-time as well as going to school full time. They came to class exhausted, their lab reports often had major holes where things were simply omitted, and they were often ill (stress-related?). I still don't know how to deal with this problem.

6. *How do you evaluate your students and how do you evaluate the efficacy of your own instruction methods?*

I evaluate the students by means of exams (some multiple-choice/matching and some short-essay questions). They also turn in lab reports, and sometimes problem sets in some classes.

I evaluate the efficacy of my instruction methods by student response (signs of life, asking questions, etc.). I have begun requesting submission of a short paragraph over material covered each class. This paragraph can be over basic concepts, their own observations relating to the material, questions they have about the material. etc. This serves two purposes --presumably they have to put at least some thought into the material to regurgitate something, and sometimes I can see areas which are unclear and that need to be approached again. Also, sometimes questions come up that are interesting and should be discussed in class. I also look at the test results to evaluate whether the message is getting through, especially the final. For more difficult classes, I sort of expect the early exams to be mediocre, but if my instruction is adequate, I expect the students to have solidified the material into a coherent unit by the end (perhaps wishful thinking).

7. *Before you began teaching, what were your biggest concerns about teaching, and which of these came true and which did not?*

I was afraid I wouldn't have enough to say to cover the amount of class time available. This wasn't true - I found I could have used twice as much class time as I have. I was afraid that my tests would be too easy - I actually overestimated the knowledge base of the students and if anything they may have been too hard.

8. *What were your mistakes during your first year(s) of teaching and how did you correct them?*

I was too concerned about the material being difficult and the students being too stressed out over it. I built too many points into the grading scheme which were for just trying. I plan to correct this by cutting back on the number of "low-cost points". Another mistake I made which is related to the first is not forcing students to deal with the material.

The first course I taught was a "senior level" course. I assumed basic knowledge of cell structure and general aerobic metabolism. Next time, I'll start the course with a hard-core review of these items before moving on to the actual course material. In addition, I'll try to find videos, film-strips, computer programs, etc. which will help present basic ideas in a more visual form to supplement written and drawn material.

I plan to assign frequent problem/question sets to try to get students to think about the material as we go. Also, I will try to incorporate concept maps to see if that help them see the "big Picture".

9. *What do you wish you had known or that someone had told you before you started teaching?*

Don't count on students having retained any knowledge from previous classes. It would have been helpful to have known what to expect from students at each level in terms of capabilities, useable knowledge they have coming in, etc.

10. *What were your best sources of information that helped you teach your classes?*

I used old textbooks (microbiology, biochemistry, ASM Manual of Methods for General Bacteriology) heavily. I also talked to people who taught similar courses about what they covered, how they evaluated students, what texts they used etc. Also, although I wasn't aware of it before I started, I found The Teaching Professor newsletter to be helpful for ideas for implementation in future classes.

11. *What are your most successful teaching techniques, methods, strategies, and activities?*

Oral or poster presentations on primary scientific literature seemed to work well. The first time I tried this I had students turn in titles well in advance of their presentation. However, a few students didn't even look at the paper until the night before the presentation and (surprise, surprise) they didn't understand their paper and the presentations were disastrous. The next semester I had them turn in the title early as before, but I also required an outline of the paper several weeks before the presentations. This seemed to work well. Most chose to do posters (options were an oral presentation or poster) and seemed to enjoy it. I used the flier ASM sends out on slide/poster presentations as a guide. Several of the basic concepts we were discussing in class came up for discussion during the "poster sessions".

One course I taught had three sets of laboratories which were considered individual projects (pairs of students took a problem and designed their own exercise within the limits set). One thing I added to this that I will use again was to let them re-plan the first exercise they did and actually repeat the project. The results were much better the second time around, most made much better choices of media and isolation techniques after learning from the first exercise.

12. *What was the greatest help to you in preparing for your teaching position?*

Talk to other instructors both at the institution at which you will be teaching and at other institutions to get ideas on course organization, resource material, problems to expect, useful strategies that they use, etc. As far as possible, use course format which was used before (assuming it is not a new class), implement a few of the things you think are important, but try to not recreate the course the first time you teach it. After the first time through, implement a few more changes. It is too difficult to try to restructure a class while you are going through it the first time.

13. *What information would have been useful to you as you began your teaching assignment?*
   a. 101 fun demonstrations illustrating basic biological principles
   b. List of videos, films, computer programs etc. which are particularly good
   c. Sources of supplementary materials which are available for student purchase. (For instance, when I was an undergraduate we purchased collections of reprints for class use).

14. *What else?*

When you start teaching, there will probably be a lot of things that you don't like about the organization of labs, purchasing of items, equipment available for lab use, procedures for getting items xeroxed, budget available for classroom use, etc. Be patient. Prioritize and pick your battles carefully. Make changes where you can, but if you can't, keep plugging away (progress is often slow). Try to develop a support group. There are others who are frustrated by the same things you are. If a group works together, accomplishments come quicker and easier.

Henri Maurice, Barat College

1. How would you describe your first year(s) teaching?

Time-guzzling hell, but gratifying. The first year consisted of three different courses each semester with lab. None had multiple sections. The second year was also a six course load, with only two being repeats from the first year. The teaching load was only a part of the responsibilities during the first year. Additional responsibilities were: Faculty Governance Organization meetings (I served as secretary), Committee Meetings (served on Academic Programs), how to order stuff, where to find everything, Science Club, Director of the Science Fair, and advising students. All of this was coupled with a move from Long Island to rural Iowa and final preparations to defend the dissertation.

Some responsibilities were laid on by virtue of the person I replaced. Several students expected me to be exactly like the person I replaced which I refused to do and eventually told the students in no uncertain words that they were not dealing with Dr. X. By year three, everything was together and running quite smoothly.

Youth was not necessarily all good here. At the age of 26, I was running the show. A large number of students were my age or older, so the authority question came up a few times, but only with certain individuals. To fit in and suggest a bit more authority, I needed to look and act older. The unwritten dress code set limitations on how to dress. Expected: tie and nice dress pants/shirt, i.e. "professional." The Dean was quite surprised to see me lecturing in plant physiology in dungarees and sweatshirt one morning. The look he gave was enough to cause me never to dress that way again when teaching a class.

2. What is the best thing about teaching?

Seeing the lights come on in students and knowing that they have been successful because I helped them. Seeing those "darn freshmen" mature into competent, young men and women walking across the platform to obtain their degree in Biology is simply indescribable. Hearing from them while in grad school, medical school, or at their megabucks research and development jobs leaves a great feeling inside. The very simple "thank you for all your help, Dr. Maurice" and "I am so glad to have been a student in your course" coming from a student makes you feel good. You really did touch at least one person in your life and that person feels you made a difference in their life. Some students are friends, indeed colleagues, for life.

3. What is the worst thing about teaching?

Multiple things: prepping labs (when there is no one to help or anyone to tell you how it is done), grading exams, and actually giving grades. Lab preps can be a real chore, especially with a class that does not appreciate the beauty and satisfaction of doing experiments and emulating, in part, what happens in science. Grading exams and reports is time-consuming especially when there is a large class and some essay questions are the norm. How do you grade these equally fair for each student? It is not easy, and one has to think about a structured system so that every student who says one thing gets x points and if they say something else they will get y points. One shouldn't have a coronary after getting off-the-wall answers: students sometimes did not understand what YOU were saying or asking. You must go back and look at the question carefully.

Giving final grades is perhaps most difficult, especially for certain students in the class. Most earn a grade they deserve and you can live with. Others are lazy but do well regardless and some try so hard, but do not make the grade. These are a concern since they often come from a poor background but have clearly learned so much, yet they do not pass. A person who can manage a D+ in General Biology I without having any course in Science in high school has done remarkably well and progressed very well though below the expected mark. Due to questions of fairness to all students and to minimize the possibility of lawsuits, however, all are graded on the same scale. If you earn this many points you will get this grade. No questions asked. It is absolute.

4. What were the most surprising aspects about teaching on your own?

- You have to be able to improvise and troubleshoot which are not always easy.
- Putting a syllabus together, even in your specialty area, is NOT an easy task.
- Finding the right text and lab manual (do you even use a lab manual?) for a course is NOT easy. With labs you often have to make modifications to the point where it is easier to write your own. Some fields do not have texts and/or lab manuals at all! Choosing the right text for the particular students you are dealing with takes time.
- You do not need all your lecture notes written out; outlines work well if you know what you are doing. The outline just keeps you on track and

helps remind you of those important things you want to get across.
- You learn quickly.
- Student demands concerning quizzes and exams. They wanted MORE! Some wanted a major exam every two weeks!! My response was NO WAY.

5. *What were your students like and how did you deal with their problems?*

The average ACT was 16. Some higher, many were lower. Poor skills in written and oral communication, math skills essentially non-existent in many (the majority, about 65-70%) was the norm. Most students were from rural Iowa and the first in their families to go to college. A large number of students were non-traditional and had families and jobs to balance, but there were usually the best students overall. The typical male student (Biology Department had 80% males) was most interested in hunting and fishing, to the point that it was an obsession and blocked learning. Most students were very polite, non-competitive, and willing to help each other. In general, these students needed lots of encouragement. They had the capacity but were unable to see it and often were never stimulated to do better than average. The amount of time taken outside of class to encourage students and show them they CAN do it was so large one could never keep count. Some had been "Average" for so long that when they did well and started to blossom as students they could not believe themselves. It was their opinion that my standards had softened but that was hardly the case.

Using very concrete examples was also important for overcoming obstacles to understanding key concepts. Most importantly, listening, carefully, to the student and working one-on-one or in very small groups was critical. Listening and understanding what I heard was the crux. Being honest and open with the students enabled them to express their difficulties. They could count on me to have an answer or refer them to a source that did. This happened at the academic and the personal level.

6. *How do you evaluate your students, and how do you evaluate the efficacy of your own instructional methods?*

My Students:
Evaluation of the student depends on the course, but there are two important components in our courses: lecture/discussion and lab. 40-50% of the points come from the lecture while 50-60% comes from the lab.

Each thing the student does for evaluation has a certain number of maximum points. The number of points associated with lab is so high in my courses because so much of the time, effort, and learning occurs in the lab.

In General Biology I and II, the flagship course sequence of my Department at Barat College, students are given a major exam at the end of each unit studied (3 or 4 exams a semester); a comprehensive final exam; weekly on-line quizzes based on the previous week's lecture material; written lab quizzes on techniques, experimental design/data analysis, problem solving (some traditional practicals); critical thinking case studies, discussion questions, problems to solve; instructor evaluated written reports based on student designed experiments; peer evaluated oral reports on student designed experiments; answering questions on lab topics which introduce techniques before the students investigate their own topic of interest introduced in that lab. The quiz load is less in upper level courses but the emphasis on designing experiments, interpretation of results, critical thinking problem solving, and communication play even greater roles than in General Biology.

In all courses, lecture exams consist of multiple choice (in some cases students must explain the reason for choosing a particular answer over the other choices), matching, short answer/essay (problem solving, distinguishing between related terms, describing processes, etc.), true/false (students explain why a statement is false or must make a false statement true).

My Methods:
Read students faces: look for expressions of confusion or lack thereof. Ask and Listen. Students will tell you (written or orally) if you ask them. It helps if your Dean gets evaluations forms back to you before the start of the next semester. Look carefully at exams and see where student difficulties lie. Also, hear what the students tell you when you ask them to answer a question, or see what they write in their reports. If something did not get through, it becomes crystal clear. There are three alternative explanations for why students may not be doing well on a particular question or exam: 1) the students did not study; 2) you did not explain, describe, etc. clearly enough so there is a flaw in the technique; 3) a combination of 1 and 2. Close analysis of the situation is warranted and, yes, it is NOT always the students!!

7. *Before you began teaching, what were your biggest concerns about teaching, and which of these came true and which did not?*
A. I will be a failure (like Dr. X when I was in college who was well educated, but was incapable of transferring ideas)
B. This stuff will be too complex
C. I will be too demanding
D. Cheating in class
A. Did not come true. There are some, especially non-majors, who would say otherwise. However, in the same group of students, with the same backgrounds many do very well (A's and B's) while others fail. In some cases, those who earned the F had too good of a time in class, or in other cases there was a lack of effort. This is NOT a failure on my part.
B. This did come true. Getting some ideas across is really difficult. In some cases I changed the approach each year for a few years to find a way to get the point across.
C. I am demanding, but reasonable. These are college students. Many believe they can memorize everything, but not in my class. You need to know your stuff and be able to analyze and think. Students say exams are hard. When pressed for a specific reason, most say they were challenged to think. I expect students to perform. They (or their parents or someone's tax dollars) are paying me for a reason, and it is not just to do nothing. I demand work be done in a specific way and exams and/or quizzes are used to keep the students on their toes.
D. This has happened: duplicate lab reports, completely incorrect calculations on some lab due to a single error in a mathematical operation, exams. Against my nature, I have had to conclude that students cannot be trusted on exams. Watch them like a hawk. Catching them cheating and accusing them of such can be quite a problem and may open you to legal problems. Actually observing cheating and having witnesses of this is not always enough proof/evidence. When you do catch duplicate lab reports or reports that are identically wrong, students do not see this as cheating! Students become quite nasty when called on the carpet about this and threaten to take action against you for accusing them of cheating (even though the word has not been used). Rather than accuse, I simply ask why papers are identical. Before doing this, I have shown other colleagues and they have all concluded that some

element of cheating was at work. The Dean has not always been so helpful in these cases and has often sided with one student for whatever reason.

8. *What were your mistakes during your first year(s) of teaching and how did you correct them? (How does an instructor improve?)*
    *   Text in some courses was too difficult
    *   There is a number of exams that is too few and too many for the typical student at your college/university.
    *   Do not be too easy. Students will push, but do not give in. Once standards are set, that's it. No exceptions.
    *   Did not write enough on the board.

9. *What do you wish you had known or that someone had told you before you started teaching?*
    *   It is OK to say NO! If you do not, people will take advantage of you.
    *   Labs do not appear at the blink of an eye or the twitch of a nose. There are recipes and instructions for growing organisms and prepping certain solutions which are not written out everywhere. You may have to search. There are suppliers for some organisms, but you must search. Labs that worked in your undergraduate lab oratory that you saw work as a TA may have been home grown. Where are the specific instructions?
    *   Students view time differently these days than you do and how you did as an undergraduate.
    *   Do the best you can to hide that fact that this is the first class you have ever taught alone.
    *   If you look young, dress or do something that makes you appear older.

10. *What were your best sources of information that helped you teach your classes?*
    *   Instructor's manuals with lab prep recipes
    *   A model instructor in the department
    *   Various publications from AIBS, *American Biology Teacher*, BSA
    *   The Biologists Resource Book (published by Macmillan)

11. *What do you think are (were) your most successful teaching techniques, methods, strategies, and activities?*
    *   Hands-on labs: working with balances, pH meters, spec-20, centrifuges, liquid measuring tools, chromatography (paper, TLC, gas),

electrophoresis, etc.   Students do lots of experiments
- Investigative labs
- Independent projects for a course requiring the whole semester with subsequent presentation in the format of a scientific meeting (paper evaluated) and written paper (instructor evaluated). This is the investigative lab taken to the extreme.
- Computers for simulations, data analysis, and review/instruction
- Pointing out "THE TAKE HOME MESSAGE"
- Not reading from text or notes: telling a story rather than reading the story.   You must, however, stay focused. Know the material so well it is second nature. Maintain eye contact and move around while lecturing. Do not sit or stand at a podium.

12. *What as the greatest help to you in preparing for your teaching position?*
- Opportunity to teach several different courses, albeit labs, as a TA with people who were EXCELLENT teachers helped me greatly.
- Look at the instructors you liked and did not like.   Think about their techniques.   Use the best of each one you liked. Avoid the methods of those you did not like.
- Always check mechanical equipment.   Does the overhead projector really work?
- Think ahead and plan. Have objectives in mind and stick to them. When allotting time, always add more. If you expect 1 hour, plan for 1 hour and 15-30 minutes. If it takes you 45 minutes to take an exam you have written, figure 75-90 minutes for your students.
- Expect the unexpected with labs. Run the lab before the students do it.   Anticipate procedures where students may have difficulties.
- Jot down outlines for your lecture. Fill in as you actually lecture. Do not read the text (students hate this) and do not read your notes as a newscaster might. Know the material so well it is second nature.
- Be honest if a student asks you a question you cannot answer. Offer what you feel is a good hypothesis or tell the student you will try to find the answer or perhaps direct the student to a source which might have the answer.
- Be relaxed.

- Know, intimately, the type of student you are dealing with.
- Keep a diary of what works and what does no work. Jot down any brainstorms you have.
- Keep your mind open to learning new strategies, etc. all the time.   Also, students have LOTS to teach you.
- The best you can do as a teacher is to take the students from where they are at to where they want to go. You cannot do anything if a mind is closed and refuses to open.   This it NOT a failure on your part. You do have limitations and the limit is set by how far the student really wants to go. You can successfully push the student limits farther, but only to a certain point.
- It is OK to be demanding and challenging (students do not mind) as long as you are fair, understanding, and reasonable.   If students know the expectations they usually work to meet them.

13. *What information would have been useful to you as you began your teaching assignment?*
- How does one construct and evaluate a fair, meaningful exam?
- There are alternatives to cookbook labs
- Where do I find how to make some solution/reagent for lab? How do I grow this organism for lab?
- How do you put a whole course, with lab, together?   Where do I start?   Can I do everything? If not, what do I cut?

Don Streubel, Idaho State University

1. How would you describe your first years of teaching?

Lists, facts, data, basically a transmitter of information rather than a listener, a pauser, a reflector with students, or a questioner, and less willing to take a risk than I am now. Barely ahead of the student.

2. What is the best thing about teaching?

Excitement of sharing enthusiasm and "turning a student on." Seeing their interest stimulated by the classroom experience. Preparing thoroughly, thinking, reflecting about teaching. Receiving positive feedback - some years later. Knowing that you can improve.

3. What is the worst thing about teaching?

Interference with teaching, time constraints and other responsibilities. Class sizes grew at my institution very rapidly. This creates constraints. Students who have no motivation, nor care for their own future, nor come to class.

4. What were the most surprising aspects about teaching on your own?

How much I knew compared to the students. How little students seem to carry over from previous coursework. How much time teaching takes—it's not something you can do as a "side activity." How much fun it can be. How much time writing tests can take.

5. What were your students like and how did you deal with their problems?

Friendly, some receptive, some not interested, diverse, but seemed to respond favorably to a caring attitude. Quick to complain about too much work. Unwilling to come and see me in my office (All of this relates to a certain segment of the population, not all!)

6. How do you evaluate your students, and how do evaluate the efficacy of your own methods?

Class size, with no TA readers, precludes many essay questions, mostly multiple choice exams. In-class, "time out" essays (short), summaries, "tell me what you know" type questions. Handed in and graded very liberally. I use this as "pretest"...I give students 10-15 mins of class time to complete these assignments.

It's important to create an informal, non-threatening, non-authoritative atmosphere in the classroom. Talk to students before and after class, ask them if they understood such and such, etc. They will open up. Student evaluations should be done early in the semester rather than at the end, or do them twice. Once the course is over you can't go back and change things. Invite a colleague or a graduate student to sit in and critique your teaching. Buy them lunch and discuss it informally.

7. What were your mistakes during your first years of teaching and how did you correct them?

Talked too much, not enough questions, "covered" too much - not enough focus on important concepts and misconceptions of students. Seriously consider teaching. Read various materials, talk teaching with colleagues, attend workshops such as Chautauqua workshops, and converse with students. Consider a sabbatical leave that focuses on teaching/science education. Ask colleagues to sit in your course.

8. What do you wish you had known or that someone had told you before you started teaching?

Very little emphasis on teaching in academia, few colleagues to discuss teaching with. How unimportant and ineffective textbooks are.

9. What were your best sources of information that helped you teach your classes?

Teaching Professor, Science News, Jossey Bass series, *American Biology Teacher*, J. College Science Teaching.

10. What was the greatest help to you in preparing for your teaching position? (What advice would you give to first-year instructors?)

My degree and my position at ISU. It forced me (willingly) to consider teaching seriously and to attempt to create innovations in the classroom.

Advice, consider teaching seriously. We have awesome power and responsibility to shape the future of our students. The biological sciences are important and will become probably more important in the future. We need an informed public, which our students become. Have colleagues, etc., critique your teaching. Video-tape yourself. Solicit your students' input.

11. What information would have been useful to you as you began your teaching assignment?

Taxonomy of cognitive domain. Specific examples and practice with writing questions and objectives.

Sue Harley, Weber State University

1. *How would you describe your first year(s) of teaching?*

My first years of teaching were very time intensive. I taught five different courses the first year, including two outside my main area of training (plant physiology) that required more prep time than the other three. As one of these two courses was a lecture class that met four days a week, I was barely one step ahead of the students the first time I taught it. Just when I had taught the courses often enough that my prep time was settling down, other things came along that demanded my time--faculty senate, an accreditation review subcommittee, and students working on projects.

2. *What is the best thing about teaching?*

What I enjoy the most are the labs. If you like to putter around the lab, trying various techniques, teaching someone how to do things, then teaching labs are the place to be. The labs let you bring out the interest of students who are curious about how plants work. These are rarely the best students, as determined by exam scores, but they are the most enjoyable students because of their enthusiasm. There are also students who drop by after they have graduated, and it's fun to catch up with them and hear how they finally realize why they had to learn "x" for their degree. My favorite moment was a student who, at graduation, gave me a "Thank you teacher" mug, even though he had to take Plant Physiology twice.

3. *What is the worst thing about teaching?*

The worst thing is students who want a degree without learning anything or spending time on course work outside of class. In general, this group has the worst perceptions and most complaints about grading, mostly because they do not see poor grades as related to anything they have or have not done. They assume that any essay exam is graded arbitrarily. Multiple choice is no better because they suspect that you have written trick questions. Taking off points because a student has not followed format instructions for reports or notebooks is also viewed as unfair. If you catch them plagiarizing or cheating, they get mad that you caught them, but there is no acknowledgment that they have done something wrong.

4. *What were the most surprising aspects about teaching on your own?*

I expected grade distributions and student personality types to be basically the same from quarter to quarter in different sections of large general education classes. But the different sections have never evened out. One quarter, no one in my section of general botany failed, but the next quarter 25% did. Some quarters I have a lecture full of enthusiastic students, asking and responding to questions, contributing their own observations. Other quarters the only time I get anything from students is on exams.

A minor surprise has been the number of students who ask for definitions of "regular" words (not technical terms) during exams. Also, students do not make associations between different courses. A prerequisite course is viewed as something to have waived, not a body of knowledge to be called on in the next course. Even within a course, they do not link subjects. For example, in general botany, which at Weber State is taught in a series of ten modules, most students do not make a connection between the modules on reproduction and genetics. I have also had a difficult time finding textbooks for two upper-division classes. For one, I have been using review articles, and in the other, I supplement the most appropriate genetics textbook I could find with additional material.

5. *What were your students like and how did you deal with their problems?*

Weber State is a comprehensive undergraduate institution and most students commute to campus. Many are first generation college students; the majority is classified as non-traditional. Most students work at least one job and must meet minimum GPA requirements and course loads to maintain their eligibility for financial aid. Students want high grades, but their other commitments do not allow for the study time that high grades require. I point out the consequences of their apparent priorities, and some realize they need to make decisions about how serious they are about getting a degree. Unfortunately, others are unwilling to accept the responsibility of choosing between commitments and demand that exceptions be made for them. This latter group also seems to have a constant string of crises because there is no room for emergencies. These students assault you with a constant barrage of demands for make-up exams and assignments, extra credit (which I never allow on the grounds that if someone cannot do the assigned work, he or she has no business doing extra), incompletes, and waivers. There is very little you can do for them unless you are willing to give up your standards.

For many students, a science course is the first really demanding course that they have taken in college. It might also be the first science course they have ever taken, particularly for non-traditional students. The basic difficulty is not the specific course content but the fact that they do not know how to study for a science class. I have found that taking some time the first week of class to go over general study habits and some science-specific hints that I have picked up (see question 10) can head off some problems.

6. *How do you evaluate your students, and how do you evaluate the efficacy of your own methods?*

Students in general botany take weekly essay quizzes and two multiple-choice exams. I give unannounced quizzes in economic botany and plant genetics, as students have a tendency not to keep up their studying with the former or their problem sets with the latter without a graded incentive. Exams in economic botany are mostly multiple choice, with three or four essay questions for 20-25% of the points. The exams for my upper division classes are all essay or problem-solving questions. The problem that I have seen with exam questions, multiple choice or essay, is a student reading more into them than is there. When multiple choice exams are graded, I get a printout showing how many students missed each question. I use that to identify ambiguous questions and errors in the exam key. I also check to see which wrong answers the A and B students were giving. This helps me identify poor questions or badly explained concepts. When students have problems understanding a question, they ask for clarification. I use this feedback to revise the question if I decide to use it again. In upper division courses, students do a lot of project work. For oral reports on these projects, the botany department has put together an evaluation form. I have prepared a similar form for poster presentations. My upper division students keep lab notebooks that are checked at the start and end of each lab period for completeness. I collect them at midterm and the end of the quarter for a more thorough evaluation. Lab students are directed to use their notebooks as a place to record not just data, but also comments and reflections on the labs. I have also just asked students what they thought about labs, textbooks, etc. and for their suggestions for changes. Courses are evaluated at the end of the term with specific sets of questions for major and general education classes. Most faculty agree that these evaluations are rarely useful for improving your teaching. For useful feedback, I watch students during lecture, trying to identify "barometer students" who will frown when things do not make sense or nod when they get something.

7. *Before you began teaching, what were your biggest concerns about teaching, and which came true and which did not?*

A concern that came true is the amount of time that grading takes and the time required for non-teaching duties. Another concern I had is that my background is in biochemistry and cell biology, and I am in a department where everyone else specializes in organismal botany and field work. This has caused some problems in that the required courses that I teach (plant genetics and plant physiology) are the only ones that have extensive prerequisites (e.g., two years of chemistry) outside of the department. Another concern was teaching two classes outside of my area, economic botany and plant genetics. Plant genetics has become my favorite course. I enjoy the math, and the challenge of working outside my primary field keeps my interest. In contrast, I am still not thrilled about teaching economic botany. I know this is due more to the class format (large lecture, four days per week) than to the course content. This brings up another concern I had, teaching large lecture courses. While I can do it, there are other instructional methods I find more comfortable and enjoyable.

8. *What were your mistakes during your first year(s) of teaching and how did you correct them?*

For general botany and economic botany, I started with existing department syllabi as these are multi-section general education classes taught by most of the faculty in the department. Many things about these initial syllabi did not work for me, but I was reluctant to make too many changes the first year, especially in the economic botany class where, at best, I was one chapter ahead of the students. As I have gained confidence with the course material and found alternative activities to lecturing, I now make changes faster when I encounter approaches that do not work. I am also looking for more ways to engage students in my courses. I explain more to students as to why a certain educational approach is used. For example, on the first day of general botany, I used to just explain how the course, which is audio-tutorial, is set up and what activities the students were to do on certain days. Now, in addition, I go over why the botany department has used this method of instruction for over 20 years.

9. *What were your best sources of information?*

The American Biology Teacher is good. I have enjoyed reading back issues, especially articles from the decade or so after WWII. When you read concerns then about how to increase hands-on opportunities, depth vs. breadth of coverage, and investigative vs. cookbook labs, you see that nothing is really new. I have also found *J. of Biological Education* and *J. of Chemical Education* helpful. I also like scanning journal articles for things useful or adaptable for student labs. In this regard, library budget cuts leading to shifts from journal subscriptions to reliance on interlibrary loans and document delivery services are frustrating. These things work fine for specific articles but do not work for browsing. I also look at lab manuals (old or new) I find.

Weber State has two "across the curriculum" programs, writing and speaking, which provide suggestions and feedback on pedagogy. Because of these programs, I got to hear a report from a communications professor who decided to take a human anatomy course after an accident while riding a mountain bike. Her comments on learning how to take a science class, when she thought that surely by now she knew how to study, were very useful and enlightening for me. Chatting with colleagues about teaching is also helpful for generating ideas and solutions to problems. The American Society of Plant Physiology always has a section of teaching posters and a teaching booth at its annual meeting. I have also found the Council of Undergraduate Research conferences good for ideas on incorporating research opportunities into undergraduate education.

Books particularly relevant to the development of my lab classes include Robert Day's *How to Write and Publish a Scientific Paper* and Howard Kanare's *Writing the Laboratory Notebook*. A book that has provided lots of good examples and warnings is Darrell Huff's *How to Lie with Statistics*.

10. *What are (were) your most successful teaching techniques, methods, strategies, and activities?*

To check on student understanding of chi-square analyses in Plant Genetics, I have them find papers in *Journal of Heredity*. Each student must give two oral presentations, work the chi-square analysis from the paper, and then explain the statistical support for the conclusions drawn about the genetic trait being studied. When students prepare for their first report, I find out quickly who does not understand.

I have students do several investigations on induction of nitrate reductase in plant genetics and plant physiology. As most students take these two required courses in sequence, this gives them a connecting point between the two courses as well as familiarity and confidence with an experimental system which they encounter so often but in different guises.

I do not let students leave lab early. If students have finished collecting data before the three hours of lab are up, I have them start on the analysis. Many students will now stay an hour or more after lab to finish the analysis while the lab is still fresh in their minds and their lab partner is still there (and I am around to answer questions). I am almost done microscaling labs in my upper division classes. Since the microscale labs are faster to run than most conventional scale ones, students can *really* complete a lab (with analysis and conclusions) before they leave even without staying late. The microscale labs have also increased student awareness about hazardous waste generation and disposal problems.

General botany is taught by the audio-tutorial system. Now I give the rationale for the department's use of this instructional method. My drops the first week skyrocketed, but my late term drops are lower.

To get students to appreciate the different kinds of writing in science and the assumptions authors make when addressing specific audiences, I have my sophomores in research design read and then answer questions about papers in research journals compared to those in *Scientific American, Natural History,* etc.

11. *What was the greatest help to you in preparing for your teaching position?*

I taught general botany at the University of Oklahoma as a sabbatical-leave replacement before getting my tenure-track position at Weber State. This gave me a much better idea of what teaching is like than a teaching assistantship ever did.

Start a collection of labs you want to try, papers you think would be good for a journal club, interesting things you find on the World Wide Web, etc. Graduate school and postdocs are very good at narrowing your focus on a particular subject. You need to broaden out, especially if you teach general education classes. Good periodicals to read are *Natural History, Scientific American, Discover, Smithsonian* (which had a great article on tomatoes just as I got to them in economic botany one term), *American Scientist,* and *BioScience.*

12. *What information would have been useful to you as you began your teaching assignment?*

Anything on pedagogy would have been useful. I did not even know the word existed until I started teaching. A "new faculty" orientation as to the functions and locations of the various student services offices would have also been welcome.

13. *What else?*

You might have been hired primarily to teach, but that is not going to be sufficient for promotion and tenure. Be aware of what other activities you need to engage in. You cannot "just teach" if you expect to remain in the system. At a large research institution, there might be faculty with expertise in a particular area, each with several postdocs and graduate students. At an undergraduate teaching institution, even though it might have an enrollment over 10,000, you could be the only person in your speciality. If you are replacing someone who has just retired, make it clear that you are not his or her second coming. Also, any papers from your thesis or postdoc need to be written before you start your teaching position.

In a small department, you will be the only person in your area of expertise. You may teach courses, both upper and lower division, borderline to that area. Many science departments/colleges/schools are still very low in percentage of women faculty. I was only the fourth woman faculty member in the College of Science at Weber State and first in Botany — a situation that warranted a write up in the campus newsletter when I started working there. Because of low numbers, women faculty get tapped disproportionately to serve on committees (at all administrative levels) where gender balance is wanted.

When you ask for letters of reference, make sure the authors know what type of job you are applying for. Supply written information to the references on your experience and rationale for this position. A copy of the ad is useful, too. For example, you don't want letters that stress your research skills when you are applying for a primarily teaching position.

Jim Nellessen, University of Oklahoma

1. *How would you describe your first year(s) of teaching?*

I would describe them as busy, anxious, exciting, interesting, feeling good about some presentations, feeling inadequate about other presentations, getting better the second time around, glad when students do well, asking what went wrong when some students did not do well, finally realizing some students do not care how they do, and feeling satisfaction from those students who do care and ask questions and come to me for help.

2. *What was the greatest help to you in preparing for your teaching position?*

The greatest help probably came from my past experiences as a laboratory instructor. Giving 15 minute lab introductions and then helping the students through lab is definitely helpful but is still quite different from actually teaching day after day. Giving departmental seminars was probably also important to a certain extent. To be perfectly honest, the only way to gain preparation for a teaching position is to teach!

3. *What were the most surprising aspects about teaching on your own for the first time?*

Probably the lack of questions received from students in a number of class periods and consequently going through the material at a faster rate than was anticipated leaving me to purposefully slow down, or to go into material I had planned for the next day, or to let students out early. When I was a student myself I recall many times when the class had no questions, but to be in front of the class and get silence was obviously a new experience and perspective.

4. *What was the best thing about teaching?*

Having fun talking about things I like and am interested in and getting some response from the students in the form of questions. Even if all I get are simple facial expressions saying "that is interesting" or "that sounds unusual, amazing, or new to me" is positive feedback that makes the teaching a good experience. Answering student questions and leading them towards a better understanding of the material is also a rewarding component.

5. *What was the worst thing about teaching?*

A few times making a stupid mistake on the blackboard by writing the wrong term or something similar, not having any students catch my mistake and my not realizing it until after the class is over. Then I have to make a clarification/correction the next day. Sometimes stumbling over my own words in an attempt to explain something and consequently feeling like a stupid idiot is another example.

6. *What advise would you give to first-year instructors?*

Be well prepared for your lectures. You will have to spend at least twice as many hours outside of class preparing yourself as you will spend in class. Have a definite agenda for each lecture of points you should cover but at the same time be flexible and be spontaneous because you may get students interested in certain topics that they may want to spend more time with. I would like to stress having a definite outline for each lecture because I found that students really appreciate an organized approach (e.g. having topics, subtopics, and even numbered points) because it can make things so much clearer to the students.

7. *What were your best sources of information that helped you teach your classes?*

The best sources of information came from people who had taught the course before. By obtaining previous course outlines and topics and occasionally consulting with other instructors on specifics I was able to plan better and feel better about going into the class.

8. *What were your biggest concerns about teaching, and which came true and which did not?*
   A) Making mistakes - which did come true.
   B) That I would receive bad evaluations from students at the end - which did not come true, in fact I received pretty good evaluations.
   C) That I might give tests that were too easy or too hard - this also did not come true.

9. *What do you think are (were) your most successful techniques, methods, strategies, and activities?*
   A) To be very organized with presenting the material such that the topics came in "apparently neat packages" whenever possible. In other words Topic X is divided into subtopics A, B, C, D, etc. Specific points are covered under the subtopics and then at the end of Topic X summary points can be made, point 1, 2, 3, etc. Although in reality most of the information from the beginning of the course to the end is going to be interrelated at least it gives the student a framework to follow.

Creating a synthesis of different but related topics can be done when necessary.
   B) To give real examples of how plants function in the world, to identify how humans use some plants and why, to give examples of how we are impacted (e.g. with fungi I always mention the Irish potato blight changing history, and that the potato itself is not of European origin).

Linda Watson, Miami University

1. *How would you describe your first years of teaching?*

Despite being in a similar position at the University of Oklahoma for several years, I was surprised at how challenging it was to move to Miami University with a heavier teaching load and a stronger emphasis on teaching skills. My first two years at Miami are best described as hectic. I did not request release time my first semester at Miami, which was a mistake because preparing lectures and developing courses is time-consuming. My lack of preparation and experience was apparent to me and the students. Overall, I felt somewhat disoriented, barely keeping one step ahead of the students at times. I did not feel that I did a particularly good job the first year.

This hectic schedule has continued, in that after two years I have yet to teach the same class twice. I have found preparing for entirely new courses each semester frustrating. In two years, I have taught five different courses, ranging from the 100-level to the graduate-level; and ranging from fewer than a dozen students to over 200. I still find it difficult at times to know the level of the students' understanding and expectations, which I think is related, in part, to not having had the opportunity to have the same level of students more than once.

Each course has had its own set of difficulties. For example, I was not prepared to teach a large section of non-majors in a 100-level course, particularly my first semester. These students exhibited little interest in the subject matter, and were critical of my presentation style, the rigor of the course, and my expectations of them. The most difficult aspect was dealing with their disrespect for me and for the material. At the graduate level, I have been disappointed in some students' motivation levels, I expected motivation to be intrinsic to all of them at this point in their educational training. In part, I feel that my expectations of the students and myself have been too high in some respects. I don't know if this is true, but I have been told that this is a common mistake in early stages of teaching.

My teaching has become markedly less hectic. While I taught new courses my second year, I began to understand the Miami system, and learned where to locate teaching resources, and where to find moral support and guidance within the department. I also had developed more self confidence and ease by this time, which the students easily perceived. And I learned how much time is required to prepare for class. My goal now is to improve my teaching skills, and worry less about writing lectures and classroom presence. Despite sounding negative, the first two years were enjoyable.

2. *What is the best thing about teaching?*

The best thing about teaching is the student interaction. I enjoy interacting with students in the classroom and during office hours. I get a great deal of satisfaction when the students learn and express their own satisfaction and interest. It is particularly satisfying to hear them say that they got more out of the class than they ever expected, and that the course opened up a new world for them. I have also enjoyed relearning the material myself, from a different perspective.

3. *What is the worst thing about teaching?*

The worse things about teaching are the constant and never-ending demands. I am constantly writing lectures and preparing for class. I do not like dealing with excuses and last-minute requests of students, or dealing with a student who could care less. I also do not like writing and grading exams, and dealing with gradebooks, scores, and final grades. I also get tired of all the mid-semester grade requests from various departments, athletics, fraternities, and the like.

4. *What were the most surprising aspects about teaching on your own?*

There weren't too many surprises, although I was surprised at how much I enjoyed teaching. I thought the students would be a little less critical towards the instructor and would be more accepting of their own responsibilities towards their learning. I also thought they would be more mature and would act like adults. I was also a little surprised that preparing for class would take so much of my time.

5. *What were your students like and how did you deal with their problems?*

Miami students are pretty uniform in general, being from the white, upper-middle class. Few have had major problems or have not come forward with them. Not surprisingly, the non-majors have been less interested than the majors and have expressed a disappointment in the science classes being too rigorous. I did not deal with this effectively and basically told them to quit whining. This only resulted in low morale in the classroom, and I wish I had handled it differently. The majors are more interested, but so keenly competitive that they focus too much on points earned and grades, rather than material learned. I had been told how exceptional the students were at Miami and expected them to all be Honors students, which turned out to be an unrealistic and naive assumption. They are good students, but no more so than other state institutions.

6. *How do you evaluate your students and the efficacy of your own instructional methods?*

To evaluate students, I use a combination of methods including traditional exams (multiple choice and short answer for large classes, and essay for smaller ones). The students do better on essay exams, but almost all of them express a dislike for an essay format. Sometimes I tell them one question in advance that does not have a single correct answer, so that they can think about it before hand. I also try to give them a choice in answering four out of six questions, so they feel empowered. I also try to have them write at least one term paper or complete one research project. I have found that a brief presentation early in the semester allows for better classroom discussion throughout the semester. For graduate students, I tend to have them write term papers and open-book essays which they are free to discuss with each other, rather than giving in-class exams. It is surprising to me how much the grad students complain about this though, saying they would prefer a standard test. I also try to have the grad students conduct a research project, sometimes as a group and sometimes independently. I try to make sure it involves gathering and analyzing data to test a particular hypothesis or answer a specific question related to the course. I try to emphasize the most appropriate type of data to collect, and the most meaningful data analyses.

I use both student and peer evaluations for myself. The student evaluations are typical forms used at all institutions, and the students' responses tend to be negative and critical. I try to ask them to respond to two to three specific questions related to the course, so that they feel more empowered. This helps it become a more positive response. Sometimes I do an unofficial mid-semester evaluation, so I know what the students are thinking and how they are perceiving me. Not only does this make them feel good about providing input, it also lets me know if I need to adjust my methods. I also have two to three faculty members evaluate my teaching each semester, who visit the classroom and observe. In a small classroom, their presence can inhibit the students though. Many of the faculty have been very helpful in providing strong feedback related to content, presentation, presence,

and interaction. Others are less helpful, however, and some never show up as they promised. I have yet to have myself videotaped, but feel that would be a useful exercise.

7. *Before you began teaching, what were your biggest concerns about teaching, and which came true, and which did not?*

One of the biggest concerns about teaching would be that it would be all-encompassing, leaving me little time for research. This has been true for the most part. The time pressures and constraints have lessened some from experience alone, and I feel it will get better once I get more repetition into my schedule. But for the first two years, I got little else done. Had I not had a strong research program in place before I started teaching, I don't think I would have been very successful at either.

Another fear was that I would not be an outstanding teacher and would be just average. I have learned not to worry about this so much and to focus more on the class (the students, classroom exercises, content) and less on my performance. I have found that I have improved vastly, just in having more consistent classroom experience.

I was also afraid teaching would be boring and monotonous and that it couldn't measure up to research. This I have found to be absolutely false. I am amazed sometimes at how much fun teaching is, and how much I look forward to going to class because I am so excited about presenting new material to the students.

I worried some that I wouldn't know my subject matter in the detail that would be necessary, or that I wouldn't be able to recall information that I once knew. I have learned that it almost always comes back from the depths of memory, or that it isn't that important anyway.

8. *What were your mistakes during your first years of teaching and how did you correct them?*

In many of my first classes, I did not encourage classroom discussions as much as I would have liked, and now I work toward it regularly. I wish I had asked a peer evaluator to observe me during the early part of my first semester to head off some of the minor problems which became exaggerated. For example, I was perceived as being unorganized, which could have been easily corrected by having an overhead with an outline of the lecture on it kept up during class. Some overheads could not be seen in the back of the room, but the students did not bring this to my attention until the end of the semester. These were easily correctable problems that went uncorrected until the second semester and were reflected in my evaluations and in student note-taking. Morale was low in this same class, which stemmed primarily from the students thinking that my relationship with them was adversarial. This was primarily related to low test scores on the first exam. To curve this set of exams (by 10 points) would have meant a 1-2% effect (10/500 total points) on their final grade. I now feel it would have been better if I had curved the exam and for them to feel that I cared about them as students so that they could move forward, rather than worry that they would perceive me as a pushover and them holding bad feelings towards me.

I have tried to cover too much material in just about every class I have taught. While I understand less is more, it is still difficult to omit areas that I feel are critical to a course/subject. But I am making progress towards presenting less information and not worrying that I will be finished lecturing in half the time allotted.

I am quick to say that I don't know the answer to all questions, which I strongly feel is the right way to teach. However, it can be difficult to do without losing credibility sometimes. I have tried not to worry about it and have learned that it is the way it is said rather than what is actually not known. I think this is in part because students expect answers to be black and white, and we as instructors need to emphasize the gray area sometimes. We don't always express that well.

I feel I have not yet been entirely successful at conveying to the students their own responsibilities. Some students tend to view their score as the instructor's fault. For example, their lack of preparation for class, particularly as it is related to discussions, is often viewed as the instructor's inability to teach. I am working towards conveying to the students that teaching and learning are a partnership between the student and the instructor.

9. *What were your best sources of information that helped you teach your classes?*

At Miami, we are fortunate in having many areas of support services and resources available on campus, including peer review and formal mentoring programs. In addition, I have found a few departmental members who have been willing to provide peer review and to share information on previously-taught courses and teaching methodologies. I find a lot of information in a variety of textbooks, and

in laymen's journals for undergraduate courses. Experience has been the single largest factor that has improved my teaching.

10. *What do you think are your most successful teaching techniques, methods, strategies, and activities?*

Every class has been different, and I have used different strategies and methods for each one. I try to target my techniques to the level and the size of the class. For smaller classes, I try to do more interactive learning and have more discussion groups, and to have hands-on activities when a lab is not part of the course; while for larger classes, I tend to lecture more frequently. For graduate level courses, I try to have the students lead the discussions and make presentations, rather than me doing it. Some students respond well to this, while others are critical of it. I have the students prepare a list of 10 discussion points that they must give to me one week before their discussion. I edit it and give it to the remainder of the class a few days before class. This helps the students focus on the topic to be discussed, and requires that they prepare adequately for class.

CHAPTER III. WHAT TO DO BEFORE YOU GET TO YOUR JOB

When you interview for a faculty position, you may be asked to present a lecture in a biology course as well as a research seminar. These are two different beasts. While you should consult with your major advisor and colleagues about your seminar and lecture, you should also look at the chapter on lectures (Chapter 10) and consider organizing your presentation based on the suggestions there. If the inviting department asks you to present both a research seminar and a lecture, faculty in that department probably consider teaching a major component of your position. Thus, you should spend time preparing your lecture–don't assume a good research seminar will land you a teaching position. While it is difficult to judge your long-term success as an instructor based on one teaching seminar, your formal presentation is usually the most important part of the job interview. The following is a list of suggestions to consider as you prepare for your teaching seminar–based on a recent, and unsuccessful, candidate's mistakes.

PREPARING FOR YOUR TEACHING SEMINAR

1. Make certain you find out if the course in which you will demonstrate your teaching skills is for majors or non-majors and who will be attending the lecture (undergraduate students and faculty, or graduate students and faculty wanting to see how you would do in front of a class.) Adjust your presentation accordingly.
2. Make sure you are familiar with the name and area of research for all faculty members of the department you visit. Most departments will have a web site that you should check before visiting. Faculty members are looking for colleagues with whom they can work with for many years. Show an interest in different areas of research and teaching. Also, you may meet administrators who have a totally different agenda than that of faculty, so expect different questions from these people.
3. Don't try to cover too much information in your presentation. Give a focused lecture with good, appropriate visual materials and, if the course is small enough, perhaps try to engage the students in a discussion. This, however, can be very tricky because the students don't know you and may be reluctant to participate with a new person and several faculty intruders in their course watching

your (and their) performance. One way to overcome these potential problems is to write several types of questions, some that require short responses, some that are open-ended, and to consider possible answers and subsequent questions based on the student responses. You may also want to review the chapter on discussions (Chapter 11). Regardless, make sure you have a focused, interesting, and dynamic lecture.

4. Practice, practice, practice. Ask your host how long your seminar should be and **never** go over the recommended time. Keep track of your time while you are speaking, and leave time for questions at the end.
5. Make sure that you thank your hosts for giving you an opportunity to speak to them.
6. All of your slides and overheads must be legible by people in the back of a large room. Check these out before you go on your job interview. Check your slides before your presentation to make sure they are in the proper order and orientation.
7. Define all of your terms while you speak--do not assume that your audience will be familiar with your topic or the organisms to which you refer. This is especially true if there are undergraduates in the audience.
8. When answering questions, don't put a lot of background information in the answer. Go immediately to the heart of the question--be succinct first, and then, if there is time, elaborate.
9. Show that you are enthusiastic and interested in the subject you are presenting.
10. Relax!

QUESTIONS A JOB APPLICANT SHOULD ASK WHEN APPLYING FOR A FACULTY POSITION

The following questions are not equally important, and some may not be relevant to your situation. Make sure you get important parts of your agreement IN WRITING.

1. Rank (Assistant, Visiting Assistant, Research Associate) Do you have to have your degree in hand before you arrive?
2. Salary (9- or 11-month basis; is there a chance for a raise each year; when will your first paycheck be disbursed; what is the estimated net pay?)
3. Benefits (Who is covered on your insurance; what percentage does the university contribute to your retirement package; is the pension transferable if you leave; are there loans for housing or is there faculty housing?)
4. Start-Up Offer (How much do you get for research and teaching equipment; will you get all the money when you arrive?)
5. Office and laboratory (Where are they located; do you share an office; what equipment does the department already have; is there a chance to build a lab for you; does the department provide a personal research microscope?)
6. Research support facilities (What plant growth, animal care, or microbial growth facilities are available to you, e.g., greenhouse, growth chambers, incinerators, autoclaves, fermenters, culture and media prep center?) Do faculty share major pieces of research equipment?
7. Course load (What course(s) are you expected to develop; how many courses are you expected to teach per semester; what constitutes a course-- e.g., does leading a graduate seminar count as a course; how are labs counted toward your teaching load?) What efforts can give you release time from teaching--for instance, if you get a major grant, can you be released from teaching one or more of your classes?
8. Course budget (Are there lab assistants, or a lab prep person to organize laboratory materials for the instructor; how many students are there per class and laboratory; what equipment for teaching does the department already have?)
9. Participation in basic courses (What is the size of classes; is there team teaching; what books are used; how often do you teach the basic course?)
10. What kind of student teacher evaluations are given? How are they used in the annual evaluation of the faculty members?
11. Students (What are their backgrounds; how many majors and non-majors, what is their interest in science, and what is the racial makeup?)
12. Summer school teaching? (Is it required or optional; what is the salary for teaching in the summer?) What opportunities are there for interdisciplinary studies, e.g. Honors Program?
13. Research supplement (Is there summer support for faculty members; is there money for travel to meetings or research sites; are institutional grants available?)
14. Number of faculty members and ultimate size of department (Is there a fixed number of full and associate professors; what subdisciplines are emphasized in the department, e.g., ecological, physiological, molecular).
15. Organization of the department (chair or head; permanent or rotating; is there a departmental executive committee?) Do junior faculty members have a voice and vote equal to senior members on department matters?
16. Starting time (When are you expected on campus; when are you expected to teach your first class; can you negotiate a contract in which you don't have to teach during the first semester so you can set up your lab?)
17. Assistance in moving expenses (negotiable?)
18. Leave (Sabbaticals, leaves of absence, how often, what requirements?)
19. Tenure (What is the method of annual evaluation; length of time to achieve tenure; how considered; what is expected of you to achieve tenure in terms of teaching, research, and administrative duties? How is teaching viewed in comparison to research in terms of tenure, promotion, and raises? Will any of your work experience count toward tenure?) Ask for a copy of the unit's tenure policy.
20. How are research accomplishments measured? (e.g., a) by grant dollars received or number of grants; b) by number of papers or the quality of the journals; c) by the quality of the graduate students trained by the faculty member; or d) the significance of the research to the discipline?)
21. Length of academic year (Holidays, starting and stopping dates, dates of finals). Ask for or buy a class schedule.

22. Promotion and salary increments (Is it systematized or irregular; across the board or by merit?)
23. Grad school status (When can you be appointed to graduate faculty--when can you have graduate students?)
24. Support for graduate students (How many TAs and RAs are there; does department or university support travel and research of all students; are visits to the department by potential grad students paid for by the department or university?)
25. Funds for minor research needs (Who pays for mailing of business letters, reprints and reprint requests, faxing, long distance telephone calls, duplication of printed materials, minor/major repairs of equipment?)
26. Grant development support (Does the department or university provide word processing support or budget development personnel to help you write a grant proposal?)
27. Availability of transportation (Is there a university car pool; department field vehicles?)
28. Computer facilities (Will department provide you with a personal computer; is your office or department connected to the Internet; what type of system does the office staff use; what kind of printers are available to you; what statistics packages are available for your use?)
29. Office support (What can you ask the office staff to do for you--type letters and manuscripts, mail out reprints?)
30. Technical support (Who orders supplies; where do you get materials for lab and your office such as "typing" paper; who troubleshoots and fixes equipment in the department; where can you go to get some special equipment made for you? Is there any institutional support for teaching development?)
31. Library--check out journal listings while you are on campus. (How easy is it for you to get interlibrary loans; what reference materials are available and how are they available, i.e., hard copy or CD-ROM; what is the library budget?)
32. A-V equipment (What is in the classrooms and labs; are there computing facilities for students?)
33. Spousal support (Can your spouse be hired in the department; what are job opportunities and benefits available for your spouse?)
34. Campus environment (What is parking availability and cost; is there mass transportation; how are the bookstores and restaurants; is there a credit union for faculty?)

35. Personal considerations (What is the cost of living, availability of housing, schools, access to campus, safety, cultural centers, nature of the community, availability of tickets to sporting and cultural events, health facilities?)
36. Make sure you purchase a local newspaper to check costs of homes and rent and types of local entertainment. If your visit is successful and you are offered the position, ask if the department could support (at least partially) a second visit to the area to look for housing. There are web sites that allow you to compare the cost of living in one part of the country with another--check them out before you visit.

THINGS TO DO BETWEEN ACCEPTING AND STARTING THE JOB

1. Get a list of the courses you will be teaching your first year. Talk to people at your current institution who teach those courses about what works and doesn't.
2. You may teach lower division/general education courses that are already taught by people in your new department. With luck, all of the instructors have agreed to use the same textbook. Get a copy of the book and the syllabi from those who have taught the course. If different texts are used, get copies and try to select one that is already in use. There is probably a department-generated workbook or lab manual. Ask them to send you a copy if one wasn't provided when you interviewed.
3. Start reviewing textbooks for your upper division (specialty) courses.
4. If you don't have a statement of teaching philosophy, write one now. This will help tremendously when you write your syllabi.
5. Read broadly--you will be asked questions outside your area of expertise. Also, you need to build up a supply of odd examples and interesting exceptions for your class. *Natural History, Sci. American, Smithsonian, Discover, Am. Scientist,* and *BioScience* are good sources.
6. Read the classics in your field (e.g., in biology, *The Double Helix* and *Origin of Species*).
7. Start a lab collection. Look at back issues of *American Biology Teacher, Journal of Biological*

Education, Journal of Chemical Education, etc., lab manuals (old or new), and methods journals.

8. Arrive at your job as soon as possible, especially if you are teaching an upper division lab class the first term. Select your labs and run through them before school starts. Identify equipment and procedure bottlenecks and adjust the labs accordingly. Consider that students will take 2-5 times longer than you will to weigh samples or reagents, pipet liquids, and adjust a microscope.

9. If you haven't done so, concentrate on finishing your dissertation or postdoc. Write any papers before leaving for your new teaching job--you won't have time after.

10. Get a copy of the university's mission statement. Often, the department or college will have one as well.

11. Start making a list of what will have to be ordered for your lab and your courses. If there is a lab prep person, check with him/her and see if a list of deadlines has been already established for you to use. (adapted from comments by Sue Harley).

SELECTING TEXTBOOKS

A Good Textbook:
presents difficult material in different ways so student learning is enhanced (written explanation, illustrations, and examples)
elaborates main concepts using examples and material that is relevant to students
gives contrasting material
helps students distinguish what is important from what is not
keeps students interested in learning
presents the subject matter clearly
helps students apply what they have learned to new situations
understands how students learn
has clear and appropriate illustrations
is interesting to read

What to Consider When Choosing a Text
For your first year, you may not have the responsibility of selecting a textbook. If you do, however, there are several considerations. The basic criterion in selecting a text ought to be the extent to which the text helps an instructor accomplish the course's goals. One of the keys to success is to start early--the choice of a textbook takes several weeks. Don't select a textbook if a review copy is not available.

Criteria for textbook selection
Reviews: has been evaluated favorably in professional journals
Author: knowledgeable in subject field
Instructor's Manual: useful teaching aids, test questions, supplemental materials, suggested teaching strategies
Student Workbook or software: materials that supplement text
Assessment Materials: assessment devices or test items included
Bibliography: current and appropriate
Sources: properly documented
Content: accurate, consistent, up-to-date
Topics: topics correspond with course objectives
Sequence: arrangement is appropriate or adaptable
Bias: contains no bias (gender, racial, etc.)
Reading level: appropriate for level of students
Student experience: appropriate for student background in subject
Organization: titles, headings, and subheadings

give visual organization; table of contents, index, and appendices are accurate and complete

Illustrations: close to text where discussed; accurate, captioned correctly; clear and easily read graphs, maps, tables, and charts

Type: clear and easily read

Price: appropriate for its use in the course

Durability: well constructed

Other: Does a glossary appear within the text? Does an overview precede or summary end each chapter? Are questions to test understanding, additional notes and suggestions for further reading provided at the end of each chapter? Would the majority of readers find the reading interesting? (adapted from Hemmings and Battersby, 1989; Johnson, 1990)

Initial textbook selection steps

1. Collect publishers' catalogs, sales representatives' business cards, and professional copies of textbooks from colleagues in the department.
2. Contact publishers and request copies of every textbook that seems to fit the course objectives.
3. Review textbooks that were considered for the course in past semesters. Sometimes "revised" editions are greatly improved.
4. Use staff in the college bookstore to facilitate obtaining desired copies of textbooks. Sometimes a call from a buyer gets a faster response. (adapted from Doyle, 1983; Davis, 1992)

Reasons to Change A Textbook

The problems, questions or exercises are no longer challenging to students since the answers are so widely known.

The content is outdated or incorrect.

The cost has escalated unreasonably.

It is no longer appropriate for the student population, i.e., minorities or females are under-represented in the text.

Physical changes in the textbook are undesirable, i.e., print style, font, graphics.

IMPORTANCE OF MENTORS

An important relationship for you to cultivate is that between you and a mentor at your new institution. If there is an experienced faculty member who is willing to befriend you and to help you organize your course, then you should consider accepting that person's assistance. As you begin your job, you should:

1. **Observe somebody else teaching**. Attend the class of your mentor. Discuss instructional styles and strategies.
2. **Observe each other teach**. Do it more than once, and do it with two objectives: First, offer your colleague input, and second, learn from your colleague about your own teaching.
3. **Interview students from each other's classes**. Hold an office hour and encourage students to come individually or in groups to tell you about their learning experiences in your class. Brainstorm alternative strategies, and use the good ideas.
4. **Have your exams reviewed**. Your mentor and graduate students can provide you with input on the clarity of the questions, scope of the exam, and length of the test given the period in which it is to be completed.
5. After you've taught a course a number of times, it becomes so familiar, so commonplace. **Get input from a colleague about your course and assignments.** Subscribe to a general science/biology magazine to help you keep up, such as *Science News*.
6. **Read a book or journal article about teaching**. Agree to discuss a chapter a week over lunch with your mentor. Take the text apart, agree, disagree, or come to other conclusions. (See Literature Cited for possible material to discuss.)
7. **Collect, review and discuss new evaluation data from each other's classes**. Help each other explore what the results mean, and more importantly, what you ought to do as a result of them. (adapted from Holmes, 1988)

Develop a list of tasks you must accomplish to make it possible for you to teach your class, then arrange them in the order in which they must be completed. Which activities require ordering equipment and supplies, which require collecting information before you can begin planning, and which depend on the work of others who must be contacted? Now is the time to make a time-line so you will be ready on the first day of class. Using your list, work backwards toward a reasonable date to begin acting on each task–don't be caught by the time crunch once teaching begins. Never say to yourself–I can worry about this later because I don't have to teach until next semester–next semester is too late.

CHAPTER IV. MODELING EXCELLENT TEACHING

The role of the teacher is to facilitate learning, to help students get excited about learning, and to them understand concepts. Teachers should interact with students enough to recognize what students think, what they know, and how they know what they know. Exemplary teachers actively monitor student behavior by moving around the room and speaking with students, maintaining control at a distance over the entire class (Tobin, Tippens, and Gallard, 1994). The key to teaching with understanding is verbal interaction with students. Exemplary teachers use a range of verbal strategies, including asking questions to stimulate thinking, probing student responses for clarification and elaboration, and offering explanations to provide additional information.

Excellent instructors emphasize inquiry rather than facts, and foster student independence and curiosity. They use concrete examples to illustrate abstract concepts, and analogies and examples from outside the classroom to facilitate understanding. These instructors anticipate areas of content likely to give students problems, and at the conclusion of a lesson, they highlight and reinforce the main points of the class. Exemplary teachers have extensive knowledge of how students learn as well as what to teach and how best to teach it; these teachers understand the content of their discipline--in fact the result of an instructor's lack of content knowledge results in an emphasis on students memorizing facts instead of understanding the processes of science.

Think about the best teachers you ever had and the best courses you ever took. What was special about them? Consider the following list of characteristics of excellent instructors as you think about how you might modify your own teaching style. If you have never seen yourself teach, one of the best exercises you can do is to videotape yourself as you teach a class. Review the tape with your mentor or with someone on campus who is qualified to do so. Whatever you decide to do, work to correct your weaknesses, feature your strengths, and don't try to teach in a manner that is completely foreign to your own personality. You will teach best when your teaching capitalizes on your skills and attributes.

CHARACTERISTICS OF EXCELLENT INSTRUCTORS

Based on a number of evaluations of instructors of different disciplines by students from many backgrounds, there are six characteristics that students constantly express as desirable in their instructors. These six are:

1. **being prepared and organized;**
2. **being enthusiastic about teaching;**
3. **presenting information clearly;**
4. **being able to stimulate students' thinking;**
5. **being knowledgeable;** and
6. **enjoying teaching and working with students.**

These six characteristics are interconnected, but they are related mostly to being prepared to teach and liking what you do. If you are prepared to teach, you can present the information clearly and appear knowledgeable, and you can focus on ways to stimulate your students' thinking. In addition, if you are prepared, you will also be more enthusiastic about teaching and will enjoy it more because of the positive feedback you receive from students. But, one of the most difficult parts of a new position is keeping ahead of the game. So, try to do as much as you can *before* the school year begins—once it starts, your time will be eaten up by more responsibilities than you can imagine.

Developing a Rapport with Your Students

Related to the above six characteristics, the following is a list of characteristics of outstanding professors in the classroom that helps them develop a rapport with their students. Such behaviors include:
1. being strongly interested in students as individuals and sensitive to subtle messages from them concerning the way they feel about the material or its presentation;
2. acknowledging students' feelings about class assignments or policy and encouraging them to express their feelings and viewpoints;
3. encouraging students to ask questions;
4. communicating both openly and subtly that each student's understanding of the material is important; and
5. encouraging students to be creative and independent in dealing with the material to understand and formulate their own views.

CHARACTERISTICS OF POOR INSTRUCTORS

At the opposite end of the spectrum are behaviors that guarantee to stifle discussion and learning in the classroom, as well as to produce negative evaluations. The poor instructor fails to recognize students as individuals; uses sarcasm, discourages student questions, is defensive about policies or procedures, and is inconsistent or unpredictable. The seven deadly sins of teaching are:

1. arrogance;
2. dullness;
3. rigidity;
4. insensitivity;
5. vanity;
6. self-indulgence; and
7. hypocrisy.

Academic arrogance (thinking you are better than the students or that the students are all stupid) can come from the nature of specialized study in graduate school that places very large amounts of detailed information in people of very limited experience in dealing with students. Such arrogance may also stem from insecurity. Many people also think that "anyone can teach." Certainly this is just as true as thinking "anyone can conduct research." But to be competitive in academia, you have to teach and/or conduct research *well*.

Dullness disregards the need for attention to students and destroys interest students may have for the discipline. No teacher can escape the necessity of providing discipline, however, it is a mistake never to deal with people on an individual basis. Listening carefully and responding to students' concerns will prevent the appearance of insensitivity. Problems of vanity may occur if you are more concerned about how an activity may reflect on you rather than if it will help students learn. Self-indulgence may be exhibited as laziness once a person achieves tenure. Hypocrisy has to do with saying one thing to students and demonstrating another behavior. Obviously, you want to avoid as many of these sins as possible, but you might have to fight their appearance in class if these characteristics are part of your "nature." (adapted from Eble, 1983)

INVENTORY OF MODEL TEACHING

Here is an extended list of model instruction techniques to which you can compare your teaching.

Clarity: methods used to explain or clarify concepts and principles

Give examples or analogies for each concept, using concrete, everyday illustrations to explain concepts and principles.

Define new or unfamiliar terms, and write key terms or names of organisms on the blackboard/overhead.

Repeat difficult ideas several times (3 times in 3 different ways—e.g., introduce idea verbally, show pictures, then write key points on the board).

Stress most important points by pausing, speaking slowly, or changing tone or volume of voice.

Use graphs, diagrams, or photographs to facilitate explanation.

Point out practical applications of concepts.

Answer student questions thoroughly for all students to hear—if questions are central to understanding.

Explain subject matter in familiar, colloquial language—level of language is appropriate for students.

Restate questions or comments from students to clarify for entire class.

Enthusiasm: use of nonverbal behavior to solicit student attention and interest

Speak in a dramatic or expressive way; show passion for discipline and teaching.

Move about while lecturing, walk up aisles.

Gesture with hands and arms for emphasis, but not wildly.

Exhibit appropriate facial gestures or expressions.

Make eye contact with students.

Tell jokes or humorous anecdotes; smile or laugh.

Do not read lecture from prepared notes or text.

Interaction: Techniques Used to Foster Students Participation in Class

Treat students with respect.

Encourage students to ask questions or make comments during lectures.

Respond constructively to wrong answers.

Praise students for good ideas; be generous with approval.

Ask questions of individual students as well as the class as a whole and encourage students to answer difficult questions by providing cues.

Provide time for student answers and refrain from answering your own questions.

Incorporate students' ideas into lecture.
Present challenging, thought-provoking ideas to stimulate discussions.
Allow relevant student discussion to proceed uninterrupted.
Show tolerance of different points of view and respond constructively to student opinions.
Require student thought and participation.

Rapport: Building Quality Interpersonal Relations Between Teacher and Students

Learn the names of all students in class.
Take a personal interest in students' success; seek out and help students who are having difficulties.
Be sympathetic toward and considerate of students and sensitive to their feelings.
Direct students with learning problems to appropriate help on campus; announce your availability to help students.
Talk with students before and after class.
Solicit feedback and listen carefully.
Do not deprecate ignorance or misunderstanding or make students feel inferior.
Recognize when students do not understand or are confused.
Treat students equitably and encourage mutual respect.

Organization: Ways of Organizing or Structuring Course and Subject Matter

Use headings and subheadings to organize lectures.
Put outline of lecture on blackboard or overhead.
Clearly indicate transition from one topic to the next.
Give preliminary overview of lecture at beginning of class or major concepts during class.
Explain how each topic fits into the course as a whole.
Review topics covered in previous lecture at beginning of each class.
Summarize main points at the end of class.

Efficient Use of Class Time

Begin class on time in an orderly, organized fashion.
Do not dwell excessively on obvious points.
Ask if students understand before proceeding to next topic.
Stick to the point in answering students' questions.

Disclosure: Explicitness Concerning Course Requirements and Grading Criteria

Advise students how to prepare for exams.
Provide sample exam questions.
Tell students exactly what is expected of them on tests, essays, or assignments.
Remind students of test dates or deadlines.
State objectives of course as a whole.
Be fair and impartial in dealing with all students.
Return assignments/exams quickly with meaningful feedback.

Speech: Characteristics of Voice Relevant to Classroom Teaching

Speak clearly and at an appropriate volume.
Speak at appropriate pace, but vary pace occasionally.
Avoid annoying habits such as saying "um" or "ah."
Vary voice through lecture.

Presentation: Lecture or Leading Discussions

Create a non-threatening atmosphere.
Do not "hide" behind the podium.
Write in large and legible letters on blackboard or overhead.
Talk to the entire class, not the board or windows.
Use a variety of media and activities in class.

Credibility and Control: Being an Authority Figure Without Being Authoritarian

Respond to distractions effectively, yet constructively.
Appear comfortable and competent with the content, speak with confidence and authority.
Respond confidently to student inquiries for additional information.
Use authority in classroom to create an environment conducive to learning.
Admit errors and/or insufficient knowledge (have students explore answers outside of class).
Respect constructive criticism.

Content: Appropriate Subject Matter

Expect a great deal from students; challenge students intellectually--but not just the challenge of memorizing lots of information.
Integrate text material into class presentations.
Relate current course content to what's gone before and what will come after.
Relate current course content to students' general education.
Present background of major ideas and concepts.
Present up-to-date developments in the field and contemporary examples.
Help students appreciate and recognize importance/relevance of your discipline.
Help students identify main points and relate them to each other.

Active Learning: Laboratories, Field Experiences, Student Research

Clearly explain directions and goals of the activity.

Have materials and equipment necessary to complete the activity.

Give prompt attention to individual problems.

Make safety supervision obvious.

Allow sufficient time for completion and clean up.

Schedule time for discussion of results.

Require skills reasonable for the course and students.

Allow opportunity for independent investigations.

Promote student-centered vs. teacher-directed activities.

Critical Thinking: Developing Thinking Skills in Your Students

Help students gain new viewpoints and appreciations.

Help students recognize good and poor reasoning or arguments in the field.

Help students approach information/ideas from a variety of perspectives.

Help students understand how their biases may influence their understanding of content.

Help students appreciate the importance and relevance of course activities.

Differentiate between concepts of greater and lesser importance.

Let students compare, analyze, synthesize, and/or apply the information covered in the course to novel situations.

Provide opportunities for students to think and act independently and to accept personal responsibility for their choices.

Ask questions that stimulate critical evaluation and application of the course content and provide sufficient time for students to respond.

Use writing to stimulate critical-skill development.

Encourage students to evaluate the course.

Address multiple learning styles of students: *auditory* (use discussions, questions, and lectures); *kinesthetic* (use hands-on activities, role playing, simulations, and case studies); and *visual* (use writing, demonstrations, displaying information on blackboards and overheads, and videotapes).

(adapted from OSU, 1990; Bonwell and Eison, 1991; Haley, 1992; Weimer, Parrett, and Kerns, 1992; Ludewig, 1993; Lumsden, 1994)

Chapter IV

   Before you continue, consider how you will specifically incorporate model behaviors into your class or modify your own teaching style. What are your major teaching strengths--how can you best feature them in your course? What are your weaknesses, and what specifically can you do to overcome them?

CHAPTER V. HOW STUDENTS LEARN

There is a large body of science education literature that describes how people learn. It is not the intent to review this literature here, however, it is important to understand that students learn in different ways. Thus, the key is for you to **teach the major concepts in several different ways**. By teaching in different ways, you build in repetition, but you also address the multiple learning styles of your students. For instance, provide a short article about a biological concept such as photosynthesis, write key points of the process on the board, show a film and slides with diagrams, and then discuss the entire concept with students. By doing so, you reinforce what students have gained from each method, help students to synthesize their knowledge, and reduce confusion. Related to this, repeat the important messages, information, and content to your students, especially if you are lecturing. **Learning is the most important outcome of a curriculum and instruction. A focus on how to get students to learn is much different from a focus on what to teach.** While focusing on learning, instructors must address the needs of students who have diverse backgrounds and interests. How can one develop an effective biology program for a group of diverse students, and what must be included in a program to bring about learning?

PRINCIPLES OF LEARNING

Learners are not simply passive recipients of information; they actively construct their own understanding. The following is a list of a few principles of learning.

Principle 1

If information is to be learned, it must first be recognized as important to the student. Help students understand why the information you present is important and then to identify what is essential from what is not. (Never say that something is important because "I say so." You might explain how this information forms the foundation for related concepts.)

Principle 2

During learning, learners act on information in ways that make it more meaningful to themselves. So, use examples, images, elaborations, and connections to students' prior knowledge to make information more meaningful and to help form a bridge between what they know and what they don't know. (Analogies are useful. This is also related to the issue of relevancy to students. Bring to class news articles that relate to the concept being taught in class.)

Principle 3

Learners store information in long-term memory in an organized fashion related to their existing understanding of the world. So, provide an organizational structure for students, or they will build their own structure and may simply memorize the information. (Get students to understand the "big picture" before they begin learning any of the detailed information related to it.)

Principle 4

Learners continually check their understanding, which results in refinement and revision of what is retained. So, provide opportunities for students to check on their understanding—by asking them to write about the information or by class discussions. (Ungraded pop quizzes also work.)

Principle 5

Transfer of learning to new contexts is not automatic, but results from exposure to multiple applications. So, expose students to concepts in different ways and then help them see how concepts can be applied to new situations. (Being able to apply knowledge to a new situation is an important measure of student learning.)

Principle 6

Learning is facilitated when students are aware of their learning strategies and monitor their use. Students need to learn how to learn. (**Get students to think about how they know what they know.**) (adapted from Svinicki, 1994)

CONSTRUCTIVISM

In recent years, cognitive psychologists have shed some light on the learning process and proposed a model that accommodates all students, a model called *constructivism.* **Learning is a process of making sense of new experiences in terms of a person's existing knowledge.** Students redefine, reorganize, elaborate, and change their initial concepts through interaction between themselves and their environment and other individuals. The learner interprets objects and phenomena and internalizes the interpretation in terms of previous experiences. Such changes often require the instructor first to challenge the students' initial conceptions by showing these conceptions to be inadequate or inaccurate. To avoid leaving students with an overall sense of inadequacy, however, there must be time and experiences to reconstruct a more adequate conception than the original one (BSCS, 1994). So, *learning is an act of construction* when pupils generate new meanings from incoming information by linking it with prior knowledge (Gunstone and Champagne, 1990).

To help students construct concepts, when preseningt new information I assume that my students know little, if anything, about the subject I'm talking about. I start with basic information about the concept and then move through the material quickly or slowly depending on how much students know and how quickly they learn. Starting with the basics is especially important in a non-majors introductory biology course where students may have heard of scientific terms, but may have forgotten their exact meaning (or never understood them in the first place). If your students do have a firm grasp of the concept, then move quickly through the basic information to the next, more complex, level.

By starting with basic information, you can make certain your students have a point of reference, a firm foundation, on which they can build new information. Without this reference point, most of what you say and do will probably be lost on your students. For instance, if I were to tell you that I live in Norman, Oklahoma, and you didn't know where that was, I could tell you that Norman is 5 miles north of Noble. This information is useful to you only if you know where Noble is located. If, however, you lack this reference point, then that information and the location of Norman is still a mystery to you--and your ability as a student to learn where I live is lost.

If, however, as an instructor, I find a reference point that you already possess, I can help you build upon the knowledge you have. If I choose a broader reference point, then there is a better chance you will possess that basic knowledge and be able to understand what I am trying to "teach" you. For example, if I say that Norman is 15 miles south of Oklahoma City, then you might have a better idea where my home is, unless you don't know where Oklahoma City is located. So, perhaps I should state that I live in Norman, which is located 15 miles south of Oklahoma City, which is in the middle of the state.

In a similar way, if you begin to teach a new topic such as plant physiology and you tell your students that *chlorophyll is a photosynthetic pigment located in a chloroplast,* this information has meaning only if students know what a pigment is, what photosynthesis is about (at least in general terms), and if they know what a chloroplast is. If a student doesn't possess this information, then it is difficult for them to come to a full understanding of what chlorophyll is and does, and why it is important.

Rule of thumb: Make sure your students have a firm foundation of basic information and a good overview of a concept *before* attempting to add new detailed information to their knowledge base.

CONCRETE VS. FORMAL THINKERS

You have probably heard about students being "concrete" or "abstract or formal" thinkers. A concrete thinker is one who can reason, but only about tangible (concrete) events and objects. Most of these students think that all problems should result in a single, right answer. They also have difficulty with symbols such as A>B. In the transition to formal operations, students can reproduce the results of abstract reasoning to solve problems and begin to use symbols, but they often need concrete examples to function well. They may have trouble applying one principle to another example. Students who are formal thinkers are able to construct testable hypotheses, see multiple possible answers, and use abstract reasoning to see the application of principles to other examples. They can use symbols to guide their reasoning. Most college freshmen have not reached the stage of formal thinking--about one-third use formal operations consistently over a variety of problems, about half are in the transitional stage, and the rest are concrete thinkers. This means that most of our entering students will have trouble designing an experiment using a scientific method of investigation or comparing and contrasting two different ideas. Therefore, we must provide students with ample opportunities to move to the formal level and help them do so.

What this boils down to is whether a student can visualize what you are talking about just by what he or she is hearing or reading (formal thinkers), or if he/she has to work with the subject in the form of physical objects. You can make an abstract thought concrete by allowing a student to manipulate materials physically—thus the importance of a hands-on laboratory. "Hands-on" manipulation of materials also must include "minds on" experiences in such forms that require students to draw analogies, provide opinions based on evidence, make independent decisions, and analyze new information.

So, how can you help students learn? Start with basic knowledge and work your way up, using analogies and examples and moving from the familiar to the unfamiliar. Analogies are good, as long as the students understand the analogous object, and examples are essential to give a student a reference point to which he/she can return when reviewing the information. Also, give them the opportunity to work with the materials and processes of scientific investigation.

FRONT LOADING

It is important that all of your students are on the "same page" when you begin your lesson. If your students aren't all talking about, thinking about, or listening about the *same* information at the same time, then your point is lost to many. To insure that all students are together, repeat, at least twice, the message to students that you are "now talking about chlorophyll," or that you are "now looking at the diagram of the carbon cycle," or whatever. This is related to the idea of "front-loading." Read the following poem just once to your class and ask students to write down what the poem is talking about (without any discussion).

> With hocked gems financing him
> our hero bravely defied all scornful laughter
> that tried to prevent his scheme.
> Your eyes deceive he had said, an egg not a table
> describes this unexplored planet.
> Now three sturdy sisters sought proof,
> forging along through calm vastness.
> Days became weeks
> as many doubters spread
> fearful rumors about the edge.
> At last welcome winged creatures appeared
> signifying momentous success.

Now, clearly say the words, "Christopher Columbus" and read the poem aloud again. Ask students what difference it made in the way they were able to understand the poem. Images should pop into their head as you read the poem the second time. This is an example of front-loading and why it is important that all students are informed about what the topic of the moment is. Try to keep all of your students on the "same page" as you throughout your lesson. (If you let students read this poem themselves, they can "figure out" the meaning because they have the time to go back and review words—which does not happen when you are lecturing to them.)

MISCONCEPTIONS

Students come into your class with a lot of misconceptions, or alternative conceptions, about biological/scientific principles and information (Wandersee, Mintzes, and Novak, 1994). If these misconceptions are not identified and broken down, then this inaccurate knowledge forms a shaky foundation on which new information is laid. It also guarantees that your students are on "different pages" and thus not thinking about the same information as you. For instance, suppose I tell you that I live in Norman, and that Norman is 5 miles north of Noble. If you are thinking about Noble, Indiana, then this puts me in a whole different location. Likewise, if your students believe that plants obtain much of their food from the soil (as many of them do), then the importance of chlorophyll to the life of a plant, and them, might be lost.

How do you know how much basic information or what misconceptions your students possess? Try to determine this before you start instructing. You can just ask them—it is better to talk to individuals or small groups of people. You can also give them a short quiz in lecture or lab that is not graded. Small-group discussions, writing, and concept mapping could be used to gain information about students' current explanations of concepts. These explanations would then become a baseline for instruction as you help students construct explanations aligned with current scientific knowledge.

Another way to assess basic knowledge in your students is to use a multiple-choice question in the following way. I hand out four, colored 3 X 5 cards to each student (red, white, blue, and yellow) in my large lecture section. I then put a multiple-choice question with four choices on the overhead projector and ask students to give me an answer—all students at the same time. I tell them that if they choose answer "a," then they should hold up the red card. If they choose answer "b," then they hold up the white card; blue for "c"; and yellow for "d." They hold up the colored card that corresponds to their choice, and I can immediately determine if students understand that concept by the number of cards of different colors. If a majority of students answers correctly, then we move on; if more than a third of the class gets an incorrect answer, then we spend more time on the subject. We work on student misconceptions about the subject based upon which incorrect answer they chose.

STUDENT PROBLEMS WITH LEARNING

Unfortunately, many students who enter college are not prepared for learning. The following list is what you might *expect* your students to be like, but the truth is that they probably won't have many of these skills or attributes. The key is to help your students identify what their weaknesses are and to work cooperatively to improve on or eliminate these problem areas.

Learners Capable of Autonomous Learning Will Characteristically:
be methodical/disciplined;
develop individual plans for achieving goals, stick to them and modify them as necessary;
establish personal priorities;
pay close attention to details of an ongoing project;
be reflective and self-aware;
decide what knowledge and skills to learn;
understand his or her own values, interests, abilities, and knowledge;
demonstrate curiosity/openness/motivation;
be curious, with a continual need to learn;
confront questions and problems willingly;
be flexible;
be able to learn in many situations--e.g., from observations, conversations, reading, listening, taking notes, and reading;
be able to accept or reject material based on its merit;
be able to achieve or abandon goals based on their appropriateness;
be persistent/responsible and have a tolerance for frustration;
detect and cope with personal blocks to learning;
have developed information-seeking and -retrieval skills;
identify, and intelligently select and use, most relevant sources of information;
have knowledge about and skill in "learning processes";
be able to report what they have learned in a variety of ways;
have developed skills in taking notes, remembering, and relating; and
participate in evaluating their own progress.
(adapted from Candy, 1991)

HELPING STUDENTS BECOME SELF-DIRECTED LEARNERS

One of the goals of your teaching should be to help your students become lifelong learners. Grow (1991) suggests that this process has four steps or stages, and that different kinds of teaching can facilitate the movement of students through these stages.

Stage 1: Students are dependent learners, and teachers are coaches. Dependent learners need an authority figure to give them explicit directions on what, when, and how to do something. Learners at this stage respond best to instruction that is clearly organized and laid out for them.

Stage 2: Students are interested learners, and teachers motivate and guide students. Here, students respond to efforts from instructors to motivate them. These learners respond positively to personal interaction from the teacher who persuades students to participate and achieve, while being highly supportive and reinforcing students' willingness to learn and their enthusiasm.

Stage 3: Students are involved learners, and teachers facilitate their learning. Here students begin to see themselves as participants in their own education and to realize that they can learn from interacting with others. Students at this stage respond to a teacher who guides them through unfamiliar territory, offering appropriate methods for investigation, listening, encouraging, and supporting students' efforts.

Stage 4: Students are self-directed learners, and teachers are consultants. At this stage, students set their own goals and standards. Here the instructor does not teach subject matter, but cultivates students' ability to learn and select problems for investigation, monitoring progress, making suggestions, and giving feedback.

BIOLOGICAL LITERACY

A great deal of recent discussion has centered on scientific or biological literacy. One outcome of the many reports detailing problems with American science education and scientific literacy was the publication of several books describing what people should know about science--to help people become scientifically literate (e.g., Hirsch, 1987; AAAS, 1989; Hazen and Trefil, 1990; Flaste, 1991). Unfortunately, these books are content-oriented, and expectations of people achieving scientific literacy after reading one or more of them may be unfounded. Similarly, we must ask if students in our science courses can become scientifically literate after simply reading their science textbooks or hearing our lectures. Educators use the phrase "scientific literacy" to express the major goal of contemporary science education, an aim recognized for **all** students. However, before we can help students become more scientifically literate or can develop a course or curriculum in which all students contribute to this goal, we, as scientists, teachers, and educators must define scientific literacy and understand that achieving that goal is a complex and multifactorial problem. Biological literacy is not an endpoint that can be attained within a single biology course, but a continuum over which a person's understanding develops throughout life. The following pages outline a four-level continuum of biological literacy for college students, clarify some of the characteristics of students at each level, and suggest teaching strategies that will promote continued development of biological literacy.

The Dimensions of Biological Literacy

It is essential for biologically literate students to know and understand the characteristics of scientific knowledge, the values of science, and the methods and processes of scientific inquiry. The following are characteristics of a biologically literate individual. A biologically literate individual should:

understand
- biological principles and major concepts;
- the impact of humans on the biosphere;
- the processes of scientific inquiry;
- historical development of biological concepts;

develop appropriate personal values regarding
- scientific investigations;
- biodiversity and cultural diversity;
- the impact of biology and biotechnology on society;
- the importance of biology to the individual; and

be able to
- think creatively and form questions abou nature;
- reason logically and critically and evaluate information;
- use technologies appropriately;
- make personal and ethical decisions related tc biological issues; and
- apply knowledge to solve authentic problems

Most discussions of biological literacy use the term as a goal that one either achieves or does not; that is a person either is biologically literate, or is not. It is much more appropriate to recognize that each individual occupies a position somewhere along a continuum of biological literacy for different biologica concepts. Accordingly, the task for biology educators is to move students to a different position along the continuum and a richer understanding of biology.

A MODEL OF BIOLOGICAL LITERACY

The model of biological literacy on page 49 reflects different levels of understanding a student has about biological concepts, and a student (or faculty member) may be at different levels of literacy at the same time. For instance, while a student may possess a nomina or functional level of literacy about photosynthesis anc cellular respiration, that same student may possess a structural or multidimensional level of literacy about dinosaurs because he or she has studied them since grade school. A student may, but does not necessarily have to, pass through each level on the way to multidimensional literacy, and most students may never reach this level. As instructors, however, we should help our students move away from the nomina and functional levels and toward the structural anc multidimensional levels.

Nominal biological literacy. Many students recognize the domain of biology and certain words anc concepts as belonging to the realm of biology, as opposed to other disciplines such as art or politica science. For instance, students might be able tc identify the term mitosis as being "scientific" in nature, but have little knowledge of its meaning or use. *Students often come to class with a nominal level of biological literacy*, that is, they are literate in "name only." Students may have heard a biological term or concept before but did not develop an understanding of the information presented to them. To students who are nominally literate, most biological terms, principles, and concepts have little or no meaning, and they may possess misconceptions about all of these.

At the nominal level of literacy, students can only recognize information and concepts as being scientific. In biology classrooms this inability to understand and explain ideas is promoted by the use of textbooks and teaching that emphasizes facts and by multiple-choice exams where students choose answers simply by recognizing "correct" information. Students should bypass this level of literacy, and instructors should identify the misinformation, misconceptions, and misunderstandings of biology that their students possess. Once problems have been identified, an instructor should then use activities that break down student misconceptions and help them construct appropriate understandings of biological concepts. For instance, many students believe that plants obtain much of their food from the soil. By comparing the growth of albino and normal corn plants in both washed sand, which has no nutrients, and in nutrient-rich potting soil, students can easily see that plants without chlorophyll do not survive, no matter what kind of soil in which they are grown, while green plants grow, at least for a while, if given only water and light.

Functional biological literacy. *Students may memorize an appropriate definition of terms or concepts, which results in functional biological literacy.* With this type of literacy, students can accurately define certain biological terms or concepts but have limited understanding of or personal experience with them. Unfortunately, technical vocabulary is often emphasized in biology classes and textbooks and by instructors which leaves students at this level of biological literacy. Students at this level have no understanding of the conceptual structure of biology as a discipline and no feeling for the excitement of scientific investigations. Just as people described as functionally literate can "get by" in life, students who have a functional biological literacy may be able to get by on certain objective examinations about biology.

Students may be able to pronounce the terms and memorize what they have read, but with limited understanding. Teaching and learning at the functional level recognizes and supports the importance of biological vocabulary, but educators should help students develop other dimensions of biological literacy. Biologically literate individuals should be able to read,

comprehend, explain, analyze, and work with information in their textbook. Biology programs should de-emphasize rote memorization of terms and use a variety of assessment strategies that promote the understanding and application of knowledge. For instance, students could be given more problems to solve and essay exams, asked to build three-dimensional models of biological parts or processes, or to find, read, and report on a newspaper or magazine article that relates to a subject that has been taught in class. Any activity that rewards students for not simply memorizing information and that gets students to practice their critical thinking skills will move students toward a structural level of biological literacy.

Structural biological literacy. Students should understand the major conceptual schemes of biology, those ideas, such as evolution, that help organize all of biological thinking. One can think of these schemes, or unifying principles, of biology as branches on a tree that has evolution as its trunk and the "facts" of biology as its leaves. An understanding of the trunk and branches of the biological tree constitutes structural biological literacy, whereas functional literacy focuses on the leaves alone--and when the leaves fall, the facts are gone and forgotten. Continuing the tree metaphor, for students to reach a structural level of literacy, they also should understand the processes of growth for the tree, that is, the nature and methods of scientific inquiry. *At the structural level of literacy, a student understands a biological subject well enough to explain it to another person in his or her own words and can place the subject within a greater scheme of biology.*

Students are willing to learn more about biology if it is meaningful and interesting to them. One way to engage students is to use hands-on, inquiry-oriented experiences that generate excitement and enthusiasm while introducing students to biological concepts and teaching them about the processes of scientific investigation. Empowering students with tools to identify questions, pursue open-ended investigations, and propose explanations of natural phenomena on their own is important to promote biological literacy. In addition, instructors should help students see the personal connections between biological concepts and themselves. For instance, although photosynthesis may be taught as a series of chemical reactions represented by an equation, students should learn and appreciate the significance of the process to their lives--that the oxygen they breathe, the food they eat, and the clothes they wear are byproducts of photosynthesis. Similarly, memorizing the phases of mitosis provides some understanding of cell division; relating uncontrolled mitosis to the development of cancer, however, can interest students in mitosis because the study of cancer is more relevant to them.

Identifying the personal significance of biological concepts addresses the common student question, "Why do I have to study this?" When confronted with a personal problem, an illness, a physical problem, or even the purchase of a major consumer item, many people are compelled to learn as much about the problem or purchase as they can because they have become engaged in the subject at hand. For these people there is no prescribed amount of information to find or learn, but an amount that is limited only by their own imagination, resources, or continued interest. The major concepts in biology are all relevant to the lives of students, if only indirectly so, and highlighting these relationships by using current events, interesting natural phenomena, or human-related examples should promote an increased appreciation for their study.

Students demonstrate structural biological literacy when they understand how biological facts, explanations, and theories were developed, when they are able to apply information about the subject to novel situations, and when they know and appreciate the significance of the information to biology and to themselves. The structural level of biological literacy is a foundation on which the understanding of other, related biological concepts is based. For instance, a student may be sexually active and develop an interest in sexually transmitted diseases. He or she may develop an understanding of the cause of AIDS and thus be able to understand why certain behaviors are more risky than others, why the virus cannot be controlled with antibodies, and why a cure for the disease eludes scientists. This understanding, in turn, may lead to learning about other health issues, about differences between bacteria and viruses, and about biomedical technology.

Multidimensional biological literacy. This dimension of biological literacy represents a broad, detailed, and interconnected understanding of a subject in biology. Each area of biology, for example, has a history, is influenced by a variety of social and global issues, may incorporate technology, and is related to conceptual schemes and major biological concepts. *As students develop a fuller understanding of a biological subject and its connections to other subjects and disciplines, they develop multidimensional biological literacy.* Few professional biologists, not to mention students, fully achieve this level of literacy in all areas of the discipline, hence our view that biological literacy is a continuum. A scientist may have multidimensional literacy about the life histories of temperate birds, but have only a functional level of literacy about the molecular biology of plants.

Students may reach the multidimensional level if they continue their study of a subject, if their personal interest remains high, or if they are confronted with a problem related to the subject. For instance, a student may be functionally literate about air pollution. If, however, he or she faces the possibility of giving up driving because automobile exhaust contributes to local air pollution, that student may see a need to act on the problem or to discover enough information to make an informed decision about driving. This may be followed by a willingness to act or to investigate further the issue of environmental problems in general.

Students initially may not be willing to organize and undertake a plan of action to investigate a biology-related problem. Such students may be drawn into action if they develop a commitment or a relationship to the subject. For instance, in northern California, students who studied a bog as a class assignment developed a fondness for the natural area, and when a developer proposed destroying part of it to construct a parking lot, the students became committed to saving the bog. They were willing to protect the bog and began a plan of action *on their own* that required detailed information about the bog's physical and biological attributes as well as its economic importance to members of the human community. In a classroom setting, it is important for the instructor to find some topic or local issue, such as a land-use problem, that can propel students along an open-ended study in which they try to investigate as much as they can about a specific problem or to answer a specific question asked of them. You might be involved in a research project in which students can be used to collect and analyze data. Such projects are ideal ways of involving students in open-ended investigations--as long as they are not merely data collectors.

Multidimensional biological literacy involves the ability to investigate a problem concerning a biological concept, to collect related information, and to apply this knowledge to the resolution of that problem. Students discover that this intensive investigation requires the interconnection of many ideas and much information. Once they begin a long-term study, students should recognize the types of information and skills required to answer a question or solve a problem, and they should realize that biological knowledge might have to be integrated with that from other scientific, mathematical, social, political, and economic disciplines. The multidimensional level of literacy cultivates and reinforces lifelong learning in which individuals acquire the abilities to ask and answer appropriate questions and develop and retain a need to know.

Recommendations to address problems of scientific literacy in undergraduate science courses include: (a) downplaying facts in favor of concepts and higher-order intellectual skills (Holden, 1989); (b) providing more hands-on activities and spending less time on lecturing (Raloff, 1988); (c) teaching science using skills of observation, deduction, and analysis (NRC, 1990); and (d) using methods of scientific inquiry and reasoning (NCEE, 1983; NSF, 1989). Use of these recommendations would help instructors promote higher levels of literacy for all students, moving students beyond the nominal and functional levels. If biological/scientific literacy is truly a goal for all American students, then we must understand that literacy is not an objective that can be achieved within the limited time of a semester or within the confines of a textbook or lecture hall. We must expand our classroom to include the world in which students live and provide students with the skills, background, and interest in science that will carry them through a lifelong development of their biological literacy. Do we want students simply to recognize scientific information and memorize it, or do we want students to understand biology and to use their skills and knowledge to solve problems and conduct further investigations? If we want students to become biologically literate, we must determine what type of literacy we want our students to reach and how best to help them do so. Biological literacy is a continuum along which individuals continually progress, with structural and multidimensional levels of biological literacy as goals for all students. (Adapted from BSCS, 1994)

Characteristics of Students at the Four Levels of Biological Literacy

Nominal Biological Literacy
Students can identify terms and questions as biological in nature, but
possess misconceptions, and
provide naive explanations of biological concepts.

Functional Biological Literacy
Students use biological vocabulary,
define terms correctly, but
memorize responses.

Structural Biological Literacy
Students understand the conceptual scheme of biology,
possess procedural knowledge and skills, and
can explain biological concepts in their own words.

Multidimensional Biological Literacy
Students understand the place of biology among other disciplines,
know the history and nature of biology,
can ask and answer their own discipline-related questions, and
understand the interactions between biology and society.

Developing Biological Literacy

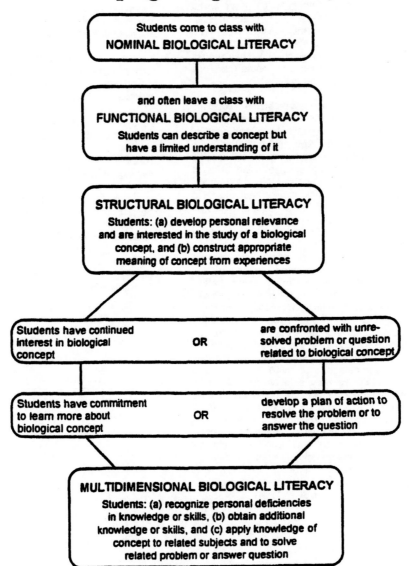

Students come to class with
NOMINAL BIOLOGICAL LITERACY

and often leave a class with
FUNCTIONAL BIOLOGICAL LITERACY
Students can describe a concept but
have a limited understanding of it

STRUCTURAL BIOLOGICAL LITERACY
Students: (a) develop personal relevance
and are interested in the study of a biological
concept, and (b) construct appropriate
meaning of concept from experiences

Students have continued
interest in biological
concept   **OR**   are confronted with unresolved problem or question
related to biological concept

Students have commitment
to learn more about   **OR**   develop a plan of action to
biological concept   resolve the problem or to
answer the question

MULTIDIMENSIONAL BIOLOGICAL LITERACY
Students: (a) recognize personal deficiencies
in knowledge or skills, (b) obtain additional
knowledge or skills, and (c) apply knowledge of
concept to related subjects and to solve
related problem or answer question

AN INSTRUCTIONAL MODEL

There are many different models of how students learn. The Biological Sciences Curriculum Study (BSCS) has produced a learning model with five phases based on constructivism that can be incorporated into any curriculum. A feature of each of these phases is the focus on student actions; each phase is defined in terms of what students must do in a science activity. The first phase is to *engage* students in the learning task. Once students are engaged, they need time to *explore* ideas through common, concrete experiences on which they build concepts, processes, and skills. Next, students must *explain*--develop common explanations for their explorations. They then should *elaborate* the concepts, processes, or skills that have been explained. Finally, students need *evaluation*--feedback about the adequacy of their explanations. The following sections describe the five phases of the instructional model. You can use the model to organize a semester-long program, units of the curriculum, or single lessons.

Engagement. The first phase engages students in the learning task. Students mentally focus on an object, problem, situation, or event. The activities of this phase make connections to past and future activities. The connections may be conceptual, procedural, or behavioral. Ask a question, define a problem, or show a discrepant event to engage students and focus them on the instructional task. Show pictures related to your subject, show students how the subject is relevant to their own lives--even if the relationship is only tangential. The role of the teacher is to present the situation and identify the instructional task. This is a hook--how can you get students interested in what you are talking about? Successful engagement results in students being intrigued by the activity and motivated to learn.

Exploration. Once engaged, students need time to explore ideas. Exploration activities are designed so students have common experiences upon which they continue building and discussing concepts, processes, and skills. This phase should be as concrete and hands-on as possible. The instructor initiates the activity and allows the students time and opportunity to investigate objects, materials, and situations based on each student's ideas of the phenomena. As a result of their mental and physical involvement in the activity, students establish relationships, observe patterns, identify variables, and question events. If called upon, the instructor may guide students as they begin constructing (or reconstructing) their explanations. The use of historical examples depicting the development of biological concepts serves as an excellent exploratory activity. The historical examples often align with and subsequently challenge the students' current explanation of concepts.

Explanation. The word *explanation* means the act or process in which concepts, processes, or skills become clear and comprehensible. Explanation, therefore, requires that students and teachers use common terms related to the learning task. In this phase, the instructor directs student attention to specific aspects of the two previous phases and formally introduces scientific explanations to bring order to the exploratory experiences. The explanation phase is instructor- (or technology-) directed using a variety of techniques and strategies including verbal explanations, videotapes, films, and educational software. Students ultimately should be able to explain in common terms their previous class experiences. The key to this phase is to present concepts, processes, or skills briefly, simply, clearly, and directly, and then to move on to the next phase.

Elaboration. Once students have developed explanations, it is important for them to extend, or elaborate, the concepts, processes, or skills. Some students still may have misconceptions or may understand a concept only in terms of the exploratory experience. This phase involves students in new situations and problems requiring the application of similar explanations. Generalization of concepts, processes, and skills is the primary goal of elaboration.

Evaluation. At some point, it is important that students receive feedback on the adequacy of their explanations. In this phase, teachers administer tests to determine each student's level of understanding and to allow students to evaluate their own understanding using their newly acquired skills. The instructional framework proposed here parallels processes involved in the scientific enterprise, and the methods of scientific inquiry are excellent tools for students to use as they test their explanations. (adapted from BSCS, 1994)

PHASES OF AN INSTRUCTIONAL MODEL

Engagement	The engagement phase initiates learning. The activity should: (1) make connections between past and present learning experiences, and (2) organize students' thinking toward the learning outcomes of current activities.
Exploration	The exploration phase of the teaching model provides students with a common base of experience within which current concepts, processes, and skills are identified and developed.
Explanation	The explanation phase focuses students' attention on particular aspects of their engagement and exploration experiences and provides opportunities to demonstrate their conceptual understanding, process skills, or behaviors. This phase also provides opportunities for teachers to introduce concepts, processes, or skills.
Elaboration	The elaboration phase challenges and extends the students' conceptual understanding and skills. Through new experiences, the students develop deeper and broader understanding and adequate investigative skills.
Evaluation	The evaluation phase encourages students to assess their understanding and abilities and provides opportunities for teachers to evaluate student progress toward achieving the educational objectives.

(BSCS, 1994)

CHAPTER VI. INQUIRY INSTRUCTION

Inquiry is a teaching method that allows students to discover or construct information for themselves instead of an instructor *telling* them that information. Inquiry has been identified as the central strategy for teaching science (NRC, 1995). This method can best be conducted in the laboratory and discussion sections of your class or as investigations in and out of the laboratory setting. However, versions of inquiry can even be conducted in the lecture.

Think about when you read a murder mystery. After the murder and before Holmes identifies the criminal, you try to put together all the pieces of evidence and throw out the red herrings tossed at you. Your mind is engaged in an inquiry investigation. Imagine, however, if you were told who committed the crime on the first page (or you read the last chapter first)--how much fun and how much thinking would your mind be engaged in? Probably little. Likewise, when you tell students about a biological concept first instead of letting them figure it out for themselves, they don't have much fun, their minds are not engaged, and not much thinking happens. Thus, if you want to allow your students to practice critical thinking, use inquiry in your class, and don't tell students what is going to happen and what to expect before they conduct an investigation. Let them discover for themselves what the principle or major concept the lab is presenting, constructing their understanding of the concept based on their previous knowledge of the subject and their experience in class.

Does inquiry work? There is much supporting evidence that suggests students taught using inquiry learn as much "factual" information as do students taught in a traditional lecture/lab class. Inquiry students, however, retain more information longer, have a more positive attitude toward science, and improve their critical thinking skills compared to traditional students (Gabel, 1994). Think about your own research, which is an inquiry-based activity. Will you ever forget how you conducted the last experiment for your dissertation, or what the evidence was to support your conclusion, or what your main conclusions were? You asked the major questions of the investigation, helped develop or select appropriate procedures, conducted the investigation, and interpreted the results--and so it is easy for you to revisit the experiments and results in your mind. You have learned very much about your particular research topic because you were actively involved in the work from start to finish. While we can't

expect that every lab experience or discussion be equally rewarding for your undergraduate students, it is important to mimic, as much as possible, an investigative procedure in your class, so that students have the opportunity to remain actively engaged in different aspects of "science as a process."

You can make your class inquiry-oriented by asking more questions, asking certain types of questions, and by focusing on **how** science is done rather than the subject matter. Ask open-ended questions, and ask for examples, the source of an idea, a summary of what has been read or discussed, an assumption that may have been made, comparisons, interpretation of data, and for supporting data. See the list at the end of the chapter for a variety of inquiry-oriented skills you might want your students to possess.

TYPES OF INQUIRY

Inquiry means different things to different people. Inquiry is what scientists do, as well as a way to teach science and a way for students to learn science. When you teach using inquiry, you select learning strategies that provide opportunities for students to practice their critical thinking skills (see later this chapter and Chapter 7). When students practice inquiry, they conduct investigations and learn about the content of science while experiencing the process of science.

All inquiry-oriented investigations share the characteristic of active learning focusing on the process of scientific investigations. One kind of inquiry is *guided inquiry* in which instructors guide students through their investigations and projects, asking them focused questions, giving them suggestions and ideas, and acting as a supervisor of students' work. This approach might be most useful at the beginning of a course with scientifically naive students. A second form is **open-ended inquiry** in which instructors facilitate independent studies by students who design, conduct, modify, and report on their own experiments--mostly working on their own. This kind of project could follow guided inquiry. Even inexperienced students can do such open-ended projects given enough time, support, and adequate experience. A third kind of inquiry is **collaborative inquiry** in which students and teachers work side by side in authentic investigations for which neither party knows the outcome of the research. These projects usually are of interest to both instructor and students and may have a local relevance--such as a land use issue. These projects require a lot of class time and may become the focus for the entire course (adapted from D'Avanzo and McNeal, 1996).

THE INQUIRY PROCESS

Inquiry can be conducted in any class, even a lecture. In a typical inquiry-oriented class, students:

1. are confronted with a question, problem, or observations of some natural phenomenon;
2. propose explanations to the natural phenomenon, generate possible answers to the question (hypothesis-making), or develop solutions to the problem (experimental design);
3. conduct experiments, collect data using scientific methods of investigation, analyze and interpret data;
4. evaluate possible answers or solutions based on data, and identify the main concept; and
5. apply concepts learned to new situations and problems. (adapted from Grambs and Carr, 1979; Moll and Allen, 1982; Uno, 1990)

KEYS TO SUCCESSFUL USE OF INQUIRY INSTRUCTION

For inquiry to be successful, have students conduct as many hands-on and mind-on activities as possible to help them discover and construct biological concepts for themselves. This means that students should be allowed to manipulate materials and equipment but should also be thinking about why they are doing what they are doing. Provide students with an introduction to a concept and enough background information so they can work out the rest of the idea. Begin with the familiar and move toward the unfamiliar.

Incorporate elements of a scientific method of investigation as often as possible in your class. Allow students to observe, form hypotheses (but see below), and make predictions, test hypotheses through experiments or demonstrations that illustrate experimental results, analyze and discuss data, draw conclusions based on results, and relate major concepts and ideas together. This doesn't mean that your students have to participate in *all* of these activities each day, but they should be able to conduct parts of an investigation as often as possible. Discussion is an integral and essential part of any inquiry investigation. Students need to be able to discuss with each other what they are doing, what they have found, and what they think the results indicate. Refer to the chapter on discussions (Chapter 11) for ideas about how to promote better interactions among your students.

You might consider having your students deal only with predictions and questions and avoid the word "hypothesis" completely. Many students have problems dealing with the idea of hypothesis formation, especially null hypotheses--they get tangled up in the terminology and miss the whole point about the question under investigation. Students will also develop a hypothesis "out of thin air" without any logical reason for doing so. Ask students to *predict* what might happen if you treated plants with Agent X--and *why they think that might happen*. A final note, do not use inquiry all of the time--students will become tired of responding only to questions. So, use a variety of teaching methods.

QUESTIONS TO IMPLEMENT INQUIRY IN YOUR CLASS

The following questions might help you begin an inquiry-oriented discussion in your class.

1. What do you think will happen, given this set of conditions, if, for example, X is added to Y? (Prediction forces students to draw on past experience.)
2. What actually happened? (Focuses the attention on the precise details of the event.)
3. Why did this happen? (This is an opportunity to speculate and to allow that speculation to lead to further investigations.)
4. How did it happen? What hypotheses can you propose? (Establishes that there may be a cause and effect relationship.)
5. How can we find out which of these hypotheses/predictions is the most reasonable? How would you test them? How do you know that? What is the evidence? How does that conclusion follow from your data? Is that the only way these results can be interpreted? If you make an interpretation, what are you assuming? (Demonstrates that interpretation and conclusions must be supported with evidence, such as observations or data, and must be related to evidence by a line of reasoning.)
6. How can you relate the investigated ideas, concept or principle to your daily lives? (These questions promote conceptual understanding by developing a student's ability to analyze, synthesize, evaluate, and relate to everyday life.)
7. Is there an alternative explanation to the one you proposed? Do you need more evidence? How do you account for an explanation that is different from yours? (Shows experimental results can have several equally valid explanations. Challenges students to see the big picture and to link ideas in biology.) (adapted from Cherif, 1989; NRC, 1995)

SUGGESTED INQUIRY ACTIVITIES

1. Allow students to design, conduct, and carry out an independent research project. This can be simple and inexpensive, but should allow students to hypothesize and predict, correctly design an experiment, collect data, and interpret the results. Plants make good experimental organisms in these projects because they can be subjected to a wide variety of conditions with minimum expense. Give your students pots, soil, and seeds, and see what they propose to study. (Look at the Independent Project guidelines later in this chapter.)
2. Provide data in the form of tables or graphs and have students determine trends or identify main points. Introduce them to the use and importance of statistical analyses, which then may be used with their independent projects.
3. Have students explain a complicated or difficult subject via essays, demonstrations, presentations to other students, posters, artwork, or student-produced films. A lot of learning takes place as a person attempts to understand a concept well enough to explain it to others.
4. Show students natural phenomena and have them make observations about them and speculate as to what factors contribute to their occurrence. For instance, show a tree with bare ground underneath it, or a plant showing phototropism or geotropism. In natural areas, plant-animal interactions are good sources of questions for an investigation. You can also use short video presentations that provide realistic observations of demonstrations, experiments, and simulations.
5. Provide students with sets of materials that can be compared; for instance, a group of ferns versus a group of cycads, or a group of arachnids versus a group of insects. What are the similarities? What are the differences? What makes a fern, a fern? What do spiders and insects have in common?
6. Give students a scientific journal article to review. Have them comment on experimental design, methods of investigation, results, and whether they agree or disagree with the author's conclusions.
7. Have students measure objects or natural phenomena, discover trends within their measurements, and note sources of error. For example, students could collect and measure the size and weight of acorns or grasshoppers, comparing those from one locality to another. Is there a genetic basis for the variation seen? For

acorns, is there any relationship between weight of the acorn and the rate of germination?

8. Have students study a local ecosystem, such as a pond or field, investigating the kinds of plants and animals there, the interactions between them, and the physical factors that affect them. Compare the plants next to the sidewalk with plants two meters from the sidewalk, or the kinds of animals that feed on a plant at noon versus those that feed at dusk.

9. Instead of explaining a concept to students and then having them conduct a laboratory that simply reinforces the idea, allow them to conduct the laboratory first with a minimum of introduction (e.g., how to use equipment properly). Follow this with a discussion of class results, the development of the concept, and an opportunity to conduct further studies.

10. Present students with a real environmental issue in your community concerning land use or energy and water conservation. Let them investigate the problem and suggest possible solutions to it. (adapted from Uno, 1990)

EXAMPLE OF A LESSON USING INQUIRY

Although there are many ways to teach inquiry, consider the following example of an inquiry activity about leaf anatomy (see Uno, 1990).

Inquiry step: Begin teaching a concept by showing students some natural phenomenon.
Sample Activity: Have students observe and sketch a cross-section of a privet leaf.

Inquiry step: Ask students to observe the phenomenon and then speculate what caused it to happen or suggest its significance.
Sample Activity: Students draw representative tissue samples and notice gaps between spongy parenchyma cells. Ask: Are gaps formed in slide preparation (are they tears in leaf tissue) or are the gaps real and filled with water or gas? Could there be a vacuum between the cells?

Inquiry step: Choose one question and develop a hypothesis, prediction, or speculation based on the observations.
Sample Activity: Students predict that the gaps are real and filled with liquid or gas.

Inquiry step: Design an investigation to test the hypothesis (or prediction or speculation).
Sample Activity: Squeeze the leaf or heat the leaf and observe what comes out.

Inquiry step: Allow students to conduct the investigation to test the hypothesis, or provide them with information about such a test.
Sample Activity: If students can't decide on a procedure to test their prediction, suggest that an intact privet leaf be placed in hot water--when this is done, tiny bubbles form, but only on the bottom of the leaf.

Inquiry step: Analyze and discuss the data. Allow students to draw conclusions about the hypothesis or prediction and the nature of the phenomenon.
Sample Activity: Students discuss ideas and suggest that the gaps in the leaf cross-section are real and filled with gas because bubbles came from the heated leaf.

Inquiry step: Apply newly gained knowledge to new situations.
Sample Activity: The observations also suggest that there are holes, located mainly in the leaf bottom, through which gases can pass, but not on the top of the leaf. This leads to discussion on diffusion and photosynthesis and should be linked to discussion of leaf anatomy.

HOW YOU CAN CREATE INQUIRY ACTIVITIES

You might want to review the section on "An Instructional Model" in Chapter 5 which relates directly to inquiry activities.

1. **Identify the main idea/concept** that you want your students to "discover" or investigate. Focus on processes, form and function, and cause and effects. Focus on understanding and not terms. Limit the scope of your concept to study.
2. **Look for a pattern in nature, a misconception students have, or some observable natural phenomenon** that is related to that main idea/concept. You must understand the idea/concept yourself first before you can develop inquiry activities. Where did *you* have difficulty understanding the subject? Students will probably have the same difficulty as you, so how can you help them understand? Develop an activity mimicking the thought processes you went through as *you came to* understand a subject.
3. **Provide students with some background information** that lays the groundwork for an investigation but does not reveal the concept.
4. Ask a question or **have students conduct a specific short activity that leads them to discover part of the whole story**--to discover the pattern, to challenge the misconception, or to begin study of the cause of the natural phenomenon. This might include making careful observations of the phenomenon and speculating what is happening. (Give only enough directions or information so that students can conduct the activity and so they have a general idea why they are doing what they are doing. However, don't give them the answer to the story.) Let students "play" with the lab materials and get them to ask questions themselves. These questions may lead to the discovery of the concept on their own.
5. If students don't come up with a question themselves, supply additional information or **direct students to conduct another activity(ies) that leads to the main point** of the investigation or reveals more of the story.
6. **Allow students to review** what has been investigated and to tie the story together.
7. **Encourage students to go beyond what they have just learned**--provide them with an opportunity to apply their knowledge in the study of a related question of their own choosing or an experiment of their own design.

Review the following two examples of developing inquiry-oriented activities.

An Example of the Development of an Inquiry Activity: The Donner Party.

I needed a lab on human physiology. I happened to be reading about the Donner Party in an article from *Discover* where they listed the name, age, and gender of the people in the original group that left the Midwest and began their trek through the mountains of California. In the activity based on this article, I asked students to make some preliminary observations of the Donner data. Students were given a little hint (prompt, clue) if they couldn't figure out a way to look at the data which, when analyzed, clearly shows a trend that many survivors were young women. This leads to a discussion as to why this might be so, and then to a discussion as to the evolutionary significance of the differences in the physiology of males and females. A follow-up activity is about competitive endurance races, such as marathons, and what it requires to participate in one.

An Example of an Inquiry Activity: Cell Cycle

Our introductory biology class needed a more "minds-on" activity on the cell cycle. We still use a static prepared slide of *Allium* root tips, however, students are asked to determine what is the number of cells in the different phases of mitosis and interphase and then to use this number to estimate the length of time each of the phases takes. Because you find a disproportionate number of cells in interphase, students should be able to deduce that this phase lasts the longest in the cell cycle. Likewise, because there are so few cells in any other phase, we should speculate that these phases last only a very limited time and make up a small part of the overall process. Indeed, in onion root tips, while the cell cycle lasts approximately 20 hours, interphase takes up about 19 of those 20 hours. We then discuss the significance of the length of time spent in interphase as opposed to the other phases.

AN INDEPENDENT INVESTIGATION

The following is a handout that is given to introductory botany students at the University of Oklahoma for a semester-long independent project on plant growth and development. This investigation can replace the lowest midterm for any student. Students are asked to turn in a one-page proposal describing exactly what they intend to do. This proposal must be approved before students can obtain materials for their project.

Background

How can you tell if your houseplants need fertilizer? How well would your plants grow if you added *twice* the recommended amount of fertilizer to those growing in your house or in your garden? What plants are the birds eating in your backyard, and are they eating seeds or fruits? How hot does the soil get in the sun next to a tree compared to the soil in the shade, and how does this affect root growth or germination of seeds dispersed there? These are questions that you could ask every day about phenomena you see in the world around you. But how might you answer these questions? The independent investigation is your opportunity to study some small part of your natural world and to answer one of your own questions.

There are four main steps to your project:
1) select and outline a research problem.
2) design an investigation.
3) conduct the investigation.
4) write the project report.

Your investigation can be either an experiment or an observational study. In an experiment you will answer a question while using a setup with a control and variable component. For an experiment, you will manipulate part of the environment you are studying. In an observational study you will not change the conditions of the environment nor create controlled or variable situations. For instance, if you observe the kind and number of individual insects that visit a particular species of plant in a field near your house, you are doing an observational study. However, you are doing an experiment if you remove petals from some flowers and not from others of the same species to determine if insects are attracted to the flowers by their petals.

Either kind of study, observational or experimental, is satisfactory for this project. Whichever you choose, there are several skills you need to develop and use. The first skill is to formulate a research problem that you can answer based on your observations of the world. You are not expected to win a Nobel prize with your work. It is important, however, that the project be well-designed and conducted properly and that you choose a project that is of interest to you. Once you have an idea for a research problem you would like to study, decide on the method of investigation. You must be able to complete your project with limited materials and time. Your proposal to me will discuss in detail what you are going to study and exactly how you are going to set up your investigation. Set up your study and then begin collecting data systematically and thoroughly. The data you collect will be processed, interpreted, and then incorporated into a write-up of the results of your investigation. The final skill involved is the writing of the report.

Selecting and Outlining a Research Problem

First, choose an area of interest. Do you like to work indoors or outdoors? Do you like ecology, physiology, or cell biology? Do you like to work with flowers or with leaves? Next, observe and ask questions about a situation related to your area of interest. Select one question and form your research problem based on this question. A good research problem is simple, specific, and feasible in regard to your time and materials available. The entire project will be based on your observations.

There is an infinite number of projects from which you could choose. Consider plants and the soils in your community. Do all kinds of soil absorb rainfall at the same rate? Do all soils hold the same amount of water? Is the amount of water that can be held related to any particular characteristic of the soil? Does soil type make any difference in plant growth? What happens to the size of individual plants if they are crowded in a pot with limited space? All these questions can lead to different independent investigations. See the end of this handout for additional ideas.

Research Questions

Consider the following research questions. Some of them are workable, some of them are not.

Question 1: What kinds of seeds are found in the soil near the canopy of maple trees--are only maple seeds found here, and do you find more seeds the closer you get to the trunk of each tree? Either question is acceptable--both are simple, specific, and can be completed with your background, materials, and time. The questions, however, must be more clearly outlined.

Question 2: What will happen if I play soothing music versus rock-and-roll to my plants--will plants grown in rock-and-roll music be as healthy as plants grown in soothing music? This question is unacceptable. All conditions in a project must be the same except for that one being tested. This means that plants exposed to the different kinds of music must be kept in identical, but separate, rooms with identical amounts of sunlight, identical temperatures, identical humidity, and cared for in an identical manner. This is an impossible task. If you kept plants in the same room and then moved them into other rooms just to play music to them, you create other variables that destroy the precision of the experiment (moving the plants, leaving plants in the sun for different lengths of time, etc.)

Question 3: How do different amounts of fertilizer affect the growth of corn plants--would the plants with the most fertilizer given to them be the largest? This is acceptable as long as the experiment is set up properly. Include a pot with no fertilizer given to the plants to see if fertilizer has any effects at all on plants.

Designing Your Investigation

You will turn in a proposal for your investigation. Your proposal should focus on what you intend to study and how you will go about it. It should begin with an *Introduction* that includes the general problem, background information, and question you are attempting to answer. Following this should be a *Methods* section with a detailed outline of the materials and equipment needed to complete your project. In this section, you should also include a description of each of the methods that you intend to use. Use the following checklist to evaluate your proposal.

INTRODUCTION
What is the specific question you will study?
What is your rationale for choosing the problem? i.e., What first made you think of this idea?
MATERIALS AND METHODS
Where are you going to work?
How are you going to investigate your problem? Give detailed descriptions of your methods and how you are going to set up your study.
What are you going to measure (height, number of leaves, size?) and how often are you going to measure or sample?
Do you have enough samples to allow you to average your results?
What materials and equipment do you need to complete your investigation?
Will the data you are going to collect actually let you answer the question you have asked?
Are your control and variable(s) setups clearly defined?
Does your schedule allow you enough time to complete the project and to write up the report?

Conducting Your Investigation

Keep a notebook with all of your observations and measurements. Make certain that you write everything down--do not think you will remember the information. Date each entry and include other references such as which pot or plant you are observing. You should average your data and graph it for easy interpretation. For instance, measure the height of each plant in one pot, add the heights together and divide this number by the number of plants in the pot. Do the same for each pot, and then plot these results on the same graph. Do this two or three times a week for the entire project. Remember there is a difference between raw data (numbers that you collect throughout the investigation) and processed data (the same numbers totalled and averaged).

Writing The Final Report

There should be four sections to your report: Introduction, Materials and Methods, Results, and Discussion. The *Introduction* and *Materials and Methods* sections should be similar to what you included in the proposal. However, you should include any changes that resulted while conducting the project.

The *Results* section should begin with an overall picture of all the results that you have found and the general trends that have shown up (e.g., birds ate more red berries than blue berries during the morning hours). In this section, you should include your tables and graphs, but not your pages of notes you kept throughout the project (attach these to the end of the report). Avoid analyzing the significance or apparent meaning of the data in this section--leave that for the *Discussion*.

In the final section, the *Discussion*, you should refer back to the data that you present in the *Results* section, but do not repeat the data. How do your results help explain what happened in your study--how do your results help answer your original question (or why they don't help). Avoid making unjustified conclusions--restrict your conclusions to the experiment you completed. Do not try to make broad, all-encompassing generalizations based on your results. For instance, if you find that lettuce seeds germinate at a faster rate in red light than any other color, do not generalize that all kinds of seeds will germinate at the greatest rate in red light. Finally, do not make unjustified speculations, e.g., because the lettuce seeds germinated at a faster rate in the red light, lettuce plants also will grow better in red light than in sunlight.

You may want to use this checklist to help organize your report.

Does your title indicate the content of the report?

Have you clearly stated the problem or question you have studied?

Have all your methods been described concisely and accurately?

Have measurements or observations been made adequately for all variables in your project?

Have you left out all interpretations and conclusions from the results section?

Have all the results related to the research problem been reported in a concise manner?

Have the data been processed in a useful form (graphs or tables) and have you left your raw data out?

Are your graphs, pictures, and tables drawn and labeled clearly and properly?

In your discussion, have all your reported results been interpreted and discussed in relation to your original question?

Have you stated your conclusions based on your results?

Have you pointed out possible errors or biases?

Have you written all of your sections in the most concise manner possible?

Have you checked your spelling and grammar?

Getting Started on the Plant Project

This is **not** a library report. In fact, you don't need to use any text during the project. This is an investigation on some aspect of plant life, and your observations are the most important part of it. You can choose any topic related to botany, but there are some restrictions:

1) Make certain that you can get the equipment or materials to complete your project. We will supply pots, soil, seeds (peas, beans, corn, radish, or sunflower), fertilizer, and a place to grow your plants. You may, however, want to keep your plants at home. You must supply anything "out of the ordinary." Check with us before you buy anything—we may have it.

2) Make certain that you will have time to complete the project. For instance, do not study the life cycle of an oak tree.

3) Creativity will be rewarded, however, it is **no** required. What is important is that you make **many** careful observations while your plants are growing and that you **think** about your results and what they could mean. Measurements are part of your complete set of observations. When selecting a project, do not be too ambitious.

4) You must submit a one-page proposal about your project no later than_____. It should include: a) what you are going to do, b) what materials are needed, c) where you are going to keep your plants, d) a brief schedule of completion, and how you are going to set up the project. The PROJECT IS DUE_____. The report should be 3-5 pages (not including graphs and tables). REMEMBER--A LONG REPORT IS NOT NECESSARILY BETTER THAN A SHORT ONE-- in fact, your grade will be affected negatively if you are not concise.

Important Points to Remember

1) You must grow a MINIMUM of 15 plants (in 3-5 pots).

2) You must measure _at least twice_ a week.

3) You must have the **same number** of plants growing in each pot (3-5 plants per pot).

4) Do **not** fertilize your soil (unless that is your experiment).

5) If you are going to add anything to the soil other than water, use vermiculite.

6) Keep your pots in a warm, brightly-lit place (south-facing window).

7) Water as necessary—test the soil with your finger. If the soil is moist at 1 inch below the surface, then you don't need to add water.
8) Plant seeds no more than 1/2" below the soil surface.
9) In most cases, start with seeds, not whole plants—because you need to be sure that all of your plants are the same age.
10) Start your project as soon as it has been okayed because the plants may die, and then you'll have to start over.

Examples of Independent Projects

You don't have to choose one of these--be creative. Look in your text or look at plants to generate an idea. The best way would be to take a walk outside and look at plants, trying to find anything unusual about the plants, how they are affected by their environment, or how they affect the environment or other organisms. Ask yourself what affects the growth and development of plants. Make observations and ask questions to help you think of a problem to investigate. Do not do a grafting project. Do not do a project growing plants in the light and dark. Do not do a project about talking to your plants or playing music to them.

Some Ideas

How will crowding affect plant growth?
Compare the growth of plants in:
> different types of soils, or light intensities, or colors of light, or amounts of moisture in the soil, or sources of water.

What will happen to plants grown with different kinds and/or concentrations of:
> herbicide or fertilizer?
> individual nutrients such as:
>> nitrogen, phosphorus, or potassium?
> plant hormones such as:
>> auxin, gibberellin, or ethylene?

How will the following affect plant growth:
> cigarette smoke, sugar, salt, caffeine, vitamins, pollutants, soil pH, temperature, acid rain, temperature, or humidity?

Other Questions to Ask About Plant Growth

What happens to the size of the root system if leaves are cut off a plant?
What is the effect of grazing (or clipping) on the growth of a grass plant?
Are there more seedlings of a tree nearby the mother plant or at some distance away from it?
Do larger fruits contain more seeds than smaller ones?
Do larger seeds germinate and grow faster than smaller ones?
Are there more plants of a certain kind in the sun or the shade?
Do all plants of a certain kind and age produce the same size and number of seeds?
How far do seeds of different sizes travel from the mother plant?
What kind or color of seeds or fruits do birds prefer?
Are there more algae or water plants growing in standing or flowing water?
Do certain kinds of insects visit a particular flower, and for how long? What are they doing at the flowers?
How does temperature affect the growth of yeast cells?
How does the presence of one kind of plant affect the growth of another kind of plant?
Do the same kind of microorganisms grow on different substances?
What happens to the growth of a plant if you remove the cotyledons, leaves, or roots of the seedling?

There is an infinite number of possible projects. Use your imagination, but remember to choose a project that asks just one question.

INTERACTING COMPONENTS OF BIOLOGY

Biology is a scientific discipline based on inquiry into the natural world. The discipline of biology can be divided into two parts: (a) biological concepts that have been developed through (b) the process of scientific inquiry. Biological concepts are organized around three key elements: (a) the unifying principles of biology; (b) levels of organization; and (c) the diversity of living systems. These elements are represented by the interacting matrix shown on page 61. All biological knowledge is found in the intersections of these three elemental sides of the figure. For instance, the intersection of (a) *energy, matter, and organization*, (b) *plants,* at the (c) *cellular* level encompasses many questions related to photosynthesis. Or, a scientist may investigate questions related to *patterns and products of change* in *animals* at the *population* level as he or she studies human population genetics. The three interacting sides of the figure reflect one way to organize the vast amount of biological information.

Biological information has been obtained through a systematic study of the natural world. This process of investigation is represented by the three interacting sides of the matrix shown on page 62. One side indicates a scientific method of investigation, a formalized model of the processes of science. Although scientists usually do not follow a scientific method in a rigid manner, each step contributes to a logical process of investigation. The second side of this figure represents different ways that scientists may approach their research problem. In the early stages of investigation, one describes a natural phenomenon and then conducts experiments based on the questions generated during observation. Some scientists may investigate phylogenetic relationships of particular organisms, study the components, regulation, and change involved within a system, or try to develop a model of a natural system. Still other investigators may try to determine the cause of some observed phenomenon, or the relationship between the function of a particular structure and the morphology or anatomy of that structure. The third side of this matrix includes factors that affect and are part of scientific investigations, including such influences as the historical development of a particular subject and the technological advances that might result from answering basic biological questions. Technology is not synonymous with science, although they are closely intertwined. Scientists use technology to discover explanations of the natural world and to communicate this knowledge to others. Technology is important in solving human problems and in adapting the

environment to human needs. The interacting sides of the matrix define science as an inquiry process (adapted from BSCS, 1994).

BIOLOGICAL CONCEPTS

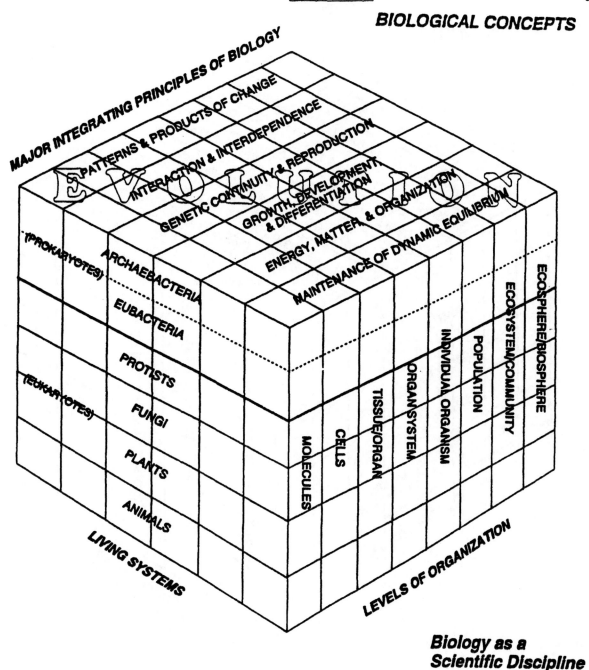

**Biology as a
Scientific Discipline**

SCIENTIFIC INQUIRY

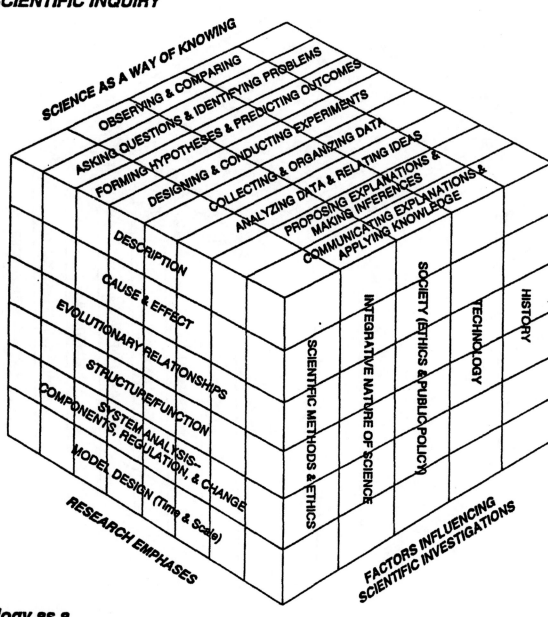

Biology as a
Scientific Discipline

INQUIRY PROCESS SKILLS

By the end of class, biology students should be able to:	
Formulate questions	• Generate a number of possible questions and use what is known about a topic to plan an investigation. • Select a question that can be explored through scientific inquiry. • Construct a hypothesis–a tentative and testable statement about what is likely to be true based on reasoning. • Predict the events that would be likely to support the hypothesis.
Plan experiments	• Identify the independent variable(s) in an experiment and explain how it will be observed and measured. • Plan to keep other variables constant and suggest appropriate controls for the experiment. • Identify the dependent variable(s) in an experiment and explain how it will be observed. • Determine whether qualitative or quantitative observations will be used as data. • Plan to avoid bias through repeated trials and random sampling. • Select a sequence for the experimental procedure that is appropriate to the specific task or problem being studied. • Select and use appropriate safety procedures.
Make systematic observations	• Select and use qualitative/quantitative observation techniques that are appropriate to the experiment such as measuring, describing, matching, or finding differences. • Select and use measuring instruments and units that are appropriate to the experiment and recognize the limitations of instruments used. • Demonstrate responsible work habits that include: orderliness, appropriate care of equipment, and avoidance of waste. • Use interpolation, extrapolation, and estimation to extend the accuracy or range of measurements while recognizing the limitations of such processes. • Have and follow a system or a plan to collect information without having to repeat observations. • Demonstrate the use of common laboratory equipment and procedures used in data collection such as: measurement instruments, compound light microscope/slides/stains, chemical indicators, separation techniques, aseptic techniques, dichotomous keys, dissection of plant and animal specimens, computer software and hardware.

Organize and interpret data	• Select patterns of organization for data that are appropriate to the question being addressed. • Organize data by developing tables, charts, graphs, matrices, summaries, diagrams, or photographs to show patterns. • Use mathematical equations and operations to calculate derived quantities where appropriate. • Determine apparent patterns or relationships among variables through examination of data. • Infer by constructing tentative explanations and cause and effect relationships that are based on data. • Identify and discuss anomalous results and explain variations in results. • Identify sources of experimental error.
Draw conclusions	• Evaluate the validity of hypotheses/predictions based on the inferences drawn from actual data gathered in an experiment. • Modify hypotheses when necessary. • Relate an experiment to other experiments. • Relate an experiment to models and theories. • Evaluate one's own inquiry process and suggest further investigations.
Communicate	• Prepare a written report of the experiment that includes: abstract, introduction, materials and methods, results, discussion, and conclusions. • Use oral presentations, graphic presentations, and telecommunications to share the results of research with others.
Use scientific inquiry processes	• Demonstrate the ability to integrate the skills above by planning and carrying out an extended laboratory or field investigation involving a range of exploratory techniques.

(Adapted from Tulloch, et al, 1994)

How might you incorporate more inquiry instruction into your course? What activities will provide your students with the opportunity to conduct open-ended investigations? Take an activity that you currently use and convert it into one that is more inquiry-oriented. What are the first steps that you would take?

CHAPTER VII. CRITICAL THINKING SKILLS

A poll in the late 1980's showed that 52% of Americans believe our schools do an adequate job teaching basic facts and skills, but only 39% were satisfied with the results in teaching students to think and reason (Magnan, 1990). Students who have recently entered a university from high school rely on the ability to memorize and recall facts during college courses but cannot formulate new questions, generate ideas and principles from information, restate a given scientific problem in a new context, or apply knowledge to a new problem (Schlenker and Perry, 1986). These studies suggest that college-level students often lack the ability to think critically. Critical thinking is an extensive concept, process, and ability that we develop throughout our lives, and that must be taught systematically (Alverno College, 1994a).

How do we convince students that improving their thinking skills is necessary? First, show how thinking and learning are connected. Emphasize from the beginning that your course has two complementary goals: to promote knowledge of the subject and to develop thinking skills. Assess thinking as well as content knowledge. If we are serious about encouraging our students to think more effectively, we must ask them to demonstrate both knowledge of content and mastery of thinking skills.

How do we teach our students the thinking skills they need? Model your own thinking processes for the students. We can occasionally work aloud through a problem or issue that is new to us. This will give students a more realistic picture of the mental efforts we must put forth when we approach novel problems or materials. If we take time to teach thinking skills, how will we cover all of the content? It may help us resolve this conflict if we view the teaching of thinking skills as an exchange rather than as "giving up" content. We will be trading a small amount of course content for skills that will foster a deeper understanding of the discipline and that will allow our students to continue learning long after they have left our classrooms.

CRITICAL THINKING SKILLS

In planning a course that fosters critical thinking, you need to consider: What thinking abilities will my students develop, how will they practice and demonstrate these abilities, and what type of assessment best measures their growth? To help students reason better, we first need to know what these thinking skills are. Thinking processes are a relatively complex group of skills including:

questioning--asking significant questions about natural phenomena;

concept forming--organizing information and labeling that information with a word or words;

principle forming--recognizing relationships between or among concepts and examining the big picture;

comprehending--generating meaning by relating what is known to what is unknown, synthesizing ideas, and identifying alternative interpretations of the data and observations;

problem-solving--analyzing and solving a puzzling situation;

decision-making--being able to select from among alternatives, making sound judgments, being open to contradictory ideas, questioning conclusions and sources of facts, and identifying critical assumptions;

researching--conducting scientific inquiry, examining for multiple causes and effects, gathering complete information, and evaluating experimental design;

composing--developing a product which may be written, visual, mechanical, or artistic, and being creative;

communicating--talking with other people and articulating ideas and information;

evaluating--assessing oneself and others, understanding biases and values, and looking for hidden assumptions;

applying--being able to solve new problems through application of biological concepts;

predicting--making predictions and supporting these with sound arguments; and

analyzing--interpreting experimental data and drawing valid conclusions. (adapted from Marzano, et al., 1988; Allen and Stroup, 1993; Alverno College, 1994b)

CRITICAL THINKING APPROACH

In a course that emphasizes and promotes critical thinking:

1. students are active investigators, not passive listeners.
2. students make interpretations of experiments, graphs, equations, and data.
3. there is a question-oriented discussion. New questions follow discussion.
4. teachers ask open-ended questions.
5. the instructor does not immediately "give the answer" to questions asked.
6. experiments are used to discover and illustrate concepts and main points. Students participate in collection and analysis of data.
7. a question introduces each new topic or concept, followed by students making observations; identifying assumptions; and looking for ways to retest conclusions and interpretations.
8. activities are student-oriented.
9. real world examples are used in class that relate to student experiences.
10. the instructor works "among" the students and does not always remain in front of the class.
11. the instructor focuses on higher-order thinking skills.
12. the instructor allots time for each concept. (A critical thinking approach will take more time than lecturing to present concepts.)
13. the textbook is a reference, not the main source of information. Class is not terminology-oriented. (If students will not use a term again in the course, or their lives, then scrap the term.) (adapted from Allen and Stroup, 1993)

BUILDING CRITICAL THINKING INTO YOUR COURSE

The following may help improve critical thinking in your students:

1. **Ask for evaluation of ideas and statements--** Use questions that require students to apply standards in order to make value judgments. The key questions require "why" and "how" responses. Require students to elaborate on ideas expressed.
2. **Ask for inferences--**Set up specific situations to work with deduction and induction. Get students to apply ideas, concepts, rules, or principles to a particular case. Give them a series of examples and have them form generalizations.
3. **Ask for causes and effects--**Have students explore relationships between biological phenomena and their causes. (What causes the bare zone to form under the maple tree?) Ask students to develop a diagrammatic representation (model) showing the relationship among concepts. Have students create a short demonstration of the problem as it actually appears in a real setting.
4. **Ask for comparisons and examples--** Comparisons result from an ability to perceive similarities and differences. (What are the main differences between a mussel and a clam?) Challenge your students to establish links between ideas, concepts, or observations.
5. **Ask for solutions--**Problem-solving provides great opportunities to use knowledge, sometimes creatively. (How would you prevent the spread of the Ebola virus?) Have students identify the specific strategies used in solving a problem and labeling those strategies (metacognition)--how do they know what they know? Seek multiple, alternative, answers to questions asked in discussions and on paper.
6. **Present relevant examples--**Make examples accurate, clear, interesting, and ones that your students can understand. Ask students to provide additional examples, analogies, and to create concept maps of the concept.
7. **Create tension around ideas--**Write a guiding question that defines a problem on a transparency or handout and ask students to provide initial answers. Require a three-minute "free write" on the issue or problem and use student writing to begin a discussion. Ask

students to free-write conclusions that reconcile what they have thought and what they have heard (post-writing). Ask students in groups of two or three to develop solutions to the problem.

8. **Scan the factual base**—Ask students to search the text for factual evidence that helps clarify the concepts of a problem. Prepare a "fact list" from the text or other sources that reflects the complexity of the issue at hand. Prepare a case study, role-playing situation, or simulation that requires evaluation of essential facts.

9. **Help your students write**—Give students a scientific journal article and ask them to rewrite the article for a general audience. Ask them to rewrite a section for their parents or friends to read.

10. **Help your students read**--Use a review to preview and work with the words (terminology). To help students read scientific literature, you can provide the following questions to them. What question was the scientist investigating? What is the significance of the question? How does this work relate to previous work and major ideas in the discipline? What scientific apparatus and methods did the scientist use? Are they appropriate for this investigation? What data did the investigator collect? How did the investigator analyze and interpret the data? Do you agree with the analysis and interpretation? Were the investigator's ideas accepted by other scientists?

11. **Other suggestions**--Wave a red flag or toss students a red herring. Challenge students to explore; push them to communicate their ideas. Guide them through stages of investigation. Emphasize through practice the three steps: (1) Apply knowledge to the problem, (2) decide what other knowledge is necessary, and (3) figure out how to obtain this knowledge. Have students work together to help them learn how to monitor the effectiveness of their own thinking processes so that they are no longer dependent solely on you for feedback. Give many practice opportunities.

Use the list at the end of this chapter to help you identify appropriate thinking skills for your students to develop. Whatever thinking skills you emphasize, it is critical to give students many opportunities to practice applying those skills to a diversity of course-related issues and problems. Set expectations that all students can and will improve their thinking. (adapted from Martin, 1989; Neff and Weimer, 1989; Magnan 1990; Alverno College, 1994a; NRC, 1995)

THINKING SKILLS

By the end of your course, biology students should be able to:	
Acquire information	• Locate and use information regarding a problem from a diversity of sources including: books, magazines, journals, talks, interviews, audio tapes, videotapes, films, laser disks, CD-ROM, electronic data bases, telecommunication networks, and laboratory experiences. • Interpret and use information regarding a problem that is expressed in a variety of forms including: written, spoken, graphic, and concrete manipulation of objects. • Cross-check information in alternate sources. • Recognize objective versus opinionated evidence. • Break problems or questions into logical parts. • Extract biases or inappropriate arguments. • Understand the purpose of problem or task.
Process information	• Develop concepts from particular examples of objects or events. • Explain concepts by linking them to other related concepts. • Classify by arranging objects or events into groups according to some system and explain the system used to explain groups. • Arrange information in an organized manner. • Search for relationships, similarities, and differences among concepts. • Relate biological knowledge to other disciplines and its societal context. • Identify patterns in information (pattern recognition). • Perform appropriate mathematical and statistical analyses. • Structure information appropriately (graphs, flow charts, tables, models, concept mapping)
Test understanding	• Assess ideas and understandings using the explanations or suggestions of peers or others. • Examine the premises, assumptions, and beliefs involved in one's own ideas. • Evaluate investigations conducted by others, distinguishing between valid and invalid claims about the explanations of natural phenomena. • Express information in one's own language (paraphrasing, making analogies). • Distinguish among types of relationships, e.g., causal (cause and effect); correlative (correlations); hierarchical; synergistic (additive).

Communicate Information	• Communicate information in a variety of forms including: writing, speaking, graphic presentations, and telecommunication. • Communicate information in a variety of situations such as: written reports, essays, lab reports, letters, debates, discussions, oral reports, interviews, film making, and collaborative telecommunication. • Engage in planning, drafting, revising, editing, and sharing of communication.
Use Interpersonal skills	• Recognize the advantages of sharing in the process of learning/working and encourage the contributions of others. • Weigh conflicting opinions and ideas and search for conflict resolution through consensus or compromise. • Assume a position of responsibility within the group and contribute fairly to the work of the group. • Work with the group to assess the effectiveness of the group process.
Apply information	• Apply concepts and knowledge to new situations and to the analysis of real-world problems and issues. • Draw (state) implications from conclusions. • Work with professionals in the community.
Argue logically	• Select (identify) relevant evidence to support conclusions and reject irrelevant data. • Present an internally consistent argument to support or refute interpretations or conclusions.
Synthesize information	• Mentally manipulate three-dimensional models and extrapolate from 2D to 3D. • Relate two or more ideas/pieces of information.
Solve Problems	• Predict effects from causes, propose possible causes from effects. • Check for reasonableness of selected approaches and conclusions (e.g., order of magnitude). • Solve complex biological problems, drawing on concepts from several areas; designing, conducting, and communicating experiments that meet standards for publication.

(adapted from Alverno College, 1985; Tulloch, et al, 1994)

Getting your students to think critically should be one of the most important objectives for you and your course. How will you get your students to think about science and biology? What do you consider to be the most important thinking skills that a student should possess?

72

CHAPTER VIII. THE TASK OF ASSESSING YOUR STUDENTS

Why is this chapter here and not later? It is important for you to organize your course around your assessment plan instead of thinking about assessing your students *after* you have thought about content and taught a section of your course. Design your program by asking: (1) What are the objectives of the program for me and my students? (2) What learning strategies (labs, activities, etc.) will help my students reach these objectives? (3) How will I know my students and I have achieved these objectives? This final question is what assessment is all about.

Unfortunately, assessing students can be one of the most distasteful parts of teaching, especially when you get to know students--how can you fail the student who comes in for help all of the time and participates in all the classes? How can you fairly grade the essay exam of the student who has just flipped you off? As you develop your own course, continually remind yourself about your goals and how to measure if your students have reached them. The major consideration in program design should be the students--how are you going to help them **learn**? Students should be able to investigate a biological question using the processes of scientific investigation and to understand and explain *major* biological concepts.

Focusing on investigative skills, critical thinking skills, and the organizational power of the unifying principles (see end of chapter) should address the complaint registered by many students that they have studied the same factual knowledge--e.g., phyla of animals--in every biology class they have taken. By selecting problems for investigation, students can discover biological information that is unfamiliar to them while using methods that can be used in all their science courses and throughout their lives.

Components of a biology program should be appropriate to the intellectual development of the students. Recognize the needs and interests of young adults who will not be scientists nor enter health-related professions but who make daily decisions related to biology, health, and other science-related issues.

WHAT ARE YOUR OBJECTIVES?

Before you think about assessing the performance of your students, you need to think about what you want your students to know, value, and be able to do by the end of your course. *Knowing* has to do with content; *valuing* has to do with attitudes toward science and biology; and *being able to do* refers to skills and thinking processes necessary to conduct investigations. (Check the lists at the end of this chapter and of chapters 6 and 7 to help you select what knowledge, skills, and attitudes you want your students to possess when they leave your class.)

As you begin organizing your course, you need to identify your course objectives. Objectives are descriptions of intended outcomes--the standards--we would like our students to achieve or surpass. Objectives describe the important outcomes to be accomplished in your course that are answered by the question, "What is worth learning?" Useful objectives answer these three questions: (1) What should the learner be able to know, value, and do (performance)?; (2) Under what conditions should the learner be able to demonstrate his/her performance (conditions)?; and (3) How well must it be done (criteria for assessment)? Your assessment, then, should measure how well your students have met the criteria for each performance under a certain set of conditions. Here are a few broad objectives for you to consider. (See also Chapter 12.)

7. **Students should experience science as a process.** This means that your course should include a truly investigative experience for all students. This experience may be a set of open-ended laboratory investigations in which students can design their own experiments, independent research projects, or inquiry-oriented activities that emphasize the qualitative and quantitative aspects of biology. Note: *cookbook laboratories in which students obtain results that simply confirm what they already know are undesirable!*

2. **Focus on a limited number of major biological concepts** that are linked by the unifying principles of biology (see later in this chapter). Get your students to **understand** basic information and the "big picture" before the details--otherwise they just memorize.

3. **Include a variety of instructional strategies and appropriate assessment procedures** that challenge students' higher-order thinking and reasoning skills (see Chapter 7). This may

require writing (and grading) essays and short answers!

4. **Provide opportunities for student discussion, explanation, and linkage** of biological principles and concepts. Short writing activities can also be used as well as traditional verbal discussions.

5. **Present information that is relevant to the personal lives of students,** and provide opportunities for students to apply this knowledge in the resolution of authentic problems. Find innovative ways to tie news stories to classroom subjects.

6. **Assess the ability of students to use the processes of science as they solve problems.** Choose local land use, environmental, or conservation problems or issues that can be investigated and discussed, and for which students can plan solutions.

WORDS USED TO DRAFT OBJECTIVES

Use the words in bold to help write objectives for your students. (These words can also be used to develop test questions for your students.) Numbers relate to different types of questions that require increasing levels of critical thinking by your students. (You might refer to Bloom's taxonomy of educational objectives, Bloom, 1975). Notice relationships to possible test questions based on these levels later in the chapter.

1. **Knowledge**: Students should be able to recall words, facts, dates, classifications, principles, and theories. **List; name; identify; show; define; recognize; or recall.**

2. **Comprehension**: Students should be able to remember knowledge or principles in order to explain or solve a problem. **Explain; put into your own words; interpret; describe; compare; differentiate; or demonstrate.**

3. **Application**: Students should be able to apply knowledge or principles in order to solve a problem. **Solve; calculate; use; manipulate; apply; state; classify; modify; or put into practice.**

4. **Analysis**: Students should be able to identify the elements, relationships, and organizational principles of a situation. **Analyze; organize; deduce; or choose.**

5. **Synthesis**: Students should be able to accomplish a personal task after devising a plan of action. **Design; support; write; report; discuss; or plan.**

6. **Evaluation**: Students should be able to make a critical judgment based on internal and external criteria. **Evaluate; judge; defend; criticize; or justify.** (adapted from Pregent, 1994)

INTERACTING FACTORS OF TEACHING AND LEARNING ABOUT BIOLOGY

What should students know, value, and be able to do by the time they have successfully completed your biology program? One can think about a contemporary biology program as a set of interacting matrices, with many factors affecting the learning and teaching of biology forming the sides of each matrix. The set of interacting sides of the matrix on page 75 defines how students learn about and how instructors teach biology. The three sides summarize the curriculum themes that may be used to organize a class, the assessment instruments, and instructional strategies used to teach the class.

The matrix on page 76 illustrates some of the desirable outcomes for students completing a contemporary biology program. Knowledge is not limited to biological content; knowledge also should include a working understanding of how scientific investigations are conducted and how all the facts of biology are united by unifying principles. Many of the desired values are incorporated in the characterization of a biologically literate individual and the information he or she should possess. Among these values are openness, curiosity, and respect for logic. Higher-order reasoning is also desirable. This trait includes the ability to evaluate critically a problem for possible solutions or a scientific statement for possible biases, incorrect assumptions, or invalid data collection or analysis. There are many interdependent curriculum components to consider for use in a contemporary biology program. Although it is highly unlikely any one program would include all curriculum components illustrated, the ability of students to attain desirable outcomes depends on a meaningful and varied classroom experience (adapted from BSCS 1994).

CURRICULUM COMPONENTS

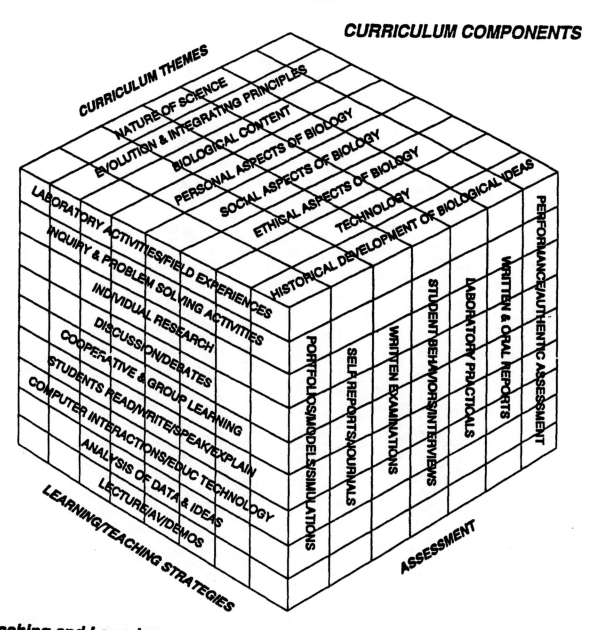

**Teaching and Learning
About Biology**

STUDENT OUTCOMES

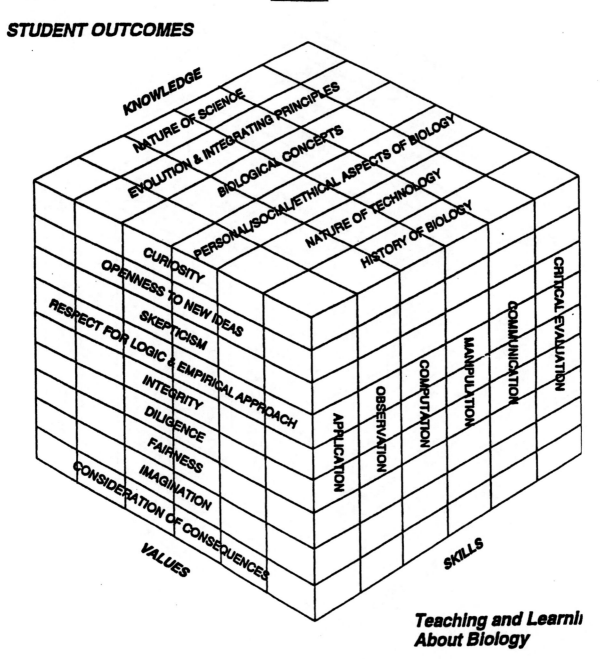

Teaching and Learni
About Biology

WHAT YOUR STUDENTS SHOULD KNOW: BIOLOGICAL KNOWLEDGE ORGANIZED BY UNIFYING PRINCIPLES

Many biology textbooks and courses are elaborate and colorful descriptions of thousands of biological facts; others emphasize major concepts or unifying principles of the discipline to organize biological information. Unifying principles should help students and instructors organize the biological content of a course. For instance, avoid a simple listing of definitions and functions of different cell parts, tissues of an organ, or growth and development hormones. Instead, use unifying principles to help students see the unity in structure and function within the diverse organisms on Earth. For example, when *Evolution: Patterns and Products of Change* is used as a unifying principle of biology, cell parts, tissues, and hormones may be seen as adaptations that have contributed to an organism's successful reproduction and to a species' reproductive success through evolutionary history. When teaching about cells (or tissues or hormones), students also can be shown how individual cell parts contribute to the organization of the whole by referring to the ideas set forth in the unifying principle of *Energy, Matter, and Organization*.

These unifying principles represent a comprehensive foundation for the biological sciences. Individual programs may emphasize a molecular, organismic, or ecological level of organization; they may give greater emphasis to inquiry or societal problems, but the unifying principles should provide the foundation for the biological knowledge in all contemporary biology programs. The principles help students make sense of the myriad biological facts and help explain living systems. The unifying principles of biology can be used as overarching constructs to organize whatever content *is* emphasized in a course (adapted from BSCS, 1994)

THE UNIFYING PRINCIPLES OF BIOLOGY

I. Evolution
Patterns of Change: *Living Systems Change Through Time*
- Forces of Evolutionary Change
- Patterns of Evolution, and Extinction
- Conservation Biology

Products of Change: *Evolution Has Produced Diverse Living Systems on Earth*
- Origin of Life
- Specialization and Adaptation
- Species and Speciation, and Biodiversity
- Phylogenetic Classification

II. Interaction and Interdependence
Living Systems Interact with Their Environment and Are Interdependent with Other Systems
- Environmental Factors
- Population Ecology
- Community Structure
- Ecosystems and the Biosphere

III. Genetic Continuity and Reproduction
Living Systems Are Related to Other Generations by Genetic Material Passed on Through Reproduction
- The Gene and Gene Action
- DNA (The Genetic Material)
- Reproduction and Patterns of Inheritance
- Molecular Genetics

IV. Growth, Development, and Differentiation
Living Systems Grow, Develop, and Differentiate During Their Lifetimes Based on a Genetic Plan and Influenced by the Environment
- Patterns of Growth
- Patterns of Development
- Differentiation
- Form and Function

V. Energy, Matter, and Organization
Living Systems Require Energy and Matter to Maintain Their Complex Organization
- Molecular Structure
- Hierarchy of Organization
- Matter, Energy, and Metabolism

VI. Maintenance of a Dynamic Equilibrium
Living Systems Maintain a Relatively Stable Internal Environment
- Detection of Environmental Stimuli
- Behavior and Movement
- Homeostasis
- Health and Disease

WHAT YOUR STUDENTS SHOULD VALUE: ATTITUDES AND HABITS OF MIND

By the end of your class, biology students will:	
Have an appreciation for life	• Value the unity, diversity, complexity, and interdependence of life. • Value the natural world as an essential resource for fulfilling physical and aesthetic human needs.
Have respect for life	• Respect each individual life. • Respect each present form of life as the only source for the continuation of that form.
Gain pleasure from understanding	• Want to know more about the natural world. • Enjoy working with biological materials and scientific techniques. • Enjoy meaningful learning as a continual process that involves establishing relationships between prior knowledge and new information. • Recognize that learning comes both from receiving and giving by sharing what is known with others.
Value knowledge as having beneficial applications	• Apply learning to their daily lives, to real life problems, and to meeting societal needs. • Value the benefits that technological advances based on scientific knowledge may have for humans. • Express concern for the potential consequences of technological change on the present and the future. • Recognize that the investment of time and resources in the search for knowledge is a worthy goal.
Respect science as a way of knowing	• Recognize that biological knowledge is: empirical (gained from observation), tentative (subject to change), historical (builds on knowledge from past), public (available to others), replicable (subject to verification by others). • Recognize that scientific knowledge should be understood in its historical, social, technological, and political context.

Respect one's own abilities	• Express confidence in one's ability to: pursue study of the natural world, pursue scientific inquiry and decision-making, work cooperatively with others, monitor, reflect on, and evaluate one's own understandings and actions. Use a diversity of modes of thinking and expression.
Respect others	• Respect the rights, feelings, beliefs, values, levels of knowledge, contributions, and concerns for others. • Value the use of investigative procedures that limit the risks to self, others, and the living and non-living environment. • Appreciate the value of a diversity of perspectives in addressing problems and issues.
Accept responsibility	• Work to make maximum use of one's own educational opportunities through active involvement in the learning process. • Recognize and accept individual responsibility for human activities and their impact on the local and global environment. • Be active in one's own long-range educational program and the educational program in the classroom. • Consider self as an active partner in creating a supportive learning climate in which all students can be successful. • Become informed about the objectives, learning outcomes, and performance standards related to the classroom.
Show skepticism	• Look for evidence or proof to support explanations or solutions to problems. • Seek alternative ways of explaining data. • Use logical reasoning and systematic investigation as a means of testing and weighing the validity of ideas.
Have an open mind	• Exhibit willingness to change ideas when new and additional information is available. • Accept ambiguity or tentative ideas as starting points for increasing understanding of the natural world. • Value original insights, unconventional ways of thinking, and careful inferences as sources of potential ideas.
Be persistent	• Exhibit self-direction and motivation in completion of both group and independent tasks.
Reflect	• Value rethinking, revising, and evaluating of one's own understanding of scientific concepts and processes for accuracy and effectiveness.
Value honesty	• Value truthful reporting of methods and findings.

(Adapted from Tulloch, et al, 1994)

WHAT YOUR STUDENTS SHOULD BE ABLE TO DO: DECISION-MAKING SKILLS

By the end of your class, biology students will be able to:	
Identify a problem	• Identify an issue and state the issue in a form that requires a decision or solution.
Identify dimensions of the problem	• Identify scientific, political, ethical, cultural, and technological dimensions of the issue.
Gather information about dimensions of the problem	• Use a diversity of resources to gather information about the dimensions of the issue. • Select information that is relevant to the issue and recognize the biases and errors of fact in the information.
Generate a list of alternative solutions	• Develop a list of alternative solutions that address all dimensions of the issue.
Evaluate each solution	• Evaluate each proposed solution in light of its scientific, technological, political, ethical, and cultural impact.
Select solution(s)	• Weigh the consequences of and values associated with alternative solutions. • Explain reasons for selecting solution(s). • Recognize when an incomplete knowledge base may result in uncertainty or ambiguity. • Evaluate decision-making processes along the way and after a conclusion is reached. • Justify and defend solution selected through written argumentation, discussion, and debate.
Use decision-making processes	• Demonstrate the ability to integrate the skills above by selecting an issue of personal, community, national, or global significance to them and using the decision-making processes above to seek effective solutions.

ASSESSMENT STRATEGIES

Assessment should outline for students the expectations for learning science. Assessment instruments (tests, projects, etc.) are most valuable when they focus on higher-order thinking skills, understanding and using biological knowledge, and the demonstration of competence in a setting that is meaningful to students. Methods of assessment should measure more complex types of learning than those measured by objective examinations alone and should emphasize what students can do with the knowledge they possess—how to apply their knowledge to novel situations. The assessment of diverse students in a classroom may be addressed by using a variety of methods, including nontraditional assessment instruments such as portfolios and student productions of simulations and models (see end of chapter).

Assessment should be an ongoing process that begins by determining the information and skills students bring to the class and continues with documentation of their progress throughout the course. Consider giving students the opportunity to express themselves through a variety of methods (e.g., oral, written, and pictorial reports). Assessment must be both relevant to the instructional objectives and reflective of the instructional process. For instance, if hands-on laboratory activities are used, then students need to be assessed on their laboratory skills as well as their content knowledge. If inquiry skills are important outcomes, then students should be given assessments that require the use of these skills and not merely the identification or regurgitation of factual information. In other words, it is important to link assessment with instruction.

The linking of assessment with instruction is the first step in creating more authentic assessments. The second step is to seek assessment strategies that reflect real-life situations, involve multifaceted tasks, and that require the integration of skills over an extended period of time. Just as learning progresses through levels of proficiency, so too should the assessments increase in complexity.

If biological literacy is one of the major goals for your students (Chapter 5), the type of assessment used should reflect the level of competency expected. To assess *functional biological literacy*, students might be required to recall, apply, and justify information through short answers and essays. More revealing information, however, can be acquired by means of assessment tasks that require students to use their laboratory skills, to apply their knowledge to resolve real-world problems, or to identify and study issues relevant to their lives.

As students develop an understanding of the subject, they can explain key concepts in their own words and can identify and describe the significance of these concepts to other concepts. At this *structural literacy* level, students should experience assessment tasks that require applications of their knowledge to novel situations. "Design-an-experiment" type of performance tasks and written reports are appropriate assessment strategies at this level of instruction. At the *multidimensional literacy* level, students can recognize deficiencies in their own knowledge and are aware of more global applications of their knowledge. Students at this level are able to connect many diverse ideas, and the assessment methods should reflect this skill. Appropriate assessment strategies are long-term research projects that require students to develop and undertake a plan of action to resolve a community issue or an independent research project (BSCS, 1994).

At all levels of biological literacy, students should be allowed to perform and exhibit their ability in a variety of tasks. The bottom line is that good assessment methods, like good instruction, have clearly focused objectives, use a variety of techniques, are relevant to the students' lives, and are responsive to individual differences. Incidentally, there is a major misconception that an "easy grader" will receive good student evaluations. Students like and respect professors who are fair, knowledgeable, interesting, stimulating, and encouraging—even if that person has high (but reasonable) standards.

PRACTICAL ADVICE FOR ASSESSING STUDENTS

These are some guidelines to consider as you plan the assessment of your students.

1. **General Considerations**
   Don't stress the trivial just because it is so easy to test.
   Use a variety of testing or evaluation methods. (See end of chapter for ideas.)
   Always give prompt feedback.
   Tests should be for learning and motivating, as well as for measuring understanding.
   Reduce the threat tests pose to students. For instance, hold a review session for students the day before the exam.
   Clarify test objectives both before and after the exam, with yourself and with students.
   Be honest, open, and fair. Discuss tests both before and after.
   Be imaginative and humorous as well as careful, balanced, and precise.
   Be generous.

2. **Developing the test**
   Check your objectives and the relevance of the means chosen to evaluate achievement. (For instance, should you use multiple choice or essay questions if you have emphasized class discussion and synthesis of ideas in class?)
   Determine the course content to be evaluated.
   Write the evaluation criteria (what constitutes a correct answer).
   Take the test yourself to see how long you need to complete it. Double this time for students, and adjust the length of the exam accordingly.
   Write the general instructions for taking the test or completing the assignment.
   Ask a colleague or graduate students for advice on the final product.
   Consider: What is the objective of the examination? Will the exam determine the skill level of students, recognition of factual information, understanding of concepts, speed of recall, problem-solving technique, or analytical assessment of knowledge? Should the examination be open-book or closed-book? An exam almost never covers all the material that you want, so priorities must be established from the list of topics you taught.

3. **Administering the test or supervising the assignment**
   Eliminate all possibility of cheating by clearly explaining what constitutes copying and cheating and by reminding your students of the established penalties. Organize the room, students, or examinations so that the opportunity for cheating is greatly reduced.
   Always proctor the exam and watch for wandering eyes. Students who are cheating often look up to see if they are being watched.

4. **Correcting the test or assignment**
   Correct systematically and impartially. Compare tests and assignments against the evaluation criteria given to students.

5. **Analyzing the results**
   Assess the successes and failures and try to determine the cause of failures. What kind of questions are many students missing? Are students misreading questions, did they misinterpret what you said, did the question ask something that students did not know was going to be on the exam, or are students just not able to apply information to new situations?

6. **Communicating the results**
   Return tests as soon as possible. If a delay is unavoidable, post a corrected copy so students can see acceptable answers. For other assignments or exercises, write down the overall grade and points for each criterion, and brief comments on these partial grades. (adapted from Eble, 1988; Davis, 1992; Pregent, 1994)

DEVELOPING BETTER TEST QUESTIONS

It is easier to *grade answers* of knowledge or memory questions, however, it is essential that you include questions that require higher-order thinking skills to answer, such as those identified in categories 2-6 below. In lower-division undergraduate courses, you might use a 50%/50% split between knowledge (or memory) questions and higher-order thinking questions. After you have written your exam, look over the questions and ask yourself, "How many of these questions can be answered by students who have simply memorized information?" Rule of thumb—**do not write an exam where more than 60% of the points require "regurgitation" of factual information.**

1. **Knowledge or Memory**: Students recall or recognize information. This is the lowest level of learning. Memory questions deal with:
    a) *definitions and descriptions*
    b) *facts*
    c) *generalizations—recognition of common characteristics of a group*
    d) *criteria (bases for judgment)*
    Also, questions where students state observations made of a system or present data collected during an experiment. Students can define, describe, identify, label, list, match, or name.

2. **Comprehension and problem Identification**: Students demonstrate understanding of the material presented in the course. The key skill is the ability to explain concepts/ideas in *their own words*. Also, questions where students identify a problem or describe the sequence of procedures they used, demonstrate the techniques or skills used, and identify the variables and controls of their investigation. Students can distinguish between different objects and ideas, estimate, explain, generalize, give examples, paraphrase, and summarize. They can also interpret charts and graphs, estimate future consequences, and justify methods and procedures.

3. **Application and Translation**: Students use what they have learned to solve problems or answer questions in another situation. They solve a "real world" problem that requires the identification of the issue and the selection and use of appropriate information and skills. At this level of learning, students can transfer information and ideas into a different form (written, oral, or pictorial). Also, these are questions that encourage students to interpret new experiences using concepts they already have learned; or give additional examples; or evaluate how appropriate an idea is to a given situation. Students can: compute, demonstrate, modify, predict, relate, solve, and use information in a new way. They can apply concepts and principles to new situations and construct charts and graphs. Rule of thumb: ask students to answer a question related to a specific example that you *didn't* cover in class, but that is similar to one that you did.

4. **Analysis and Interpretation**: Students can break the course content into its component parts so that relationships between parts are understood. They discover relationships among facts, generalizations, definitions, values, and skills, and apply rules of logic to the solutions of problems. Several kinds of interpretations exist:
    a) compare/contrast (ideas or concepts that are the same, different, related, or contradictory)
    b) implication (ideas based upon evidence)
    c) induction (application of a generalization to a group of observed facts)
    d) cause and effect (recognition of events leading to a conclusion)
    Students can diagram, discriminate, illustrate, infer, and relate ideas. They can also recognize logical fallacies in reasoning, distinguish between facts and inferences, and evaluate the relevancy of data.

5. **Synthesis**: Students put together different parts to form a new whole. Students take what they learn and use it to produce new products, such as a speech or research proposal. Student solve a problem that requires original, creative thinking. Also, questions that prompt students to put together a sequence of at least two ideas in order to explain how a system works or that prompts students to use evidence as a basis for stating relationships between variables. Students can: categorize, compose, devise plans, modify, rearrange, or revise. They can also write a well-organized paper or speech, propose a plan for an experiment, and integrate learning from different areas into a plan for solving a problem.

6. **Evaluation**: Students judge the value of information in light of given sources and biases, or the value of ideas, proposals, and solutions on the basis of specific criteria. At this most complex level, the key skill is the ability to make judgments of good or bad, right or wrong, according to standards on which you and students agree.

Students can: appraise, conclude, criticize, justify, interpret and support ideas and statements. They can also judge the logical consistency of written material, the adequacy of support for conclusions, and judge the value of a work.

If you assess your students for higher-level thinking skills, then you will find that an examination is not necessarily the most appropriate format to use. Students might be asked to develop a model, a proposal, a plan for investigation, or a plan of action related to some multifaceted problem which requires time outside of class. (adapted from Sanders, 1966; Rowe, 1978; Grambs and Carr, 1979; Jacobs and Chase, 1992)

EXAM DESIGN

Composing Short-answer Questions

1. Do not write questions on trivial ideas or information. The problem is, of course, what is trivial to one person may be of great significance to another.
2. Do not use vague language, e.g., "True or False: Wheat is important to the lives of people." Which people? What do you mean by important?
3. Make certain the question calls for a single, correct response.
4. In composing true-false questions:
   a) Do not overuse superlatives as they usually indicate the answer is false.
   b) Do not make "true" questions consistently longer than "false" questions.
5. In composing completion questions:
   a) Make sure only one response is correct.
   b) Do not put in so many blanks that the question loses meaning.
   c) Do not permit the syntax of the statement or length of the blank to hint about the answer.
6. In composing matching questions:
   a) Do not include heterogeneous subjects that reveal answers by extraneous clues.
   b) Include more items in the response column, so
      that the last questions cannot be answered by elimination.
7. In composing multiple-choice questions:
   a) Include at least four options, but do not use

obviously phony ones.
   b) Rarely use "None- or All-of-the-above."
   c) Keep all options grammatically consistent.

The Multiple-Choice Test

There are many limitations to using multiple-choice exams because multiple-choice items:

1. **are open to misinterpretation** by students who read more into questions than intended.
2. **may appear too picky** to students, especially when the options are well-constructed.
3. **deny demonstration of knowledge beyond the range of options provided.**
4. **are difficult to phrase** so that all students will have the same interpretation.
5. **take time and skill** to construct effectively.
6. **often do not evaluate higher levels of learning**--like the ability to synthesize.
7. **give students three incorrect answers** to every correct one--if exam questions are not reviewed, then students may leave class with many misconceptions. (adapted from Sanders, 1966; Clegg and Cashin, 1986; Ory, 1987)

If you still want to use multiple-choice exams, then concentrate on writing items to **evaluate higher levels of thinking**. Avoid the pitfall of writing items that test only memorization of basic factual knowledge. **Concentrate on evaluating students' ability to understand, apply, analyze, synthesize, and evaluate.** It is difficult to write multiple choice or fill-in-the-blank questions that evaluate these higher cognitive levels; but if critical thinking is what you want students to do, you will have to test for it.

ESSAY OR DISCUSSION QUESTIONS

1. Do not use essay questions to evaluate knowledge that could be tested with objective questions. For the most part, purely memory questions should not be in essay form. Rarely does a test need be wholly in essay form, because objective questions are appropriate for many categories. This allows you to do a better job in correcting a smaller number of subjective answers.

2. Design essay questions to test only one or a few specific instructional objectives per question. You must make explicit what you want to test (a necessary corollary is that you have to be clear about what you were trying to teach, i.e., expect the students to learn).

3. Give preference to focused questions that can be answered briefly. When it fits your instructional objectives, several short-answer questions will yield a more reliable score than fewer long questions. On the other hand, short answer questions may not permit students to demonstrate complex mental processes.

4. The question should clearly indicate the task(s) students are to address with respect to both content and process.

5. Use novel questions; otherwise you are testing memory. Novelty can provide interest, and may require application of knowledge, and therefore motivation, for students. (See later section for examples of questions.)

6. Before correcting the responses to a subjective question, think out as many acceptable answers as possible. Decide on elements that appear to be essential. On some subjective questions, the answers are not dependent so much on the answer students give as on how well they support their position. Refer to these key points several times while you are grading to improve the uniformity of grading.

7. Be consistent in your grading. Write out an answer key for your graders (or yourself) then read several exams before you assign any grades. Revise the key based on additional answers or points of view students may have taken during the exam.

8. Write comments and corrections on essay responses because they are more revealing than a single grade. This is a time-consuming task and accentuates the need to keep the volume of reading within reasonable limits. One essay answer carefully corrected is worth two or three read in a cursory manner and assigned a grade with no explanation.

9. Make a point not to know whose paper is being read when correcting. It is too easy to get a stereotyped evaluation in mind for each student and unconsciously give the accustomed grade.

10. Compose a guide for answering essay questions and go over it with students at the beginning of the year. A good answer to an essay question will:

    a) show understanding of the question and all its implications,
    b) show adequate knowledge of fact and theory related to the question,
    c) exclude irrelevant material,
    d) be well organized with emphasis placed upon more important ideas,
    e) demonstrate ability to write clearly,
    f) contain valid reasoning, and
    g) include originality when appropriate to the question.

11. Try to separate the substance of the essay from extraneous factors such as handwriting, writing skills, spelling, and grammar. Essay tests often provide the students with an opportunity to exercise POOR writing skills. When one considers the time, pressure, and anxiety connected with the typical essay test, it is surprising that the students do as well as they do. Most students' time in an essay test is spent physically writing. There is limited time to think, organize creatively, write a second draft, or proofread. So, give students a small break on spelling and grammar. (adapted from Sanders, 1966; Rowe, 1978; Cashin, 1987)

Strengths of Essay Tests

Essay exams:

1. **test complex learning outcomes** not measurable by other means. An obvious example is the ability to express oneself in writing.
2. **test thought processes**, students' ability to select, organize, and evaluate facts and ideas, and their ability to apply, integrate, think critically, and solve problems.
3. **require that students use their own writing skills**; students must select the words, compose the sentences and paragraphs, organize the sequence of exposition, decide upon correct grammar and spelling, etc.
4. **pose a more realistic task** than multiple-choice and other "objective" items. Most of life's questions and problems do not come in a multiple-choice format, and almost every occupation, including engineering, business, technical, and service jobs, requires people to communicate in complete sentences and paragraphs--if not in writing, at least orally. (Incidentally, the #1 attribute sought in prospective employees by corporations is the ability to communicate well.)
5. **cannot be answered correctly by simply recognizing the correct answer**; it is not possible to guess. (Students can bluff, however.)
6. **can be constructed relatively quickly.** This advantage is short-lived because any time saved in constructing the test is lost when scoring it. All well-constructed tests require time and effort; the only choice is whether you want to spend time and effort up front or after giving the exam. (adapted from Cashin, 1987)

Helping Students Do Better on Essay Exams

1. **Communicate expectations early and clearly.** Include in the syllabus: (a) why you think writing is important; (b) how your essay examinations are related to course objectives; (c) the types of essay questions students will be required to answer; (d) grading criteria; and (e) what student performance on essay exams reveals about their performance in the course.
2. **Provide an in-class lesson on what constitutes good writing.** Have students compare good and bad writing examples and then identify what makes one example better than the other.
3. **Assess student writing ability early in the course.** You might do this by assigning short in-class writings. Suggested assignment: a short reading and a short (five minutes) written response summarizing reading, and listing questions or comments.
4. **Provide students with written resources to help them improve their writing.** Construct a checklist identifying some common problems and practical advice for correcting and overcoming these errors. Urge students to use campus resources like writing centers to help them improve their essay writing skills.
5. **Write an essay that you will soon be asking your students to write.** This can help you better understand students' writing experiences, identify possible essay test problems before they occur, and develop a reflective awareness of your own expectations as well as your own strategies for writing.
6. **Give students essay questions before the test.** If you do not want to identify the questions, offer students a large list of questions from which you will choose two or three, or give them a practice essay that is similar in nature to the one you actually use on the exam. (adapted from Holt and Eison, 1989)

SAMPLE EXAM QUESTIONS

These are selected questions from Botany 1114 (Introductory Botany for Non-Majors) exams. None of the following questions were directly discussed in lecture or lab. In each case, students were being asked to apply their knowledge to new situations.

4 pts. Suppose you have a piece of DNA that is 150 base pairs long. If there are 100 "C" nucleotides, how many "G" nucleotides should there be in this piece of DNA? If this DNA is a gene, how many **amino acids** will be in the protein that is eventually formed from it? From the above information, what is the greatest number of "A" nucleotides there could be in this piece of DNA?

4 pts. Which kind of plant **parasite** do you think might kill its host sooner: a green parasite or an orange one? Choose one, and explain your answer.

3 pts. Suppose scientists soon could convert seawater into fresh water and food. Do you think we would then have to worry about the growth of the human population? Explain your answer.

5 pts. On Groundhog Day, if the groundhog sees its shadow, people are supposed to experience six more weeks of winter. If the animal doesn't see its shadow, then winter will soon end. In 10 out of the last eleven years, the groundhog has correctly "predicted" the weather. Is this an example of "cause and effect," "chance," or of a "correlation"? Explain. Also, how could you find out for sure?

4 pts. Do you think you have any **genes** that are identical to that of a plant? Explain your answer.

3 pts. If you had a tall plant and a short plant, how could you tell if tall or short was the dominant characteristic?

4 pts. Which has more energy: (a) one molecule of glucose or (b) 2 molecules of pyruvic acid? Choose one answer and explain how you know this.

3 pts. A student from last semester designed the following experiment. One bean seed is planted in each of three identical pots, with the same soil, and placed in the same location. No salt is added to Pot A. 1/2 teaspoon of salt is added to Pot B, and 1 teaspoon of salt is added to Pot C each week. Explain what is wrong with this experiment's design.

3 pts. On a quiz in lecture you saw a mouse and a plant in a glass container— and both remained alive! Explain how the situation is similar to the fish in the big, sealed-up, glass jar in lab.

5 pts. Suppose you bring home a Christmas tree and put it in a bucket of water. The water level in the bucket **never changes**, and the leaves of your tree start to fall off the tree. What do you think is happening and why?

5 pts. 100 lettuce seeds were placed on moist filter paper in a glass dish in a warm (25° C) sunlit room. Another 100 lettuce seeds were placed on moist filter paper in a glass dish in a warm (25° C) dark room. Seeds in both dishes germinated. Based on how this experiment was designed, which do you think is more important for germination: the moisture on the paper, the glass dish, or can you tell? Explain.

4 pts. Moss plants are **epiphytes**. In Oklahoma, moss often grows only on the north side of a tree. Considering the environment where epiphytes usually grow in other states, why do you think moss only grows on the north side of Oklahoma trees?

4 pts. Suppose someone gives you a plant that isn't flowering but that you know is a **long-day plant**. How could you get this plant to flower as soon as possible, no matter what time of year?

5 pts. A student added nitrogen to some corn plants and no nitrogen to others. Only one corn plant with nitrogen lived, but it grew 2 feet tall. Nine corn plants without nitrogen lived, and they averaged 1 foot tall. Based on these results, can we conclude that nitrogen helps plants grow tall? Explain.

5 pts. Flagging is one example of **genotype + environment = phenotype**. Describe another example, making sure that you indicate clearly how your example relates to each of the three parts of the interaction.

A VARIETY OF ASSESSMENT INSTRUMENTS

TYPES OF QUESTIONS OR METHODS OF ASSESSMENT	DESCRIPTION	EXAMPLES
Multiple Choice	Questions followed by four or five choices in which students recognize the correct response. Should be made to test all levels of thinking: knowledge, comprehension, application, synthesis, and analysis.	In humans, most of the building blocks necessary for the synthesis of organic compounds come from the: 1. end-products of digestion 2. products of cellular respiration 3. products of excretion 4. breakdown of white blood cells
Two-Tier Multiple Choice	A set of two multiple choice questions. The first question is knowledge-based while the second question seeks students' reasons for the prior question's response.	What is the source of energy used by animals to carry out their activities? 1. Digestion of food in the digestive system 2. Taking in oxygen and giving off carbon dioxide 3. Oxidizing organic compounds 4. The activities carried out in the body The reason for this being the best answer is: 1. The energy released during oxidation is used to synthesize ATP. 2. This is true for animals while plants obtain energy for their activities from photosynthesis. 3. In the process of respiration, organic molecules are broken down into their elements. These elements are the raw materials from which ATP is synthesized. 4. In the process of respiration, ATP is oxidized thereby releasing energy.
Free Response	Questions that require the student to complete the answer. These questions may take the form of, but are not limited to, graphing, analyzing, and interpreting data; designing experiments; identifying limiting factors; and describing problem-solving strategies.	Bromthymol blue turns to bromthymol yellow in the presence of carbon dioxide. When the carbon dioxide is removed, the solution will return to a blue color

Essay	Presented with a limited question, concept, illustration, or statement, the student is asked to respond to illustrate knowledge, depth of understanding, and creativity.	John used an insecticide to get rid of the increased number of cockroaches in his apartment. For a while, very few roaches appeared, and John stopped using the insecticide. However, many months later, the number of roaches began to increase again, and John once more applied the same insecticide. But this time the insecticide was not nearly as effective as before and the number of roaches remained high. Explain this result based on your knowledge of insect reproduction and the process of natural selection.
Concept Maps	Students are given a number of concepts that they are asked to arrange in hierarchical order showing relationships. They may have to label cross links, connect concepts, and show all relationships between terms. Examples are added when necessary. Students are not limited to just the given concepts but may add others of their own.	Using the following terms, construct a concept map. You may add terms and examples. Your map will be scored based on the number of propositions, your hierarchy, cross links and examples. Terms: adaptations, environment, evolution, natural selection, overproduction, speciation, and variation. (See Chapter 14.)
Clinical Interview	Through a series of predetermined questions (or general outline of questions), individual students are asked to explain, expand, and extend their knowledge of a particular concept. Probing questions seek student clarifications and illustrate reasoning. The interview is usually audio- or video-taped.	In many poor and developing countries, most people eat mainly plants such as rice and beans and seldom eat meat. This behavior is based far more upon certain ecological principles related to food chains than upon preferences and choice. Explain what ecological principles limit such people to their largely vegetarian diets.
Laboratory Practicals	These are standard laboratory tests that involve students demonstrating laboratory skills in order to answer questions. These skills have been outlined in the *Inquiry Process Skills* and *Decision-Making Skills* sections of this document.	Given a clear plastic metric ruler, a microscope and a prepared slide of paramecium, estimate the size of a paramecium as viewed under high power.

Long Term Investigation	This investigation should be student planned and based on observations of some natural phenomenon. Evidence should ideally be gathered from both traditional sources and electronic media that allow students to access information and communicate with experts. Also included should be: hypothesis formation, experimental design, handling of materials and equipment, gathering, processing, analysis and display of data, conclusion, and discussion including limitations of the experimental design. The student must be able to discuss and to communicate his/her procedures, results and conclusions in both written and oral forms.	Students conduct a laboratory or field study of something new to them.
Problem-Based Learning	Problems are multidimensional questions that are posed by the instructor and that require students to decide how the problem will be addressed, what information and skills are needed to answer the question, which students then obtain, and to demonstrate the methods and routes they took to study and solve the problem.	Problems can be invented by the instructor, but they also can be taken from the real world where students are asked to investigate a local problem or an issue that has been recently raised in the mass media. Conducting such investigations can approach "authentic assessment" for students.
Portfolios	Portfolios are collections of a student's work showing the growth that occurred within a given period of time (i.e., a semester) The portfolio provides evidence of the student's growth. Each student should select examples of his/her work that best demonstrates achievement in both knowledge and skills. It provides the student with a sense of accomplishment and also allows opportunities for self, peer, and teacher evaluation. Portfolio contents should be varied.	Possible portfolio contents might include: laboratory reports, journals, creative projects, papers, long-term investigations, cooperative learning projects, concept maps, or lab practicals.

(adapted from Tulloch, et al, 1994)

METHODS OF ASSESSMENT

Student Outcomes	Written Test or Practical	Inventory or Questionnaire	Group or Individual Project	Portfolio	Observation or Oral Examination	Peer Evaluation or Self-Assessment
Know Information						
Use Information						
Extend Knowledge						
Plan or Design Study						
Communicate Knowledge						
Analyze/ Interpret Data						
Have Positive Attitude About Science						
Have Interest in Biology						
Value Logical Reasoning and Problem Solving						

Matrix for Matching Format of Assessment with Instructional Outcomes. Place desired outcomes for your students on one side of the matrix and, on the top, place the method of assessment you choose to measure your students' achievement.

CONSTRUCTING YOUR EXAM

Types of Questions	Topic A	Topic B	Topic C	Topic D	
Knowledge or Memory					40%
Comprehension and Problem Identification					20%
Application and Translation					20%
Analysis and Interpretation					10%
Synthesis					5%
Evaluation					5%
	30%	20%	25%	25%	

    Completing a grid such as this allows you to develop a test with questions that reflect the emphasis on the various topics as well as the number of questions you desire at each level of thinking skills.

What do you want your students to know, value, and be able to do by the end of your course, and how will you know if they have achieved these goals? This is your chance to consider cutting back on the *amount* of information you are trying to present, to help students really understand a few major concepts and important ideas, and to help students practice science as a process.

CHAPTER IX. THE ROLE OF EDUCATIONAL TECHNOLOGY IN THE BIOLOGICAL SCIENCES

Computers play many important roles in scientific research. If undergraduate students are to understand the process of science as well as science as a body of knowledge, then it is important that they understand how computers are important tools for searching and accessing information and modeling complex systems. Networked computers and computer software for scientific research are increasingly critical vectors of information access and delivery and are powerful communication tools for scientists and non-scientists. In terms of biology education, computers enable the creation of interactive communities of scientists and students through the exchange of ideas, questions, documents, graphics, and software despite diverse geographical locations of the community members.

The methods used in teaching are often constrained by broader factors over which individual faculty members have little control. For example, introductory courses often must accommodate large numbers of students in auditorium lecture halls where the teacher-student ratio is more a matter of economic rather than pedagogical concern. In such situations, most professors adapt the traditional role of teacher as lecturer. The pedagogical assumption in lecture courses is that there is a large body of factual knowledge that is framed by the course syllabus and covered by a text. The students experience science primarily as a body of knowledge that must be assimilated and retained long enough to gain assessment points. Networked computers and innovative software offer unique possibilities for radically transforming undergraduate science education.

Technology is useful for automating and streamlining many of the tasks that are frequently part of a professor's life. Personal computers are now commonplace, and a plethora of software has been created to automate processes such as test creation and grading, and record keeping of student attendance and progress. Personal computers are a familiar sight in college dorms and in the instructional spaces of schools of higher education. Much of educational technology that was once separate (video, audio, mathematical processing) is now being integrated into the form of computer technology as the new machines and software gain in sophistication. There are, in general, five types of computer software currently used in education: (1) drill and practice, (2) tutorials, (3) simulations (demonstrations, model building and model revising software), (4) data collection and analysis tools, and (5) general productivity tools (e.g. word processors, spreadsheets). Most of the existing software that is marketed by commercial education vendors supports a transmissive (lecture) pedagogical style and consists primarily of factual information. This software, however, may be more sophisticated than textbooks because it allows for greater search capabilities and/or enables students to play and replay short animations or film clips. However, an essential question that biology educators should ask is how can the use of technology help our students to become scientifically literate citizens, and how can it be used to better prepare our students who will eventually become scientists?

We help our students become better critics of scientific methodologies if we provide opportunities where students learn to deal with complex problems similar to those being addressed by today's scientists. Jungck (1991) has provided an analysis of software that is designed to enable students to engage in the process of science. His analysis provides a critical framework for evaluating biology software. This framework serves as a useful guide for exploring the notion of "openness" and the structure of learning that occurs as a result of research investigations as opposed to learning that is rote, or more memorization-based. The following types of biology education software are critiqued below based on issues of student use and control with respect to their strengths or limits to engage students in open-ended inquiry similar to the process of scientific inquiry.

Drill and Practice
This type of software leaves little opportunity for student control. A typical drill and practice piece of software will pose a series of single answer questions. The questions might be in the form of multiple choice, true/false, or fill in the blank options. The student gets immediate feedback whether s/he is right or wrong. There is no opportunity to engage in posing problems and no need for students to consider the why's and how's behind the "rightness" of an answer. Problem solving is limited primarily to recall of appropriate responses with no deeper thought of why an answer is appropriate.

Tutorials

Tutorials are typically computerized versions of the guided learning paper and pencil forms that were popular in the 1970's. The students are expected to read a short informative description and answer a short set of questions that follow, again with immediate feedback as to whether they have chosen the right or wrong answer. The student control is greater than in drill and practice, but the choice is typically limited to simply choosing what sequence the student wishes to work through the information.

Simulations: Demonstrations, Model Building and Model Exploration Software

In academic conversations, there are many interpretations of what is meant when a person refers to a software "simulation." For educational purposes, simulations can be broken down into three types:

1) *A Demonstration simulation*
An example of a demonstration simulation is a short "movie" of a phenomena that is provided in conjunction with some supporting textual material. The purpose is to help students understand a process or concept by watching a real or animated sequence of events. The students can use a demonstration simulation to pose questions about the objects or phenomena, but conducting research to try and answer these questions cannot be performed in the simulation.

2) *Modeling simulations*
This type of a simulation models a system and allows the student to pose questions and alter parameters to test their questions. It can be argued that this type of simulation enables students to be engaged in problem posing, problem solving and peer persuasion, three important components of scientific inquiry. The depth of problem probing by students using modeling simulations is limited by the number of parameters that can be varied and the number of variations possible per parameter. The problem posing and solving occurs in a space that is limited by the model and defined by the program.

3) *Combination black box/modeling simulations*
These types of simulations mimic both sides of scientific investigation - users can identify some phenomena or problem that represents a "black box," or an unknown, unexplored territory. They attempt to generate and test hypotheses within the problem space or construct models of the black box system to check for verification of hypotheses and conclusions. In other words, in some simulations, users are given control of creating the black

box systems that can be investigated by other users without having to learn programming commands. This type of simulation offers the students the highest degree of control. They are able to chose both what they wish to investigate and design their own plan to tackle the problem of their choosing, or they can model and tinker with a particular system of their design and compare their results with data from scientific investigations of actual systems.

Data Collection, and Analysis Tools

Tools can be software for efficient data collection and analysis. Examples of such tools include pH or temperature probes, graphing and statistical packages, software that helps in the analysis of the coherence of concluding arguments, such as *Convince Me!*, programming languages for creating and modifying simulations, such as *Extend* or *Stella*, and machines controlling languages, such as *LOGO*.

Tools for Persuasion Building and Analysis

Software such as word processors, spreadsheets, graphing programs, and presentation tools are integral for the communication of the results of scientific investigations through publications, poster presentations, and presentations at professional conferences.

All of these types of software can aid in learning scientific knowledge, but only some types of software are useful in engaging scientific thinking as defined as a process of inquiry or a way of knowing. Technology should not be taught for technology's sake in science courses. Technology should be viewed as a tool that students need to address significant questions and to communicate their progress and frustrations to their colleagues. The challenge for software developers and biology professors is, as Bruffee (1993) points out, "To devise programs that help people at the computer keyboard or in front of a television screen to make contact not just with the authority that the program represents but with one another, producers and programmers will have to strive to 'lose their audience' constructively. Software writers, dramatists, writers, directors, and performers will have to find ways to weaken the bond that glues people to the tube and intensify instead the excitement, interest, and understanding that people derive from conversation about what they are seeing or have seen on the tube". In other words, the challenge is to find ways to create collaborative communities in our classrooms where students learn biology through scientific problem solving.

As educational technology grows in sophistication and diversity, it causes new possibilities for curricular change. Reflective thinking about science teaching manifests itself it many forms. A number of publications concur that science content should not be taught divorced from the process of science. These publications also reflect a dissatisfaction with traditional models of teaching in science education. There have been several recent publications featuring persuasive pieces on what science concepts all students should know (such as the National Research Council's publication on Science Standards), while others have offered a framework for thinking about how a student's learning experiences should be structured (*Project 2061, Fulfilling the Promise, Developing Biological Literacy*). Although not specifically argued in all of the publications offering a framework for thinking about improving student learning, there seems to be a growing consensus that "science should be taught as it is practiced at its best" (AAAS, 1990).

The BioQUEST Curriculum Consortium

Members of the BioQUEST Curriculum Consortium share a common belief that students learn biology best if they have opportunities to become involved in research or research-like experiences (Jungck and Calley, 1985). More specifically, the Consortium members believe that students' motivation to learn biology concepts will escalate if they are able to pose problems and decide how they will solve their problems, and they will also be more willing to write persuasive pieces where they argue the merit of their thinking. The philosophy that is articulated by the BioQUEST Curriculum Consortium has become known, in short, as the 3P's of science education: problem posing, problem solving, and peer persuasion (Peterson and Jungck, 1988). Encapsulating a philosophy in a phrase is useful for referring quickly to a larger belief system, but shortening an entire philosophy into a catchy phrase can trivialize the power of the philosophical framework.

Problem Posing. To understand science as it is practiced, students must engage in problem-posing. To appreciate this, students must recognize that much of traditional school science only provides them with experience in solving already well-formulated problems from a textbook. Many students are surprised when they realize that "one of the greatest obstacles to understanding the natural world is not knowing what questions to ask" (Moore, 1985). If students are to understand something about the process of science and reasons behind the strengths and limitations of this

process, they must have more experience posing an(pursuing research questions of their own choice. It i: important that we try to help students understand th(multiple issues involved in posing a problem, includin("interestingness," significance, and feasibility, as well a: the role of bias.

Problem Solving. After having posed a problem students need to experience open-ended problem solving. What do we mean by open-ended problen solving? Open-ended problems are ones that can b(answered by multiple logical and rational hypotheses Although traditional textbook problems are usefu teaching devices, most teachers would agree that ; disadvantage of these types of problems is that there i: usually only a possibility of a single answer. Overuse c single answer problems can contribute to a student': conception that all scientific problems have a "right answer. Real scientific problems do not have answer: at the back of the book. Students also need practice making inferences over a long series of experimenta observations where it will be necessary for them t(propose and discuss multiple hypotheses that car account for the phenomena they observe. Hypotheses are powerful tools for investigation. We as teachers need to carefully consider our students' understanding and view of the role of hypotheses in scientific investigations. Unfortunately, to students, an hypothesis is often viewed as a guess about the outcome of a demonstration of some scientific principle for which their teacher already knows the answer rather than a powerfu tool for guiding and shaping scientific investigations.

It is also important for students to study open-endec problems so they are confronted with decisions regarding when they feel the investigation is done Scientists typically do not arrive at a magical anc absolute final answer. Students should develop a sense of why and when research is abandoned and the reasons for closure, including time and resources. What are the criteria for a scientific research team to believe they are "satisfied" enough with their conclusions tc formally share them with the greater community through journal articles and conference presentations? Students can, and must, have this problem-solving experience to appreciate the nature of scientific answers and to develop heuristics for achieving closure to scientific problems.

Persuading Peers. Research is not complete, no matter how many experiments have been conducted or puzzles solved, until peers outside of a research team are persuaded of the utility of the answers. Persuasion is a social process and an essential one for students to experience in order to understand the nature of scientific theories and paradigm shifts. Therefore, all biology students should experience peer review as a professional activity. Computers are important tools that enable students to easily transfer their data, graphics, working hypotheses, and analyses into word-processing, spreadsheet, and scientific graphics software to build scientific journal-style manuscripts that can be reviewed by other students and instructors.

Changing Biology Education

Numerous educators have found that a 3P's approach resonates with their own view of teaching. They have found the philosophical discussion useful for re-examining whether or not their present instruction utilizes this approach and how they might alter their instruction to involve students in more 3P's learning. Most educators are surprised by how difficult it is to put theory into practice. Why is this so? The argument for 3P's teaching seems seductively easy. It can be argued that most K-12 teachers have little experience in participating or conducting actual field or laboratory research studies. However, it is our experience that most college and university faculty who are actively engaged in research have an equally difficult time teaching from a 3P's perspective. This is not surprising if one considers the argument behind why a 3P's approach is necessary in a science curriculum.

Researchers deal with complex and messy systems. They often have a feel for what they want to investigate, but have a very difficult time formulating questions that are answerable given their present knowledge and present day techniques and tools. Much of research time is spent trying to debug techniques in an attempt to find ways of gaining insight into a research problem. In addition, the techniques used must constantly be suspect. Therefore, a student-centered 3P's activity will most likely not fit into the traditional system that has evolved in science classrooms - namely, that the best labs are labs that "work well" in the time constraints of a lab period. Most educators will reply that a "good" lab is one that clearly and cleanly demonstrates a principle, technique, phenomena, or explanation for a phenomena and that fits conveniently into one or two labs or class periods. Ambiguity is not desirable. A scientific investigation that involves problem posing, problem solving and persuasion of peers is, by nature, messy. Students must grapple with issues related to what they want to study, their plans for data acquisition and analysis, false starts, decisions to change research

protocols or research questions as a result of their investigation, and the question of whether the research is worth doing at all. All of these issues can be intimidating to a student. It is difficult to bundle such an experience into two or three hour-long lab or classroom sessions. Therefore, it is important for biology educators to consider ways in which the use of computer software can radically transform undergraduate biology curricula by overcoming some of the traditional constraints of laboratory investigations by streamlining data collection and analysis through the use of probes and analysis tools; through the use of simulations and modeling tools; and through the use of word processors, spreadsheets, graphing, and graphics software to produce persuasive documents and multimedia presentations.

REASONS WHY INSTRUCTIONAL TECHNOLOGY IS USEFUL

In the pages above you have read how computer software can help students experience and learn about biology. In addition, educational technology can be used to:

1. do tasks that faculty cannot, such as helping students experience times, places, people, and events that cannot be otherwise brought into class.
2. do tasks that faculty can do, but better, such as helping students visualize phenomena that may be too small or too dynamic to convey effectively in print or with static models.
3. do tasks that are routine, such as helping students overcome learning differences or deficiencies best remedied through drill and practice.
4. better prepare students for the world of work where they may be required to use things such as spreadsheets, word processing, data bases, or computer-aided design technologies.
5. increase student and faculty productivity, by reducing time that routine record-keeping or communicating require.
6. reach students who are unable or choose not to attend conventional on-campus classes. (adapted from Albright and Graf, 1992)

X. THE LECTURE, AND HOW TO STOP TALKING

There are several advantages to a lecture, including that the instructor can highlight major facts, principles, and generalizations that students might overlook in their reading. In addition, one can clarify concepts and promote understanding of difficult subjects. Also, one can convey a lot of information to many students in a relatively short period of time. However, **NO COURSE SHOULD BE MADE UP ENTIRELY OF LECTURE!**

Most successful lectures begin with carefully prepared notes and some form of rehearsal. With course objectives in mind, write out your notes before each lecture. Carefully plan what you expect to accomplish, the order or your presentation, what important concepts you want to emphasize, and the amount of time you can allocate to each part of the lecture. In case of a severe time crunch, identify those portions that can be left out without a major loss in understanding. The reason for writing out notes is to make you feel more secure because you have all the information in front of you. But, **never read from the textbook or from your notes** except to provide accurate numbers or data.

Some people compare college teaching to acting on the stage. The instructor tries to give life to written words, concepts or ideas, as does an actor. The instructor must develop a rapport with the class and hold their interest, as must an actor. But, you don't have to be a good actor to be a good instructor. Just as acting is a combination of art and skill, so is teaching, and you can improve your skill as an instructor even if your artistic talents are not Oscar-worthy.

If you are teaching a large class, you are probably lecturing to your students. In such a class, students are predisposed to passivity, and most, if not all, are anonymous to you and to each other. There may be little or no individual attention to or professional relationships with students, and student questions may be discouraged. You must continually fight against these trends and against feelings of isolation among your students. To counteract this, you need to encourage questions from your students—you might set out a question box and respond to questions at the beginning of each lecture. Be aware of the diverse learning needs and preparation levels of your students. Develop ways to assess learning other than with objective, machine-scored exams so that students receive personal feedback rather than just a posted score. Adapt your style to the constraints and opportunities of large classes; most of us don't have a "big course" teaching style. Learn how to enjoy teaching in the class long-term. Also try to remove all the annoyances—what is it that drives you crazy about teaching? By eliminating major problems over which you have control, the course becomes much more tolerable. If you are teaching a small course, there really is no excuse for lecturing. Whatever the size of your course, consider the alternatives to lecturing found in this chapter.

WHAT LECTURES SHOULD DO

Lectures should:
1. provide a model of scientific activity and problem-solving approaches--not just listing the results (facts) of scientific investigations;
2. explain, clarify, illustrate, and organize difficult concepts;
3. reveal to students methods of learning and thinking about difficult topics;
4. help students analyze information;
5. show relationships among seemingly dissimilar ideas;
6. formulate and help solve problems, and develop hypotheses and predictions;
7. evaluate and criticize evidence and alternative solutions;
8. relay current research and theories;
9. summarize material from a variety of sources;
10. provide structures to help students read and study more effectively;
11. help students integrate and retrieve information;
12. challenge beliefs, misconceptions, and habits of thinking;
13. impart new information;
14. promote interest and enthusiasm in the subject;
15. provide additional examples and illustrations;
16. help students answer major questions in biology;
17. provide opportunities for students to experience concepts in ways other than the laboratory and their textbook.

Chapter X

SOME COMMON CRITICISMS OF LECTURERS

The lecturer:
1. is inaudible, or speaks in monotone;
2. is incoherent or rambles;
3. fails to pitch lecture at an appropriate level;
4. does not emphasize key points or main ideas;
5. has poor blackboard, or overhead, skills;
6. has difficult to read data slides or poor/no pictures;
7. says too much too quickly, and fails to slow down when requested;
8. assumes too much background knowledge;
9. assumes students recall information entirely and immediately;
10. forgets to provide summaries throughout the lecture;
11. does not indicate when making an aside versus making a major point;
12. has difficulty in timing the length of a lecture;
13. does not provide stopping points throughout the lecture so that students can "catch up" with the lecturer and to synthesize and organize ideas;
14. does not allow questions or time for some discussion.

DEVELOPING YOUR LECTURE

1. **Select the major topic.**
2. **Develop a question that serves as a guide.** Pos your question at the start of your lecture, the answer it. "Recall the question I raised at th beginning of today's class..."
3. **Identify key details, important data, relevan examples, and essential terms** that help to answe the question. Rule of thumb: if students will neve use the term again in class (or their lives), drop th term. Do not just recite facts and definitions—hel students see the BIG PICTURE—how does th information fit into a major principle or concept?
4. **Collect relevant media items** such as chart maps, photographs, transparencies, and slides tha will help communicate the topic. Provide illustration and examples from current events.
5. **Break lecture into major segments** with goo starting and stopping points for each segmen Make clear transitions between major sections an different major concepts.
6. **Emphasize main points** in different ways (say once, draw or write it on the board, and use pictur to illustrate the point). Repeat your main points.
7. **Summarize** each section and the lecture.

SUGGESTIONS FOR IMPROVING LECTURES

We have all experienced particularly good lecturers--think of them as role models. Also, make a list of characteristics of poor lecturers you have endured, and try to avoid their mistakes.

1. **Hit students before you lose them**--Arrive at the lecture room early and stay late. This is a good strategy if you have materials to hand out, but it also allows you to greet students, exchange a few words, and answer questions immediately after lecture when students have questions.

2. **Talk it out**--Be as conversational as you can. Your position alone, standing before a large group in a large room, establishes a certain distance between you and your class. Students are not there for a formal speech. They need information, organized and coherently presented, and the opportunity to interact with someone who knows and loves the material. Never read the lecture; instead, talk to the students from your outline. Use a tone and pattern of speech that resembles the way you would talk to one or two students somewhat informally--only louder. Speak using short sentences. Try to avoid irritating mannerisms that often result from nervousness.

3. **Look at the students**, not at the blackboard, floor, or ceiling. You pick up many cues from the expressions on the faces of the students. Can you tell who was in class without having taken roll? If not, you may not be looking at your students' faces enough. Look at your students often to show your interest in them, and watch their eyes to see if they're understanding you. Encourage student participation and questions.

4. **Think BIG**--Check your overhead and chalkboard writing from the back of the room. Speak slowly, loudly, and clearly, aiming your words at all areas of the room. Students shouldn't have to strain to hear you. Vary the pitch and tone of your voice, but try to keep it clear and relaxed. You should hit the back without overpowering the front. (You may want to use a microphone or seek advice from instructors in speech, communication, and theater departments as well as colleagues in your department.)

5. **Claim your territory**--Do whatever it takes to establish and maintain your presence in the room. But to elaborate or illustrate important points, move out among your students; don't stay fixed behind the podium. Students question the confidence and preparation of instructors who stand with white knuckles at a podium day after day. Moving around the classroom (but not pacing nervously) may make a big difference in holding the attention of those in the back. Take advantage of these excursions to establish eye contact with students in the outer regions and to ask questions of those who sit in the back.

6. **Be Prepared**--Know your subject matter. You communicate your interest in the subject by remaining up-to-date. Toss out the old examples and keep adding new information. Be prepared--but be alive, spontaneous. There is something positive about spontaneity in the classroom that keeps students attentive. It is also possible to be over-prepared to the point where you squash spontaneity.

7. Constantly **pursue answers to questions about what worked**, what didn't work, and what might work the next time you deliver a lecture. Reflect on the last class session; be aware of your overall lecturing style so that you can work at improving it. You might keep a journal of your teaching, noting what worked and what didn't.

8. **Be Humorous** (if you can)--Bring humor into your lectures because it can help students retain information; build rapport with your students; increase and maintain student interest; motivate learning; promote a positive attitude; improve class discussions; and help develop creativity and divergent thinking in your students. In addition, humor decreases academic stress; anxiety toward subject matter; dogmatism; and class monotony. If you aren't funny, collect and show science-related cartoons that illustrate biological principles.

9. **Make sure your students know to what you are referring**. During a presentation, you may start to spout off information about a new topic before students have caught up with you from the last one. To keep students on track, *continually* refer back to your outline on the board or overhead to show students with what current topic you are dealing. Point to those specific parts of a slide or computer screen presentation on which you want students to focus. (Never say, "as you can see" without pointing directly to what they should be seeing.)

(adapted from Johnson, 1990; Mangan, 1990; Bonwell, 1991; Davidson and Ambrose, 1994)

CHECKLIST FOR A LECTURE

Content
Is the information valid and accurate?
Do you have full grasp of the subject?

Main Idea
Does your lecture have a clear central idea?
Does the idea run through the whole presentation?
Is the lecture easy to follow?
Is the detail concrete, valid, and specific?

Introduction
Does the introduction get students' attention?
Does it say what the presentation contains?
Does it relate to the students' world?

Conclusion
Does it tie the presentation together?
Does it relate back to the main idea?
Does it tell your students what to do next?

Audience Awareness
Do you understand and empathize with your students as
    people who must listen to you?
Do you use their language (don't assume students
    possess a basic scientific vocabulary)?
Do you try to make contact with the audience?

Visual Aids
Are they clear and easy to see and comprehend?
Does each aid clearly support or reinforce its related
    idea?
Are they exposed long enough for comprehension
    and retention?

Delivery
Are language, diction, and pronunciation appropriate?
Are you poised and relaxed?
Is your voice clear and at a proper volume?
Are there irrelevant gestures or mannerisms?
    (What do you do with your hands?)
Are you dressed appropriately (did you check your
    fly or the back of your skirt before you stepped
    into the classroom)?
Do you look at everyone and maintain eye contact?
Do you move around the classroom?

Your Attitude
Is there appropriate enthusiasm and sincerity?
Do you seem "real"?
Are you non-egocentric?
Do you have stage fright? (a little more exercise
    and a little less caffeine can help calm your nerves)
(adapted from Davidson and Ambrose, 1994)

HOW TO IMPROVE LECTURE ATTENDANCE

What do you do if your students aren't coming to your lecture? I think I give good lectures, but about 20% of all my students don't show up to class on a regular basis. Of course, these 20% usually fail the exam because tests are based on class material. The following are activities you might try to improve your attendance—but you may still see some of your students only on exam day.

1. **Tell students you think class attendance is important** (if you do) and then ask them questions based on class material. Make your lectures more important for students to attend by focusing on material not available in the text. Also focus on processes and thinking about science instead of presenting facts that students can get from the text if they miss lecture.

2. **Take attendance**—every day or at random. Show students the relationship between attendance and performance; students who don't show up to lecture can't get the information—even if they use someone else's notes, and then they can't do well. (On exams, there is a 10-15 point difference between those who attend and those who don't (Uno, 1988)) Having an attendance record also provides great ammunition when a student comes to complain about his/her grade. (If your records show many absences, then you may be easily able to diagnose a student's problem.) You can also give points for attendance.

3. **Give pop quizzes or short assignments worth a few points**. Quizzes can compel students to keep up with the information on a regular basis instead of memorizing information the night before the exam. In addition, quizzes help you see if students understand the material. You can reduce the exam by the number of points in the quiz and use the quiz to take attendance.

4. **Review students' notes**. Look at the lecture notes of students with their first exam in hand. By comparing questions that students missed to their notes, it is easy to show them that they have incomplete notes, or have missed the main point and examples of the lecture, or have skipped over their notes when studying. This is also a good way to help them improve their note-taking and studying skills.

LECTURES AND STUDENT MENTAL LAPSES

Do not simply lecture to your students. But when you do lecture, it's important to recognize the kind of mental lapses experienced by students so you can avoid stupefying them.

1. **Short-term memory overloads.** Short-term memory functions as a kind of buffer zone where a discrete amount of information is stored before being moved into long-term memory. It takes about 5-10 seconds to transfer information from short-term to long-term memory. If you spout new ideas too fast, the buffer may overflow, and listening stops.
2. **Momentary misunderstanding.** The student doesn't immediately grasp an idea and confusion results. New information cannot be moved into long-term memory unless it "fits" with what the student already knows and understands. The lecture moves on, leaving the student behind, grappling with unclear ideas, and not attending to new ones.
3. **Translation troubles.** Instructors may use terms unfamiliar to students. Familiarity with biology makes us casual about its language and interchangeable terms. Students are much less able to make the necessary translation. As they struggle to integrate familiar and unfamiliar terms, we move on and lose them.
4. **Sidetracks.** Here, the student is at the root of the problem. You say something that triggers another chain of thought. The student pursues it, perhaps anguishing over the inability to understand. While the student is on this sidetrack, all new input passes by. (adapted from Rowe, 1983)

See the following list of *Lecture Variations and Alternatives* for possible solutions to the above problems.

LECTURE VARIATIONS AND ALTERNATIVES

1. **Lecture with periodic pauses.** This improves comprehension and retention of lecture material. Discussion helps students clarify and assimilate lecture content. Format: Lecture 12-15 minutes; pause for two minutes. Students ask questions, review, discuss, revise their notes, and clarify problem areas (repeat pattern). In the last three minutes of class, students write everything they can recall from the lecture.
2. **Energy shifts: Alternate mini-lectures and discussions.** Set the stage with a 15-20 minute lecture, followed by 10-15 minutes of discussion. A new topic is introduced during another 15 minute mini-lecture, followed again by 10-15 minutes of discussion. Give students an assignment at the end of class, and begin the next class with a short discussion of that assignment.
3. **Feedback lecture.** Format: Before class, students do "study questions" related to lecture; begin with 20 minutes of lecture; then 10 minutes for small groups to discuss questions related to the lecture; then 20 minutes lecture. After class, students do new "study questions."
4. **Feedback loops.** With this technique you elicit feedback from students during the class and modify your presentation based on that feedback. There's a disadvantage: Feedback loops guarantee detours from your nice, neat lesson plan, but they help students understand and retain interest in class.
5. **Lecture with immediate test.** Many people comprehend and retain material better when tested quickly and frequently. Format: Give a short test on that day's lecture at the end of the lecture, every time. In one study, this method doubled the retention of the lecture material on a test given eight weeks after the last lecture.
6. **Guided lecture.** The guided lecture helps students synthesize lecture material while taking better notes. Give students lecture objectives for the day and then have them put their pens down during the lecture. After spending half the class period lecturing, ask students to briefly write down all they can recall from lecture. Place students in small groups to reconstruct the lecture with their own supporting ideas. Students may like the cooperative interaction and end up with notes that are superior to those produced individually. Format: 30 minutes of lecture during which students take NO notes; for 5 minutes students take notes on what they remember; for 15 minutes small groups discuss teacher-provided

questions related to lecture and write down notes based on group discussions.

7. **The participatory lecture.** Students are encouraged to develop ideas that are then organized on the chalkboard. Devote one class per week to answering open-ended, student-generated questions about course content. List questions on the board, and let students rank them in order of importance. This list becomes the outline for the day's lecture. If you are uncomfortable relinquishing so much structure to students, ask for questions the day before.

8. **Paired learning strategy.** A paired learning strategy requires one student to answer a question, give an explanation, or do a problem, while the other plays the role of a critical listener asking for clarification, examples, or more information from the first student. These roles are alternated. For instance, give all students in the class a short article to read related to the topic of the day. Pair up students--one is the explainer and one is the listener. Without looking at the article again, the explainer tries to explain to the other student, in about 5 minutes, what the article said. The listener asks questions to correct the explanation or for clarification. The advantage here is that everyone has the opportunity to participate in a meaningful way in each situation presented. Students also demonstrate what they know or reveal to themselves where they need to concentrate their efforts. Listeners hear how other students perceive the material or procedure and are introduced to alternative ways of thinking about the concepts or doing the problems. The obvious disadvantage is that students may explain things to one another incorrectly. To counter this, provide a summary of an explanation or answer that has been assigned.

9. **Modeling analytical skills.** Students follow along in their books, handouts, or overhead projector, and watch you work through selected passages of a text or handout. You demonstrate your learning style by "walking students through the analysis of the information."

10. **Cutting large classes in half without losing control. Debates:** divide students into two groups, each supporting one side of an issue. Provide students with ample background information and materials prior to the day of the debate, or have them do the background research themselves.

11. **Smaller groups in large classes: simulations and role-playing.** After a mini-lecture, organize the students into small groups. Give each group an explicit role and a specific task to pursue. Conclude the class by discussing the solutions or suggestions from each group or instruct the groups to prepare speeches. Divide your class into groups and have them work to solve common problems.

12. **Reflective techniques.** This is an "umbrella" term for a whole collection of techniques that rely on the old, but effective, Socratic method of answering a question with a question. Help the questioner reason the answer out. (See the chapter on inquiry.)

13. **Action mazes.** Begin with a problem that has three optional solutions: one is right; one sounds right but is wrong and leads to a circuitous journey; and one is OK, but leads to a longer journey than the right answer. These experiences help students see consequences of their decisions, learning to reason through problems.

14. **Short writing exercises.** Begin class with students producing a short, informal writing that summarizes a previous lecture and that leads into the subject for the day. Ask a few students to read their writing aloud and invite class responses to them. Or, use short, in-class writings that give students a chance to explain their understanding of the material. End class with a short writing assignment that asks students to summarize the lecture or to develop specific questions about the material.

15. **Case studies.** Have students analyze a concrete problem related to a course-related subject. The case--presented by you in one or two pages--is often a real situation described using authentic information. The case leads to a crisis that requires the student to make a diagnosis or a decision based on the knowledge he or she acquires. Each student or group analyzes the problem, collects information and applies their knowledge to find a solution leading to a concrete action.

The use of cases involves learning by doing, the development of analytical and decision-making skills, learning how to grapple with messy real-life problems, the development of oral communication skills, and teamwork. Case study may strongly appeal to students turned off by traditional science courses with their heavy reliance on lecture and preoccupation with detailed content. In courses for non-majors where cases are used, 95% of the students attend, compared with 50%-65% in the traditional lecture courses. Here are several different types of cases:

Discussion Format--you ask probing questions and students analyze the problem depicted in a story given to them.

Debate format--works best in cases with two diametrically opposed sides.

Public Hearing Format--a student panel, role-playing as a hearing board, asks questions of presenters.

Trial format--you introduce the case and students role-play attorneys and witnesses.

Scientific Research Team format--students collect and analyze data, and you use results to guide discussions and to illustrate steps involved in data analysis.

Team learning Format--use cooperative or collaborative learning techniques with small groups, individuals complete readings and are evaluated on readings both individually and as a group. Answers are discussed, you offer clarification after which students apply the facts and principles to a problem or case.

(adapted from Frederick, 1986; Broadwell, 1989; Johnson, 1990; Pestel, 1990; Bonwell and Eison, 1991; Pregent, 1994)

GROUP LEARNING

Remember, you don't have to lecture. There are alternatives that actively engage students in the learning process. Many instructors use small group activities to liven up their classes, even (or perhaps especially) during a lecture to several hundred students. You can break your entire class into small groups and then bring students back together to share what they have learned in their small group. In lecture you can present a problem to the entire class and instruct the students to consult with the students sitting on either side of them for no more than 3 to 5 minutes. Individuals are then asked to report the results of their group's consultation to the entire class, and the results are recorded on the blackboard. Group projects can also involve laboratory experiments or library research. The following pages deal with group activities.

Cooperative Learning

Cooperative learning is a form of group learning that tends to promote higher motivation to learn, produces more positive attitudes toward learning experiences and instructors, and results in students who care about learning and assisting one another (Johnson and Johnson, 1987). The emphasis in cooperative activities is on negotiating meaning and arriving at consensus. Getting students to make sense of what they are learning is given highest priority, and rote learning of procedures and facts to obtain correct solutions is not encouraged.

Although not everyone views cooperative learning as a panacea, it is a potentially valuable activity because of the need for students to clarify, defend, elaborate, evaluate, and argue with one another. Cooperative learning strategies promoted higher achievement than other strategies if the task involved problem solving or concept development (Johnson, et al., 1986). However, there was no difference in achievement relative to strategy if the task involved memorization or correcting problems. Slavin (1987) reported that cooperative discussion increased the student's retention of reading material and improved student's abilities to solve problems.

The key in cooperative learning is to provide a common goal that can be achieved only with participation by *all* group members. The goal might be to design and execute a successful experiment, solve a problem, or develop a research strategy. The group product should be presented in some forum that provides practice and support for learning to function as a group. An example of group learning is hypothesis development, a brainstorming exercise that is directed at generating a wide range of possible answers. This exercise encourages students to think broadly and helps them come to grips with the notion that there are not always simple answers to most problems in biology. Show students a picture of some natural phenomenon such as a bare zone under a tree and ask them what might have caused the bare spot. Students generate a list of possible causes, each of which can then be used as a basis for setting up an experiment that can be discussed or actually conducted.

Students can also engage in collective decision-making on issues such as land, energy, or water use. Groups of students can be asked to take on the role of policy-makers who must make tough decisions requiring biological information such as where to build the next landfill in their city or town. The desire to appear responsible and rational should induce them to become experts on the issue, which will require learning information, thinking critically, and developing a creative solution (Handelsman, Houser, and Kriegel, 1994). This focus on real-world problems helps prepare students to be future participating citizens while promoting student-active learning.

Working in cooperative learning teams increases a student's self-esteem, and increases a student's motivation to learn and to help others learn. Cooperative learning decreases student dependence on the instructor and increases student responsibility for his or her own learning. Cooperative learning also models the process scientists use when collaborating.

- Cooperative learning empowers the students, making them responsible for seeking information and achieving a particular task.

- Cooperative learning strategies model features of the scientific enterprise.

- Research has shown that cooperative learning is an effective technique for involving students from groups that are underrepresented in science, such as female and minority students.

- Cooperative learning can be a powerful way to interest and motivate students who might not otherwise excel or even be interested in science.

What to do when teams do not cooperate

Cooperation might not come naturally to every student on a team. This reality of the classroom setting makes cooperative learning a challenge at times. How you handle the first signs of non-cooperation will set the tone for the class. As you plan your strategies for improving the cooperative nature of each student and team, keep in mind the following:

First, let students take the responsibility for solving problems. Avoid functioning as the source of solutions to all problems; turn problems back to teams whenever possible. Practice being a consultant. Offer a variety of suggestions from which students choose. Ask students what strategies they have tried and what alternatives they would like to try.

Second, remind students that it takes time to become proficient at cooperative learning. For students with poor working relationship skills, this could mean it will take all semester for them to praise others. Watch for small signs of progress.

Third, establish a classroom environment of respect and acceptance for each person. You can do this by modeling desired behaviors yourself. Do not show tolerance for negative remarks or put-downs. Identify strengths in each student and point those out as appropriate. Encourage students to do these things also. (adapted from BSCS, 1997)

KEYS TO SUCCESSFUL GROUP LEARNING

1. Use class time for group work.
2. Use assignments that promote both active discussion of concepts and team development. Students must learn how to cooperate, how to work with other people who might be completely different, and how to manage their teams.
3. Use a grading system that ensures both individual accountability and rewards group work. The potential gains can be completely undermined if each student is not held responsible for knowing and understanding all aspects of the project.
4. Use a group formation process that ensures that groups are maximally heterogeneous, assets and liabilities are spread across groups, and the development of cohesive subgroups is unlikely. Students must learn to work with other people whom they would not necessarily choose as teammates or who may differ from themselves in learning style, background, or ability.
5. Assign tasks that are complex enough so that a group is needed to complete it better than an individual could alone. Members of a team must rely on each other for critical pieces of information or the accomplishment of crucial jobs in order to finish a given assignment.
6. Provide feedback, repeatedly, to each team on how well it did, especially compared to other groups.
7. If students have not been exposed to this type of strategy before, it may be a difficult for some students to adjust to cooperative learning. (Your students may be interested to know that more people get fired from jobs because of an inability to work with others than because they are unable to do their work).

CHARACTERISTICS OF EFFECTIVE GROUP ASSIGNMENTS

The nature of group tasks has a tremendous effect on the quality of the learning experience they provide. To work well, group assignments should have certain characteristics. Assignments:

1. must require groups to produce a tangible output, otherwise neither you nor your students will have an idea about the effectiveness of the groups. It is **not** recommended that group term papers be assigned, however, because this task, by its very nature, is not appropriate for group activity.
2. must involve decision-making tasks.
3. must be impossible to complete unless students understand the course concepts, otherwise, students see assignments as "make work" projects.
4. must be difficult enough that very few, if any, students can successfully complete the assignments working alone. Assignments will facilitate team development when they require members to make a decision with respect to a complex set of data.
5. should allow groups to spend the majority of their time engaged in the kinds of activities that groups do well, such as identifying problems, formulating strategies, processing information, and making decisions, and a minimum of time engaged in activities that individuals could do more efficiently working alone, such as creating a polished written document.
6. should give students the opportunity to practice dealing with the same kind of issues and problem situations they will encounter in later course work or in future jobs.
7. should provide immediate and unambiguous feedback on the group's performance so that the team may make comparisons to a standard and/or the performance of comparable groups.
8. should be interesting and fun.
(adapted from Michaelsen, 1992)

PROMOTING GROUP PRESENTATIONS

1. **Limit the** number of presentations any given day or term, or spread presentations over several weeks. Limit the length of the presentations and hold students to those limits.
2. **Offer options for the groups.** Preparing and making a group presentation is a good experience for students, but so is creating a detailed poster, constructing a visual representation of the project, or making an audio- or videotape. Spell out the options clearly and let the groups decide. You may want to limit the number of groups who select each option.
3. **Teach students about group presentations.** Left to their own devices, students tend to divide presentations into equal parts, assigning each group member an individual installment. Seldom are these individual chunks related to each other or made into a coherent whole. Propose some alternative models: have some members present the larger group effort, while those not presenting prepare visuals or handouts. Stress the importance of practicing together before the presentation, in the interest of hearing what the others say and keeping within the time limits. Most basic speech textbooks include ideas and information about panels and other forms of groups presentations.
4. **Use the presentations.** Try to encourage students to learn from the presentations. Include questions on the next exam that relate to content in the presentations. Make reference to group presentations in subsequent lectures. Use the expertise of particular groups to continue to inform and enrich subsequent discussions. Have students respond to some (or all) of the group presentations with short, in-class writing assignments--two-minute reaction papers. Share a selection of those comments with the group. (adapted from Weimer, 1991a; Davis, 1992; Knoedler and Shea, 1992)

How can you make your lectures more effective, and what can you do to decrease the passivity of your students? What efforts are you making **not** to lecture—incorporate at least one activity per lecture to break up your talking.

CHAPTER XI. GOOD DISCUSSIONS

If you want your students to be active participants in your class, you need to involve them right from the beginning. The first days of class set the tone for the remainder of the course. Students should receive the message clearly and early that they are expected to participate, asking and answering questions and contributing to the discussion.

In one study of classroom activity, the mean percentage of total class time spent with students answering questions from the professor was less than 4 percent. Of those questions, 63% were memory questions (recalling specific data), 19% were routine administrative questions, and only 18% required higher-order thinking. Nearly one-third of the questions asked did not receive a response from students. These percentages are, unfortunately, not atypical. In many classes, questions are never asked of students, and students are discouraged from asking their own.

Students learn more about concepts when they have an opportunity to discuss them. Whether in the laboratory, a separate discussion, or lecture, you must get students to speak (or write) what is on their minds. More learning, however, is likely to happen in discussion than in lecture (Cashin and McKnight, 1986). A discussion focuses on two-way, spoken communication between the instructor and students and among students themselves. The following pages outline some ways to promote discussion.

DISCUSSION SECTIONS ARE EFFECTIVE FOR:

1. encouraging greater student participation and responsibility;
2. increasing student retention of knowledge;
3. developing problem-solving skills;
4. increasing motivation for further learning;
5. creating positive attitudes towards learning;
6. developing skills related to group work;
7. providing you with feedback about student learning and how much students actually understand;
8. practicing higher-order learning skills—analysis, application, synthesis, and evaluation; and
9. allowing students to become more active participants in their learning.

TRAITS OF GOOD DISCUSSION LEADERS

Remember, it is essential that students have th opportunity to discuss the ideas that have bee presented to them—to demonstrate their level understanding and to help them make the connection necessary between what they know and what they a trying to learn. The following is a list of traits individuals who lead discussions effectively.

1. **Effective Questioning:** asking different types questions, including those requiring higher-lev thought processes (e.g., analysis and synthesis).
2. **Active Listening:** hearing what a person is statin and assessing their understanding of a subject.
3. **Peripheral Vision:** seeing and hearing the entir group of students, and using this ability to determin if each student is engaged.
4. **Empathy:** seeing issues from another person' perspective in order to make students fee comfortable discussing the non-majority view.
5. **Sense of Timing:** knowing when to intervene wit a question, summary, or bridge from an earlie remark, and when to remain silent.
6. **Clarity:** knowing how to convey information in way that is easy to understand, e.g., by using th chalkboard to clarify issues.
7. **Differentiation:** separating yourself from th students to facilitate the group process withou becoming totally absorbed in the subject matter.
8. **Variability:** sensing when to be serious humorous, thought-provoking or supportive depending on circumstances.
9. **Connecting with the Group:** reaching eac participant in the discussion, accounting for th emotional and intellectual state of the individual.
10. **Self-disclosure:** willingness to share feelings thoughts, and appropriate personal information.
11. **Flexibility:** willingness to make changes in th discussion format and content, if necessary, t accommodate student interests. (Adapted fron Davidson and Ambrose, 1994)

IMPROVING DISCUSSIONS

Discussions consume more time than lectures, and thus they are not conducive to covering great amounts of content (but teaching content **should not** be your primary goal anyway). Discussions require more forethought, and you have less control. Thus, there may be some initial discomfort in getting students to talk and for you to ask questions. In a good discussion, let students tell you what they know about the subject. Then, based on what they say, ask questions and lead them to correct misconceptions, and to explain and extend their knowledge rather than lecturing to them. Also, get students to follow a logical thought process as they discuss each concept, explaining how they know what they know.

Tactics for Asking Questions

1. **Start asking questions early** in the course, and make questioning an important part of your daily activities.
2. **Avoid "yes" and "no" questions.** Ask analytical questions and give students ample time to respond. Ask questions that require inference, prediction, analogy, or synthesis of divergent ideas.
3. **Ask only one question at a time.**
4. **Frame questions simply,** using a vocabulary that is appropriate for the students, but ask questions at various levels of thinking.
5. **Acknowledge all contributions.** Let students know you appreciate their participation.
6. **Provide positive reinforcement.** Praise students in a positive, encouraging way for correct or excellent responses. However, be careful in your criticism or praise: a positive response, overdone, can embarrass as much as a negative response.
7. **Avoid the trap of stock responses:** if every contribution is "Good!" or "Excellent!" these words of praise lose their meaning. Be specific: "Good thinking!" "Unusual, but you're right." "I'm glad you remembered that." "A point I hadn't considered!"
8. **Repeat the question.** If the class looks blank, paraphrase, and offer a clue. Redirect the question to a different student or to the class.
9. **Wait for the answer.** Count to TEN with the expectation that a student will volunteer a response. Give students time to think--many good questions require time to consider as well as time to formulate answers.
10. **DON'T ANSWER YOUR OWN QUESTIONS!** If you do, students will stop thinking and let you do all the questioning and answering.
11. **Create small groups.** If students don't respond to your question, break the class into small groups and get them to develop answers. Then, bring the whole class back together and have a spokesperson from each group report on their group's discussion.
12. **Provide opportunities to ask questions.** Let students know that you value their questions, rewarding those who ask questions.
13. **Probe for explanations.** Ask, "How did you arrive at that response?" Ask this question when you receive both inadequate and good responses. **It's important for students to recognize how they know what they know.** This is also good for "know-it-all" students who blurt out answers before other students can. They might know a specific fact, but what is the logic behind the answer?
14. **Encourage more than one answer.** Ask for more information. Don't stop looking for potential answers as soon as you get a "correct" response.
15. **Invite students to elaborate.** After acknowledging an answer, elaborate or present another perspective. Take student responses and follow them as far as students find interesting and you consider worthwhile. Don't worry about getting "off the track." A discussion should not run on straight and narrow rails.
16. **Move out among the students.** Use direct eye contact. Walk close to students who are quiet or disruptive and talk directly to them. Call on students by name. Moving around may involve quiet students--when they respond, voice their response to the entire class for them. (They may be shy about speaking in front of the class, so do it for them.)
17. **Encourage a variety of students to participate.** Call on many students, not just the same few. Be careful about embarrassing students who seldom volunteer responses, and do not embarrass or scold students who give wrong answers. Determine why students give wrong answers and help correct the answers.
18. **Accept the unexpected.** When a student makes an unexpected point, don't respond with "No, that's not what I had in mind" or give a puzzled look in silence.
19. **Record student ideas,** questions, and suggestions on the blackboard. Use this visible display to tie student contributions together, to point out differences, or to wrap up the discussion. Make certain <u>you summarize</u> each discussion. Students also may remain "on task" if they know their work is to be displayed to the class as a poster or on an overhead.

20. **Create an environment of trust and mutual respect** so that discussion is not inhibited by fear. Introduce an ice-breaking activity that allows students to get to know one another. Students must be assured that it is important to explore and understand a diversity of people and opinions. Students must be viewed as individuals rather than as belonging to racial, ethnic, or gender categories.

21. **Ask students with sharp differences of opinion to explain their positions.** A listener may explain what was said by another person. When the first speaker is satisfied that he has been understood accurately, then the two can reverse roles. In this way you can build accuracy of communication and encourage mutual respect. Often differences that seemed great initially are minimized. If arguments between students start to become abusive, intervene. Take the place of the student who is being attacked and answer for him or her until tempers cool and the two initial adversaries can safely face one another again.

22. Take a moment after every class and **give yourself a grade** based on the tips suggested above. How open and flexible are you to your students? How do you encourage students to get involved? How do you deal with wrong answers or irrelevant comments? (adapted from Grambs and Carr, 1979; Weimer, 1987c and d; Neff and Weimer, 1989; Magnan, 1990; Weimer, 1990; Weimer, 1991b; Maier, 1992; Billingsley, 1993; Auster and MacRone, 1994)

WAIT TIME

One of the best ways to improve your class and you teaching is by waiting an adequate time after you ask a question in class. "Wait time" provides an opportunity for students to reflect on the question and to form an answer. When the average length of wait time was greater than about 3 seconds, Rowe (1974a and b) reported an increase in the length of student responses; an increase in the number of unsolicited, but appropriate, student responses; an increase in the number of responses rated as speculative; a decrease in the number of students failing to respond; an increase in student-to-student comparisons of data; an increase in student inferences supported by evidence; an increase in the number of responses from students rated by instructors as relatively slow learners; and an increase in the variety of positive verbal behaviors exhibited by students. **Student learning increases when you use an extended wait time in your lessons.** A rule of thumb is to count to ten under your breath after you ask a question before you rephrase the question and then wait again for responses. Remember, don't answer your own questions!

QUESTIONS TO ENHANCE DISCUSSIONS

Ask a variety of questions in your discussion. By doing so, students with different abilities and backgrounds might be able to contribute to the discussion. Categories of questions to ask include:

1. **Informational.** Questions that determine whether students have assembled information and that call for naming, identifying, and describing information. This includes identification and recall of information-- "Who, what, when, where, how?"

2. **Leading.** Questions that clue students to answers or to processes that could be used to find answers. These questions supply students with some information and ask them to infer a relationship. "Could you tell what kind of animal it is if I were to tell you how many legs it has?"

3. **Application**. Such questions should lead students to apply concepts, principles, or generalizations in different contexts. This includes organization, selection, and use of facts, ideas, and principles. "How is this an example of...? How is this related to...? Why is this significant?"

4. **Analysis and synthesis.** These questions require students to draw on the knowledge they have learned and to analyze (separate a whole into its component parts) or synthesize (combine ideas to form a new whole). This includes: Outlining and diagraming, How does this compare/contrast with...? What evidence can you list for...? What would you predict/infer from...? What solutions would you suggest...? How would you create/design a...?"

5. **Evaluation.** Correct answers to these questions depend on the ability of the student to defend his/her position with information. This includes development of opinions, judgments, or decisions: "Do you agree...? What is the most important...? Place the following in order or priority... How would you decide about...? What criteria would you use to assess...?"

6. **Problem-solving.** These questions enable students to use their creativity in devising solutions to problems. This active involvement enables students to store information in and retrieve information from long-term memory. An example: "How would you develop a plan to preserve and protect an endangered plant species while minimizing the impact on the local economy of the region in which the species is found?"

7. **Probing.** These questions often start with "Why? or How do you know?" after a student gives you a simplistic response. This forces the student to go beyond surface responses to your questions. This includes: open-ended questions searching for additional data or relationships or that encourage explanation. (adapted from Rowe, 1978; Johnson, 1990; Fisch, 1992)

STRATEGIES FOR *ANSWERING* STUDENT QUESTIONS

A discussion should be a dialogue, which means you will need to answer questions yourself. The following are ways to deal with difficult questions.

1. **The question you can't understand.** Ask the student to repeat or rephrase the question. Don't be afraid to admit that you don't know or understand. Also, you might tactfully ask other students to interpret the question for you.

2. **The question that is irrelevant.** The question might not be bad, but just inappropriate at the time. Recognize the value of the question when responding to the student, but don't get the class off track by addressing the answer to the entire class. You can answer the question but make sure the *entire* class doesn't worry about understanding the question or your response.

3. **The question for which you don't know the answer.** It's tempting to fake it, using terms and vocal authority. Don't; be honest. You don't have to know answers to every question. You can also try to reason out an answer in front of students to show how you try to answer questions.

4. **The stupid question.** Despite what you may have heard, students sometimes ask stupid questions. As long as the student is sincere, however, answer the question and then move on quickly--don't make a big deal out of it.

5. **Questions that challenge your authority.** These questions invite you to lose your cool. Stay calm, and don't start a public debate. You may deal with the issue privately. Be prepared to answer questions such as, "Why do we have to learn this stuff anyway?" There are many responses to this question, such as "Because this information forms a foundation for other concepts, or because without this information the concept as a whole doesn't make sense." Avoid answering, "Because I said so." (adapted from Weimer, 1987b)

HOW TO BUILD RAPPORT WITH STUDENTS TO ENCOURAGE DISCUSSION

You Can:
>   share relevant personal experiences,
>   admit uncertainties,
>   be open to new ideas,
>   listen carefully to students' statements, and
>   be tolerant of different points of view.

You Can Ask or Say:
>   "Can you think of a situation in which this might or might not apply?"
>   "That's an interesting idea. Tell me more."
>   "I don't know either, but that's a very interesting question. Can anyone help us unravel ourselves here?"
>   "I'm not sure I understand. Can you give me an example?"
>   "Feels to me like we've strayed from the point. Have we?"
>   "Let's not forget the basic problem we're trying to solve."

You Can Act in the Following Ways:
>   show enthusiasm when listening to student responses, nodding as students talk.
>   keep eye contact with students who are talking.
>   walk toward the student who is talking.
>   walk around the room during a discussion, so students will view people in different parts of the room.
>   look relaxed by sitting on a desk or pulling up a desk or chair and joining the class.
>   arrange chairs in a circle or other configuration so students can see each other talking.
>   stand by students who have not contributed—your proximity may draw them into the conversation.   (adapted from OSU, 1990)

SPECIAL DISCUSSION FORMATS

1. **Brainstorming**...a technique designed to encourag the development of ideas on an unrestricted basis Ask students for as many different ideas as possibl about a particular situation or solutions to a problen There are four rules: (1) evaluation and criticism c ideas by group members are forbidden, (2)   a contributions are to be encouraged, (3) an attemp should be made to create the greatest quantity c ideas, and (4) a combination of ideas and solution should be sought.

2. **Buzz groups**...the class is split into groups. Eacl group discusses an assigned topic. After a period c discussion, group representatives report back t entire class.

3. **Cases**...the entire class or subdivisions of the clas: examine a situation or problem, followed by thei suggested solutions.

4. **Debate**...as many people as desired may be involved, but at least two pro and two con. Thes people alternate speaking turns and the debate may be followed by a class forum.

5. **Panel**...three to twelve people, usually abou five...there are no prepared speeches but eacl participant may present a 5-minute introduction followed by questions from the audience anc discussion.

6. **"RISK" technique**...present in detail a proposec procedure or policy. Students brainstorm "risks' (fears, problems, doubts, concerns, etc.)...and eacl group of students decides if each "risk" is serious and substantive.

7. **Role playing**...individuals become role players Individuals or small groups discuss roles, and revised roles are identified, enacted, discussed, and generalized by class.

8. **Simulation/gaming**...students participate in a game or simulation about a particular topic. The class describes the experience and then evaluates it. The experience is linked to the everyday life of the student.

9. **Symposium**...three to twelve people give prepared speeches related to a specific topic. Questions follow each presentation, and class discussion follows all speeches.

What specific techniques will you try in your discussions that increase the interactions, participation, and learning of your students? Make it a point to get a person who has not yet contributed in class to answer a question, or to pose a question that he/she would like to ask.

CHAPTER XII.   ORGANIZING YOUR COURSE

WHAT YOU NEED TO CONSIDER WHEN TEACHING

1. **What do you want your students to know, value, and be able to do by the end of class?** (Your objectives)

2. **How can students be *actively* involved in acquiring knowledge, positive attitudes, and skills so that your objectives can be reached? How are you going to help students learn?** (Using inquiry, class and field activities, and different learning strategies--see the list at the end of the chapter)

3. **What do your students already know?** (Misconceptions you must help correct; and their various backgrounds)

4. **Are you sure all your students are "on the same page" as you?** (Proper lecture techniques, front-loading, discussions, and assessment)

5. **How do you know students understand concepts and have acquired skills related to your objectives?** (Assessment)

ORGANIZING YOUR COURSE

Should your course be a one-semester survey of all the major achievements of a scientific discipline? According to Arons (1990), courses like this are doomed to failure for two reasons: (1) they subject students to an incomprehensible stream of technical jargon that is not rooted in experience accessible to the learner; and (2) the pace makes it difficult, if not impossible, to develop a sense of how concepts and theories originate, how they come to be validated, and how they connect with experience and reveal relations among seemingly disparate phenomena. On the other hand, courses that focus entirely on some narrow topical area such as the energy crisis do not succeed because genuine comprehension of the scientific concepts, theories, and insights is an integral part of understanding the complex

problems addressed in these courses. So, what do you do? Back off, slow down, cover less, give students a chance to follow and absorb the development of a small number of major scientific ideas or concepts.

New professors who received good or excellent student evaluations reported spending from 16-20 hours per week preparing their lectures and other course materials. The personal rewards of teaching were the most frequently cited sources of self-esteem and well-being for these faculty. On the other hand, those new professors who did not fare well on evaluations often felt highly motivated but insecure in their own knowledge and skills. They spent 35 hours a week preparing lectures. They came across as stiff, formal, and generally uncomfortable in the classroom. They admitted to being humorless, non-spontaneous, content-driven, and fostering little student participation. These people were often over-prepared and, by talking fast, were determined to get it all said. They became angry, distraught, and confused with negative student evaluations and blamed students for their plight. (Turner and Boice, 1989).

What do you want your students to know, value, and be able to do by the end of your course? Rather than designing the syllabus while focusing on *content*, design your course with other desired student outcomes (such as thinking skills) in mind. Think of your objectives first. When organizing your course, focus on a few main ideas: emphasize hands-on and minds-on activities where students manipulate materials and where they have to think about what they are doing. Stress problem solving, hypothesis or prediction testing, and applying parts of a scientific method of investigation--facilitating discovery of concepts by your students. Focus on the teaching philosophy that "less is more"--teach less trivia and spend more time developing major concepts and themes.

What teaching strategies maximize learning? The following pages include strategies you might consider as you organize your course.

STEPS IN PLANNING A COURSE

1. **Determine the backgrounds and interests of your students.** (Do you need to spend time on basic chemistry for non-majors? Do you have to include more human examples for your nursing majors?)
2. **Write your objectives for the course** based on student backgrounds and on the knowledge and skills that you deem appropriate for your students to obtain (as well as on your interest and expertise). What do you want your students to know, value, and be able to do by the end of your course? (If you want students to know how to design and conduct investigations, you need to build in activities that allow students to investigate a problem of their own choosing.)
3. **Choose and develop the learning experiences to achieve the objectives.** These experiences include in-class activities such as lectures, laboratories, projects, and debates, as well as out-of-class activities such as required readings and homework assignments (see teaching strategies below).
4. **Plan assessments** of students' learning through tests, written reports, and other assessment techniques and feedback--focusing on your objectives.
5. **Choose the scope and content of the course** based on the above considerations as well as time and money constraints. (First, focus on major ideas only and the big picture--like the unifying principles. Then, fill in with only the important details.)
6. **Prepare a syllabus** based on the considerations above. (adapted from Davidson and Ambrose, 1994)

MAJORS OR NON-MAJORS?

While most faculty agree that all biology courses should include a laboratory experience and that students should be given practice using scientific methods of investigation, most faculty reduce the number of topics covered for non-majors, and have different goals and standards for majors. Faculty who teach non-majors have identified five critical problems that exist in teaching this group of students: (1) poor preparation of students in reading and writing; (2) poor preparation in math; (3)

lack of motivation; (4) inability to reason; and (5) fear of science (McIntosh and Caprio, 1990). The four-year non-major population also consists of students whose goals do not include a career in biology or related fields. They often are unmotivated by science in general even though they are otherwise good students. Non-majors may be interested in learning but not necessarily in learning about biology. Also, because faculty members often are teaching hundreds of students at one time, personal interactions between faculty and students are rare, resulting in the alienation of some students. Non-majors' courses often skimp on the activities and results of science that are needed both by the student who _might_ want to become a scientist and by the student who, as a citizen, needs to know more about what science is and how it operates. Non-major students have few opportunities to make connections between classroom information and the world outside and to participate in scientific investigations (Project Kaleidoscope, 1991). Thus, the following is a list of goals for a biology class that includes non-majors.

By the end of an introductory course in biology, non-majors should be able to:

*   appreciate and value science,
*   make informed decisions about science-related personal and social issues,
*   read, understand, critique, and discuss popular scientific information,
*   defend positions on science-related issues,
*   apply scientific processes of investigation to daily life,
*   make sense of the natural world,
*   understand the major principles of biology and science as a process, and
*   understand the role of humans in the biosphere.

The obvious question here is: Aren't all of the above objectives also desirable goals for biology _majors_? The rest of the chapter includes ideas for courses--whether for majors or non-majors--including teaching strategies and overarching structures that help organize your entire program, such as curriculum themes.

DESIGNING YOUR COURSE

Well, what should you teach? First, if you want your students (and fellow citizens) to be more scientifically literate, then you must realize that **literacy is much more than knowing factual information.** The following is what I consider important to teach in an introductory course in biology. In my opinion, students should be taught "big ideas and major skills" in biology. Big ideas are those such as evolution that unify all of biology, and major skills are those such as asking good questions and figuring out ways to answer them. I think it makes less difference what *facts* of biology you choose to teach your students as long as you also focus on major skills and ideas. However, **your primary goal should never be simply to teach factual information.** The problem is developing a course that balances process skills, thinking skills, and content. Fight your natural inclination to cram content into the course, even for majors. You can always add more content at the last minute if you can't help yourself, but conducting an inquiry-oriented lab takes planning. Here are a few big ideas and major skills to consider.

1. **Nothing in biology makes sense except in the light of evolution** (Dobzhansky, 1973). Most college students have a poor background and understanding of evolution. In fact, they usually possess major misconceptions about evolution and how it happens. Spend time developing the ideas of genetic variation, natural selection, and evolution, and demonstrate how biological information supports and fits into this overarching theme of biology. Keep in mind, "What is the significance or advantage of this particular structure, process, or function to the organism?" (Or is there any significance or advantage?) In relation to this, develop and illustrate the idea of *form and function.*

2. **What is the difference between cause and effect, correlation, and chance occurrences?** How can a person tell what has caused a particular natural phenomenon? When two events occur close together in time, did one event cause the other, or was the timing simply coincidental--such as a person whose cancer disappears after taking coffee enemas. Is a person's life controlled by the position of the stars as astrologists tell us--can a horoscope really predict your future? What is the difference between science, the supernatural, and pseudoscience, and how can you tell?

3. **Organize your course around unifying principles** (see Chapter 8), limit the content, and show how the content supports these unifying themes. Use the unifying principles to organize the major concepts you teach. This is where cell theory, metabolism, and genetic continuity (other big ideas in biology) come into play. For instance, don't just list the tissues in a leaf, but show how the structure and organization of the tissues allow the plant to obtain energy and raw materials for growth and development. **Let students learn biological information from the activities in which they participate**--let the laboratories, experiments, and projects be the source of much of the biological content for your students. Use class time to help your students develop thinking and investigative skills instead of marching them through the textbook material--which they can do on their own. Help them see connections between the information you present and how to make use of the knowledge they gain. Help them find patterns in nature and to explain anomalies.

4. **Content should not be the focus of your course.** In terms of factual information--the content-- remember that a science course is similar to a foreign language class in terms of the number of new vocabulary words given to students in a semester--in many cases, science students are introduced to *more* new terms--and, how many words do you remember from the French class you took as a freshman? So, **eliminate the vocabulary words that your students will use only once during the course,** or life, and let students learn the terms in context. If you don't build upon the vocabulary you give students, then reconsider teaching that information. For instance, my non-majors no longer have to memorize the names of different types of fruit (pepo, pome, follicle, etc.). Now, they compare size, shape, and fleshiness of fruits to decide how fruits are dispersed (focusing on form and function). You will give students terms to learn no matter what anyone says, but make a concerted effort to reduce terminology and focus on the bigger ideas in biology.

5. **Students should come away with an appreciation for what is interesting in biology, what excites you about the discipline, and the importance of basic research.** This has to do with what students should *value* by the end of your course. Certainly, being active participants in class will increase student interest in the discipline, so

have students conduct lots of activities and investigations. Expose students to living organisms in their native habitat. Use interesting or amusing anecdotes and biological trivia (there are plants alive today that began their lives before the birth of Christ). Just don't test on this trivia. This is also where the relevancy issue arises. **How does the information you teach relate to the lives of your students**, and how can the information and skills that students gain in your course be used outside of the classroom? For instance, if you teach about mitosis, discussing cancer as being uncontrolled mitosis might interest more students than if you simply describe the stages of the mitotic process. Most importantly, **students must experience biology in the way it is conducted.**

6. **Students must understand what a good investigation entails, and how to design, conduct, and report on an experiment of their own. This is what inquiry is about.** Can students ask good questions, recognize a controlled experiment, or identify what is wrong with the information that results from a poorly designed experiment? Can they use a scientific process of investigation to solve a problem, and can they recognize how this process differs from belief systems? I think it is critical that **students conduct investigations based on their interest and their own design.**

    Investigative skills also include the interpretation of data--can students draw and interpret a graph and explain information presented to them in other forms? Can they use basic scientific equipment properly to obtain appropriate and accurate data? **Use your own research** (and that with which you are familiar) **as a model for students** to see how to conduct investigations and to learn about biology. Your natural enthusiasm about your own research also may be contagious.

7. **Reliability of sources.** Does the *author of an* article have a particular bias, and does this affect the information or arguments presented? What are alternative explanations to those proposed? How does one sort through the information presented in advertisements, and what do data such as opinion polls really tell us? Can students select useful information from the morass of facts available to them? Do students rely on evidence to make decisions--**what is the evidence to support a claim or possible explanation--are they skeptical?**

8. **How do students know what they know?** To me, it is as important for students to explain how they got an answer to a question as is the answer itself. Students should understand how they solved a problem or answered a question in class so they can repeat the performance and apply the same skills and thought processes outside of class. Keep pressing students to **explain what they know, in their own words,** how one idea relates to another, and what the explanation is for different events happening.

    Can students think--can they apply information to a new situation, can they deduce an explanation from a series of observations, can they synthesize results into a coherent statement, and can they evaluate the merits of a plan based on a given set of criteria? These are also important criteria for student assessment.

9. **Help students learn to make appropriate choices in life.** What are the consequences for each action students take? What are the tradeoffs involved in situations where there are both advantages and disadvantages to a decision? Let students practice risk-benefit analysis. Students should also see how tradeoffs apply to other organisms in nature. Importantly, students should understand how they and their species fit into and affect the biosphere.

10. You must **help students develop their communication skills**, especially writing, by asking higher level, open-ended questions. Also, provide students with opportunities to become more computer literate, to discuss their ideas about biological concepts, and to work cooperatively with others in the resolution of a problem.

If you are successful in getting students to develop these skills and understand these ideas, they will be scientifically literate. Now, what do *you* really want your students to know, value, and be able to do by the end of your course, and how are you going to get students to that point?

INSTRUCTIONAL STRATEGIES

The activities of a class make up the instructional strategies, and you should use a variety of them. A variety of teaching strategies accommodates different student learning styles and provides opportunities that will help most students construct their understanding of biological concepts. Unfortunately, most science instructors consistently use one strategy, lecture. Biology education could take a significant step toward reform by using different methods while de-emphasizing lectures.

Instructional materials and curricular activities should emphasize student understanding of both concepts and scientific processes of investigation, and should lead naturally toward individual student research of biological questions. Thus, inquiry-oriented activities should be central to your course, developing in students greater independence as individual thinkers and investigators. Although laboratories and field experiences must be part of any biology course, students also need opportunities to read, write, discuss, and explain biological concepts. Instructors should consider students' initial understanding and misconceptions of biological concepts and provide ample time for students to think about, interpret, and incorporate new information and ideas, or to revise their old views. Students should debate biologically related issues that are important to them, and to work with, and possibly develop, models and simulations.

Helping Students Become Biologically Literate

Structural and multidimensional biological literacy are appropriate levels for your students to reach (Chapter 8). Focus on a few essential concepts you want your students to understand, and spend more time developing these concepts. Student interest in biology may be increased by using hands-on, minds-on, exciting activities, and by helping students see the relevance of the subject to their own lives (Project Kaleidoscope, 1991). For example, to engage students, the selection of a local environmental issue, such as the spotted owl controversy, can show students that what they learn in class (e.g., competition, resource use, and niche) has relevance and practical application outside of the classroom. In addition, newspaper and magazine articles, television newscasts, and reports from other media can illustrate that the concepts dealt with in class are related to important national, international, and personal concerns.

Students may achieve multidimensional literacy by applying their knowledge to a problem's resolution. For instance, students may be presented with a problem about a fictitious pregnant woman and her developing fetus that medical tests indicate is anencephalic. The parents of the fetus are interested in the possibility of using the fetus as a donor of organs or tissue, but have some reservations based on sanctity-of-life issues. Students must consider the implications of the medical tests for the parents, the fetus, and society, and they must determine what they need to find out to make appropriate recommendations to the parents. Students are pushed to explain and support their statements, and to think critically and to develop ethically defensible positions during their investigation. This investigative process leads students through problem identification, hypothesis building, research, synthesis of ideas, and finally to decision making. Students may be assessed on the scope and accuracy of the information they provide and fictitious advice they give, the clarity of their presentation, and their response to questions (O'Neil, 1992).

By presenting an unresolved local public issue, a bioethical problem, or a basic research question, you give students the opportunity to become directly involved in a multidimensional investigation that is relevant, in which they practice the processes of scientific investigation, *and* in which they learn biological concepts. These activities help blur the distinction between pedagogy and content and between classroom and laboratory, and help demonstrate the property of connectedness in science. Connections give the learner something to think about, and lessons lacking connections are meaningless, rote, and authoritarian (Project Kaleidoscope, 1991). An issue-centered or problem-based approach to teaching as described above organizes the curriculum around opportunities for students to practice and develop critical thinking, analysis, and decision-making skills while helping students develop higher levels of biological literacy. (adapted from BSCS, 1994)

CURRICULUM THEMES

A curriculum theme is an instructional orientation that helps organize and deliver a biology program to students (see matrix on page 75). A curriculum theme is a systematic and deliberate expression of a viewpoint about the role of science subject matter; a coherent set of messages to the student *about* science (Roberts, 1982). The curriculum theme serves as a paradigm or frame of reference to help organize the teaching of biology. Whereas unifying principles (Chapter 8) help organize instruction of the *facts* of biology, a curriculum theme helps organize the structure of the biology *program*. For example, because evolution is the central theory of biology, it serves as a unifying principle that unites all biological facts. Evolution, however, also may serve as a curriculum theme that helps to select the activities of a class. With evolution as a *curriculum theme*, an instructor may choose, for example, laboratories and activities that deal with mutation, genetic variation, and natural selection, and discussions that focus on speciation and extinction, *at the expense of other subjects*. Through the selected activities focusing on evolution, students learn the major concepts and significant facts of biology as a whole.

Alternatively, an instructor may elect to use *personal aspects of biology* as a curriculum theme. By using this theme, one can organize a course around those issues, concepts, and activities that are important to students as individuals, such as careers in the biological sciences, individual health issues, and the process and problems of human sexual reproduction. Other themes are the *nature of science*, which focuses on the basic processes of biology as a scientific discipline and helps students become competent in their use; *social and ethical aspects* of biology focusing on bioethical issues; *technology and its influence* on science and people; and the *historical development of biological ideas*. *Biological content* has been a traditional curriculum theme for many courses through the years, emphasizing the facts generated by scientific investigation. Consider organizing your biology program around one or two main curriculum themes. However, it is recommended that *biological content* **never** be the only curriculum theme of a biology program.

LABORATORIES

Your students should spend more total hours of class time in discussion and the laboratory, or the field, compared to their time in lecture. A laboratory-centered approach to teaching biology produces better understanding of the scientific process, helps achieve logical reasoning, inquiry, problem-solving and manipulative skills, and promotes more positive attitudes in students (Ramsey and Howe, 1969; Bates, 1978; Hofstein, 1988). The laboratory experience sets science apart from most subjects, providing instructors and their students liveliness and fun that are hard to obtain in other ways (White, 1988).

Rationale for Student Laboratory Work

1. Science involves highly complex and abstract subject matter. Students may not grasp science concepts without concrete props and opportunities for manipulation in the lab.
2. Student participation in investigations develops inquiry and intellectual skills. It gives students an opportunity to appreciate and understand the nature of science–how scientists work, the multiplicity of scientific methods, and interrelationship between science, technology, and society.
3. Laboratory work promotes development of cognitive abilities--problem solving, analysis, generalizing, critical thinking, applying, synthesizing, evaluating, decision making, and creativity.
4. Laboratory work is essential for developing manipulative, investigative, organizational, and communicative skills.
5. Laboratory work helps students understand the concepts that underlie scientific research, such as the nature of scientific problems, hypotheses, assumptions, predictions, conclusions, and models. Laboratories also allow one to identify student misconceptions.
6. Laboratories promote the development of attitudes such as honesty, critical assessment of results, curiosity, risk taking, objectivity, precision, perseverance, responsibility, and collaboration.
7. Students usually enjoy practical work in the laboratory, and when offered a chance to experience meaningful, nontrivial, but not too difficult experiences, they become motivated and interested in studying science. The laboratory conveys the method and spirit of science whereas

the textbook and teachers often transmit subject matter content. (adapted from Friedler and Tamir, 1990).

Consider arranging your instruction so that students first conduct lab activities with a minimum of introduction, then discuss their work and concepts learned, and finally read relevant material so they solidify their understanding.   In this way students conduct the laboratory *before they read about a concept* so that they discover biological concepts in the lab and the labs are not simply confirmational in nature.   Lectures and reading then reinforce learning and provide additional explanations of complex phenomena.   Such a lab represents a desirable guided-inquiry approach (Igelsrud and Leonard, 1988) rather than the verification approach characterizing many conventional curricula. Also, labs, discussions, and lectures may be incorporated into a single class period rather than splitting them into three different entities.   In this structure, each class period includes several activities, e.g., shifting back and forth from hands-on lab activities, to discussions of concepts, to a lecture on related topics (Uno, 1990).

MODEL LABORATORY EXPERIENCES

Compare your lab to this checklist from a model laboratory experience.

A Good Laboratory Instructor:
displays a working knowledge of the material and lab techniques.
clearly explains how to use lab equipment.
explains possible lab hazards, and insists on safe practices.
provides clear, appropriate instructions before or during the lab.
is attentive to the needs of all the students.
answers student questions and offers encouragement and useful advice.

Students:
observe natural phenomena and gain experience in designing, conducting, and reporting on experiments.
have the opportunity to do additional experimenting on their own.
are stimulated to learn and gain interest because of the lab experience.
are sufficiently challenged by lab activities so as to think and to develop their organizational skills.

Lab Activities:
add to student understanding of the course content and confront their misconceptions.
investigate problems that come up in the lecture.
produce a sense of adventure and intellectual excitement.
are not cookbook.

The lab environment:
is adequate, reliable, and safe.
has enough equipment and room for all lab groups.
is conducive to the activities.

Feedback
Questions on lab quizzes or exams involve material discussed in the lab.
Instructor feedback on lab reports is helpful.
Lab reports are graded and returned promptly.
Grading is based on well-established criteria or goals.
(adapted from Holcomb, 1988; Weimer, 1989a; Lazarowitz and Tamir, 1994)

USING THE COURSE EVALUATION TO ORGANIZE YOUR CLASS

You might obtain a sample student evaluation form from your institution to determine what your students and university consider to be important when it comes to teaching. Ask yourself how you might organize a better course by reviewing what those who will evaluate you (students, colleagues, and tenure-reviewers) consider to be characteristics of a good class and professor.

Standard Statements on Course Evaluations

The following is a list of statements that have been taken from a variety of student evaluation forms. Use the list as a guide while designing your class.

Competence of the professor

Has thorough knowledge of the course material.
Uses the board in a legible and orderly way.
Knows how to capture and hold students' attention.
Explains clearly.
Emphasizes the important points of the course.
Teaching is stimulating.
Answers student questions clearly.
Provides appropriate examples to help students understand the material.
Shows respect for students.
Demonstrates an interest in teaching the course.
Appears concerned about improving the course.
Is open to student comments and criticisms.
Encourages critical and independent thinking.
Contributes to students learning about the discipline.

Structure of the course

Each class session is well-prepared.
Generally, the course is well-organized.
The work is distributed throughout the term (e.g., all assignments are not due at the same time or near exams).
The work required by this course is justified by the number of credits.

Means of evaluating learning

Evaluation criteria are communicated to students from the very beginning.
The **weighting** assigned to each part of the evaluation (e.g., homework assignments, projects, tests) is appropriate.

Exams

Are consistent with course objectives--the instructor evaluates students on what students ought to be able to do or know.
Include questions that focus on the important points of the course.

Are written so that the intent of the questions is clear and explicit.
Cover manageable amounts of material in terms of time to study.
Are not too long to complete (and check), given the time limit of the exam period.
Require analysis and application of content and not just regurgitation of details.
When graded, include written comments that give feedback about both right and wrong answers (or at least an exam key is posted for students).
Are returned in a reasonable amount of time.
After a test, the professor reviews questions that were difficult for students.

Assignments

Produce meaningful and challenging learning experiences but are not over-burdensome.
Include a variety of activities responsive to different student interests, abilities, and learning styles.
Are appropriate to course objectives and content.
Are spaced at appropriate intervals in the course.
Accommodate students' schedules, e.g., no exam on the day after spring break.
Prepare students for more complex courses in the subject area.

Teaching material (including textbooks)

Recommended reading covers all aspects of the course.
The use of the recommended books fully justifies their purchase.
The recommended works are pedagogically well-designed (i.e., facilitate comprehension of the material). Content is presented in a logical and systematic order that enhances understanding by those unfamiliar with the topic.
Textbooks are generally acceptable in terms of departmental standards.

Laboratory sessions

Provide obvious links between the material presented in class and the laboratory.
Instructions for each session are precise and complete.
The time allotted is sufficient so students can attain the objectives of the lab.
Accompanying handouts are complete and adequate.
The requirements for completing lab reports are reasonable and match course objectives.
Laboratories focus on important concepts of the discipline.

Course syllabus

Identifies instructional resources like books and journal
   articles and where they might be obtained (e.g.,
   reserve desk of library).

Outlines the sequence of topics to be covered in a logical
   way.

Describes evaluation procedures and values.

Lists major assignments and due dates.

Contains information about the faculty member, e.g.,
   name, office address, office hours, and phone
   number.

Handouts

Are relevant additions and/or elaborations of course
   content.

Are structured so that the content is clearly
   communicated to readers.

Are neat and without spelling and grammatical errors.

Have been reviewed by the instructor and found
   appropriate before being given to students.

Visual materials

Enhance and clarify content presented in another way.

Are clear and easily read everywhere in the classroom.

Contain manageable amounts of material so excessive
   amounts of time are not required to copy down the
   material.

Overall evaluation of class

Class allows students to achieve significant learning.

Class makes students want to learn more about the
   material. (adapted from Weimer, 1987a; Weimer,

Parrett, and Kerns, 1992; Pregent, 1994)

PLANNING YOUR COURSE: A DECISION GUIDE

Here is a step-by-step guide you might follow as
you develop your course.

1. **Where are you?** Size up the situation.
    Kind of students: number, prior knowledge,
       motivation?
    Kind of learning spaces: classroom, lab, fixed
       desks/chairs?
    In what **kind of curriculum** is this course
       embedded?
    Are there external **professional standards**
       that need to be met?
    What are **your own** beliefs, values, attitudes, and
       skills as a teacher?

2. **Where do you want to go?** What are your goals?
    Ideally, what would you like students to get out
    of this course?
    Ask yourself the following questions:
    a) What do you want students to be able to DO,
        once the course is over? (Identify 3-5 general
        goals.)
    b) What would students have to KNOW in order
        to do each of the items listed in Question "a"
        above?
    c) What would students have to DO in order to
        learn each of the items listed in Question "b"
        above? (learning activities)

3. **How would you know if you/they got there?** (In
    other words, how would you know if the students
    achieved these goals? How can you assess
    student learning and achievement?) FOR EACH
    GENERAL GOAL specified above, what
    information can you gather that would tell how well
    the goal was **achieved** for each student
    individually? for the class as a whole? For which
    are multiple-choice exams sufficient? Essay
    exams?   Project   assignments?   Writing
    assignments? Other "products"?

4. **How are you going to get there?** Select a
    general strategy. What general structure of
    learning activities do you want to use?
    a. Continuous series of **lectures and reading
        assignments**, periodically interrupted by 1 or
        2 mid-terms.
    b. Sequence of **reading**, reflective **writing**, and
        whole class **discussion** (sequence repeated
        for each topic).
    c. Start with some field or lab work observations,
        followed   by   readings   and   whole   class

discussions. (Write-ups of lab/field work is sometimes included.)

d. Present **lectures**, followed by field work or lab observations.

e. Have students do assigned **readings**, followed by **mini-tests** done individually and in small groups; then move on to group-based application **projects**.

f. Work through a series of **developmental stages**: build some knowledge and/or skills (4-6 wks), work on small application projects (4-6 wks), and then on larger, more complex projects (4-6 wks).

g. **Contract** for a grade: (for example: read text and pass exams = C, + do research paper =B, + do extended project = A).

5. **What are the students going to do?** What are your specific **learning activities (teaching strategies)?** In the final step of No. 2 above, you identified several kinds of learning activities. Now examine these activities to see if they are sufficient to generate the kind of learning you desire.

6. **When are you going to do what?** Develop a **sequence of activities.** Develop a week-by-week **schedule** for the whole term.
What activities need to come first?
What activities do you want to conclude with?
What sequence do you need in the middle?

7. **Who/what can help?** Find **resources.**
What resources do you need (and can you get) to support each of the goals listed in No. 2 above? (People, places, and things, including media.)

8. **How are you going to grade?** Develop your grading system--it should reflect the full range of learning goals and activities. (Remember, NOT **everything** has to be graded.) The relative weight of each item on the course grade should reflect the relative importance of the activity.

9. **What could go wrong?** "De-bugging" the design. Analyze and assess this "first draft" of the course.
What kinds of undesirable situations might it generate? e.g., Will students be motivated to do the work?
Does the design encourage student involvement?
Are the students getting sufficient feedback on their performance?
What could you do to prevent (or at least minimize these problems)?
Make the necessary modifications in the design.

10. **Let them know what you've planned.** Now write the **syllabus.** (See Chap. 13) This should include, among other things:

General management information--instructor, office hours, phone, etc.
Goals for the course.
Structure and sequence of class activities, including due dates for major assignments/tests/projects.
Text and other required reading material.
Grading procedures.
Course policies: attendance, work turned in late, make-up assignments/exams.

11. **How will you know how the course is going? How it went?**
Plan an evaluation of the course itself and your teaching performance.
What kinds of mid-term and end-of-term feedback will you need?
What specific questions do you have about: the degree to which your goals for the course were achieved? the effectiveness of particular learning activities? your classroom performance?
What sources of information can help you answer these questions: video/audio-tape, student interviews, questionnaires, outside observers, test results? (adapted from Fink, 1994)

TEACHING AND LEARNING STRATEGIES

Laboratory Experiences	Activities in which students investigate a question in biology using materials in a laboratory setting. • Provide hands-on and minds-on experiences. • Encourage students to construct meaning from concrete events. • Should go beyond confirming what students already know to include investigations that are exploratory and open-ended. • Should include opportunities for observation, hypothesis formation, experimental design, handling materials and apparatus, recording data, data interpretation, and communication. • Should include opportunities to discuss the limitations of scientific inquiry.
Data Analysis	Students examine data collected by themselves or other investigators. • Provides opportunities for students to explain how data were collected. • Provides opportunities for analysis and interpretation of data. • Permits discussion of experiments that would be difficult for students to conduct during regular class.
Student-directed Investigations	Investigations in which the students study something new to them. • Students plan and complete a project based on observations of some natural phenomenon. • Students gather evidence and propose an explanation. • Students communicate their findings in the form of a laboratory report, poster, or scientific research paper. • Promote application and integration of scientific inquiry skills. • Should be required of all students. • May involve cooperative group work or individual work. • May involve laboratory or field investigations.
Personal and Societal Decision Making	Students study a biologically related issue to develop an understanding of the scientific, personal, societal, economic, environmental, and technological aspects of the problem. Students apply their knowledge to a real-life situation; authentic problem-solving and decision-making that has a personal or societal impact. • Stimulates students to initiate and explore questions that are meaningful to them and applicable to their daily lives. • Extends beyond the classroom, drawing on community resources to gather data and to understand local problems and issues. • Involves multidimensional investigations and promotes connections to other disciplines.
Cooperative Learning	Students with specific roles work cooperatively in a team to accomplish a common goal. • Promotes individual and group responsibility for learning. • Promotes collaborative work in the resolution of problems and issues. • Provides opportunities for student discussion, explanation, and linkage of biological concepts. • Enhances benefits of heterogeneous grouping.

Listening	Students listen and critically evaluate explanations presented by their peers, the instructor, or guest speakers, or experts on videotape or film. • Students should be encouraged to listen actively through note taking, concept mapping, or journal writing.
Reading	Students are encouraged to read about biological concepts from a variety of sources. • In addition to texts, students should read primary sources, magazines, newspapers, as well as fiction and non-fiction books related to biology topics. • Encourage active reading by having students keep journals, or prepare oral/written reports on their reading.
Communication	Students select and organize information relevant to a topic and communicate information in their own words. • Writing promotes student conceptual understanding. • Writing should be encouraged in a diversity of styles such as essays, journals, lab reports, library reports, and creative writing. • Reports may be based on lab research, field research, or library research and may use visual aids. • Students interpret or produce graphic representations of information.
Debates	Students choose or are assigned a personal or societal issue related to a biological problem. • Encourage students to recognize the role of alternative perspectives. • Help students express and experience the thoughts and feelings that arise from issues that have biological foundations.
Discussion	Instructor or student facilitates discussion of concepts and ideas. • Discussion group responds to questions generated by facilitator or by other group members. • Facilitator should be willing to examine all options proposed by students as they relate to the topic being discussed.
Field Experiences	Hands-on activities in which students investigate a question in biology using materials in a managed or natural ecosystem. • Provide opportunities for experiencing process-oriented science. • Encourage appreciation for biodiversity, the complexity and beauty of nature, and the natural history of living organisms.
Interactive Audiovisual	Programs that are stopped at appropriate points with questions for discussion interjected by instructor. • May serve as interactive visual databases that are accessed by students. • Can provide opportunity for inquiry-oriented discussion.

Computer Technology	Students use computer technology in a variety of ways that are appropriate to biological inquiry. • Computers may be used to gather, process, and graph data and for statistical analyses of data. • Computer simulations of experiments permit repeatable, short-term, applied inquiry procedures. • Telecommunication systems allow students to access information resources from all over the world. • Telecommunication systems allow students to communicate and work cooperatively with scientists or students throughout the world. • Computer literacy will be essential to the lives of all students.
Lectures	Verbal explanations of biological concepts are an efficient way to transmit information from one individual to many. • Useful to provide alternative explanations, examples, clarification, and conceptual organization of a topic. Useful after students have already had experience with the subject. • Tie into conceptual understanding of students.
Textbooks	A written resource for students. • Illustrations may be instructive and provide concrete examples of abstract concepts. • Instructor should shift away from major dependence on textbooks and toward investigations. • Instructor should place more emphasis on primary literature, popular literature, multimedia, telecommunications, and community resources such as libraries, museums, guest speakers, and computer networks as sources of information.
Demonstrations	Illustrations of natural phenomena and scientific investigations. • Permits observations that would be difficult for all students to complete during regular class.

(Adapted from Tulloch, et al, 1994)

Now that you have an idea of what you want your students to learn, what instructional strategies will you use, and how will you organize your course to help students get to where you want them? If you have already taught a course, try to add something new each semester that will help your students learn biology. It will also keep you fresh!

XIII. MAKING UP A SYLLABUS, AND THE FIRST DAY OF CLASS

A syllabus should describe the course, providing specific information to the student about how the course will be conducted. Warning: students often think of the syllabus as a contract--if they complete the specified tasks at the indicated level, then they are guaranteed to be awarded the grade as you have indicated. Once you have distributed your syllabus, it is difficult to change substantive parts of it, unless the change is in the favor of the students or unless all students approve of the change. For instance, once you establish a grading scale, you cannot raise the level for an "A" because your first exam is too easy. Or, if you have to change the date of an exam you need to make sure that all of your students know about it--which is difficult because some of your students will show up to class only on the days of the exams as indicated on the original syllabus. Of course, you may not be able to keep to the topic schedule as you have initially indicated, and so reading assignments might have to be constantly updated. (Don't worry about issuing revised syllabi--just keep students informed.)

First, find out what college/university policies must be included in your syllabus (use a colleague's syllabus as an example.) For example, you might need to include a statement for students with learning disabilities to contact you. Your department might have its own policies, such as "no make-up exams." You should definitely talk to your colleagues who are teaching or have taught the same course to see if they are imposing certain requirements on their students of which you should be aware (e.g., all tests given on the same day).

A lot of detailed information about major projects, such as an independent study, can be handed out later in the class. Don't put so much information into your syllabus that your students don't read it. The following is a list of what might be included--but not all of the information has to be included.

POSSIBLE CONTENTS OF A SYLLABUS

1. **Course Information:** Department, course title, course number, number of credit hours, location of classroom, days and hours the class and lab meet.
2. **Instructor Information:** Instructor's and teaching assistants' names, title, office location, office hours (days and times), and e-mail address. (Do not give out your home telephone or address.)
3. **Place of this course in the program:** Course prerequisites, subsequent courses, and course description/objectives. A brief course description that provides an overview of the subject and brief explanation of why students might want to take the course. The syllabus might also contain a brief explanation of how the parts of the course fit together. (This discussion could be part of your first day in class instead of your syllabus.)
4. **Course philosophy:** Pedagogical values, instructional methods, weekly requirements (number of classes, labs, or discussion hours, and expected amount of study hours). A list of course objectives, stated in terms of what the students should be able to do by the end of the course. Information about the learning experiences in the course, including in-class activities such as lectures and discussions.
5. **Textbook and supplementary reading(s):** Title, author, date, edition, publisher, cost, where available (library reserve, bookstore), extent of use (required or recommended), course bibliography, and out-of-class activities such as readings and homework assignments.
6. **Materials:** Calculators, computers, blue books, art supplies, lab or safety equipment.
7. **Course calendar:** Daily or weekly schedule of lecture topics and corresponding readings, major assignment due dates, exams, projects, or other means of assessment, and required events.
8. **Course policies:** Class participation, attendance, tardiness, missed or late exams and assignments, grading, academic dishonesty (university policy), plagiarism, lab safety, and make-up work, if any.
9. **Support services:** Library, computer center, learning center, test files, tutors.
10. **Disclaimer:** "This course outline is tentative and subject to change." A caveat that indicates that parts of the course are subject to change to meet the needs of students in the course. This allows you to slow down or speed up the pace of the course if students show a need.

11. **Evaluation/grading**: Information about how grades will be determined, including the percentage of the grade for each major element of the course, and criteria (letter grades, curving). (You may want to provide a separate handout for major assignments that includes the format for that assignment, description of the nature of the assignment, procedural steps, time frame, final due date, instructions on the form, length, or items to include in the final report, list of materials, facilities at the students' disposal, your requirements for the distribution of the assignment activities (in group work), list of times when the students can meet with you, and specific requirements (final presentation, for example).)

12. **University Rules and Regulations**: University academic policies--drop-add, withdrawal dates and procedures. (adapted from Altman, 1989; Johnson, 1990; Altman and Cashin, 1992; Davis, 1992; Davidson and Ambrose, 1994; Pregent, 1994)

THE FIRST DAY OF CLASS

First-Day Inquiry Activities

It is essential that you begin with activities (emphasis on "active") that get students engaged in the study of biology and the process of scientific investigations. These activities should also allow students to begin practicing their critical thinking skills. First-day activities that focus on scientific methods of investigation serve as the foundation for inquiry activities throughout the semester. Although it is doubtful that a single, formal scientific method exists, all investigations incorporate at least some of the following:

    1) observation of a natural phenomenon;
    2) asking questions about the cause of the phenomenon;
    3) hypothesis formation and/or;
    4) prediction about what will happen if hypothesis is correct;
    5) experimentation to test the hypothesis;
    6) collection and analysis of the data; and
    7) rejection or support of the hypothesis.

The following activities allow students to practice some or all of the above components of a scientific investigation.

Activity 1

Lead a discussion with your students. Say to them: Suppose you are an objective observer watching an empty theater before the movie begins. You observe a young woman enter the theater by herself and sit in one of the seats. A few minutes later, a young man enters the theater and, without saying anything to the woman, sits down beside her. These are your OBSERVATIONS. Now, based on these observations, ask your students what QUESTIONS they might ask about this situation.

Students give a variety of responses including: "Do they know each other?" "Is that the best chair for viewing the movie?" "Is he trying to pick her up?"

We can choose any one of these questions and study it by first forming a testable statement, a hypothesis. TO FORM A HYPOTHESIS, we can convert a question (for example, the first one asked) into a statement--*The two people in the movie theater know each other*. If this statement is true, then we can manipulate the situation and PREDICT what will happen. Ask students for suggestions, but say that they cannot ask the two people questions. Students might suggest that they could move one of the two people to a different seat and see if the other person follows. If these two people do know each other as we have stated in our hypothesis, then we predict that the other person should follow. We can now conduct the EXPERIMENT and move one of the people to a different seat. If we move the woman, and the man follows, we need to write this down as our DATA. If we continue to move the woman from seat to seat and the man follows each time, then our HYPOTHESIS IS SUPPORTED. But, that does not *prove* our hypothesis to be correct--we cannot prove a hypothesis to be true, we can only support or reject it.

Students who are asked why the results of the experiment do not prove our hypothesis to be true provide responses such as: "He could be interested in meeting her," "He could be interested in her perfume and not her," "He might be trying to find the best chair in the theater," etc. This leads to further hypothesis formation and testing.

Review the elements of a scientific method of investigation with the students and point out the steps that were used in the discussion about the movie theater. This discussion works well with college students on the first day of class because it is "non-threatening" to them-- it doesn't appear to be scientific. Point out to students that most questions, scientific or non-scientific, can be studied using a similar, logical process.

Activity 2

This activity also revolves around scientific methods of investigation. Duplicate and cut up the sheet of figures (Grouping Geometric Figures, page 134), and place one set of figures, *except* Q and R, into an envelope. Students are divided into teams of 2, 3, or 4 students. Each team gets one envelope with 17 figures (A-P and S). Students should introduce themselves and then be given the following task: "Arrange the 17 figures into groups. You can have as many groups as your team wants, but you need to write down a statement describing why you have placed the figures in each particular group."

After several minutes, teams write the letters in each of their groups on the board, but not the reasons for their groupings. The instructor chooses two interesting groupings (for example, the groupings of the Team 1 and Team 4) and divides the class in half. Then, one half of the class arranges their figures like those of Team 1 while the other half arranges their figures like team 4. (Team 1 arranges the figures like Team 4, and Team 4 arranges like Team 1.) These are OBSERVATIONS. Students now try to decide why Team 1 (or 4, whichever is appropriate) arranged the figures as they did, and they write down the reasons. This is their HYPOTHESIS. The instructor now hands out figures Q and R and the

students TEST THE HYPOTHESIS by placing Q and R into the groups they think Team 1 (or 4) would.

In a general discussion, students state why they think Team 1 (or 4) arranged the figures into their groups and into which groups they think Team 1 would place Q and R. Team 1 now reveals whether the discussion has been accurate. If so, the HYPOTHESIS IS SUPPORTED. If not, the hypothesis is not supported and must be rejected. Frequently, Q and R will be placed in the right groups, but for reasons other than those Team 1 (or 4) originally stated. In this case, the hypothesis is supported, but the hypothesis is incorrect. This is an important point for discussion. Summarize by emphasizing the steps used in a scientific method of investigation.

Activity 3

Ask students to go outside and find four natural objects (not human-made) that appear identical to each other--the four objects must look exactly like each other to the students. (Don't give them any hints, but an example would be four leaves of the same size and shape from the same tree). When they bring in these objects, they work in pairs. Each pair of students chooses one set of four objects to work with (you ask everyone to bring back four objects because some sets will not be appropriate). Students label each of the four objects with a small piece of masking tape and the letter "A," "B," "C," or "D."

Students now begin to write descriptions of each object--one description for each object. These descriptions can use any measurements that the students would like, however, the descriptions must be clear enough so that someone reading them can determine which object is being described. Make certain that the descriptions do not have the letters "A," "B," "C," or "D" next to them and that they are not in order (A-D). A key should be placed on the back of the description page so that others can determine if their selections are accurate. Each pair of students leaves their four objects with the descriptions at their desk, and other students try to determine if they can correctly identify each object by reading the four descriptions. Students move around the room looking at several other teams' work.

The main goal of this activity is to get students to make careful observations. By first challenging students to find objects that appear identical to each other and then to find differences between those same objects, you are forcing students to look for distinguishing characteristics. Students often have a difficult time seeing differences between people and objects ("all elm trees look alike to me"), and this is a way to get them to find differences through careful observations. The activity also challenges students to write clear descriptions.

Activity 4

Another first day activity is to use a cube such as the one on page 135. Construct a cube for each team of 3-4 students. Ask students to figure out what is on the bottom (blank) side of the cube. The important point here is for students to describe how they arrived at the answer and to write down their thinking. How do they know what is on the bottom side of the cube, and why? Tell students they must use all the information on the sides of the cube. This activity allows students to practice their critical thinking skills and forces them to think about "how they know what they know."

The answer is "Francene or Francine." The empty face on the cube must have a woman's name because male and female names are found on opposite sides. The number in the upper right-hand corner is the number of letters in the name, so the woman's name must be either 2 or 8--the other sides have 3-7. Finally, the number in the lower left-hand corner is the number of letters shared by the names on opposite sides.

Allow students some time to struggle with the cube. After a few minutes, stop the class and ask them what basic information they have figured out so far--this information should help the groups that have not yet found any patterns. Stop the discussion before the correct answer is revealed, and then get the groups to continue.

Activity 5

Another first day activity is to use a clear flask filled with about 20 g of sodium hydroxide, 20 g of glucose, and half a milliliter of 1% methylene blue solution per liter of water. Put about 150 ml of this solution into several 250 ml flasks, and place rubber stoppers in each. When you shake the flask, the clear liquid begins to turn dark blue and then slowly clears again. The challenge here is for students to determine what is happening and to figure out how they know what they know--what is the evidence? For the complete description of what is happening, refer to Campbell (1963).

Allow students a few minutes to play with the flasks and then stop them and ask what they have determined. They might say that a chemical reaction is causing the change in color. You might ask if the stopper might be causing the reaction, if the solution is reacting with the glass, or if the reaction is caused by the mixture of a gas and the liquid--and how they know. If a chemical reaction is involved, what might happen if you heated up the flask? If a gas above the liquid is involved in the chemical reaction, what do they expect will happen to that gas as it is being used up (a vacuum might be expected to form)? How might students detect this? They can remove the stopper slowly and perhaps be able to hear a suction sound, or more likely, they will be able to see drops along the side of the stopper being pulled into the flask. The point here is not to talk about kinetics, but to challenge students to try to determine what is happening in this multi-reaction demonstration using their observations of the system.

Grouping Geometric Figures

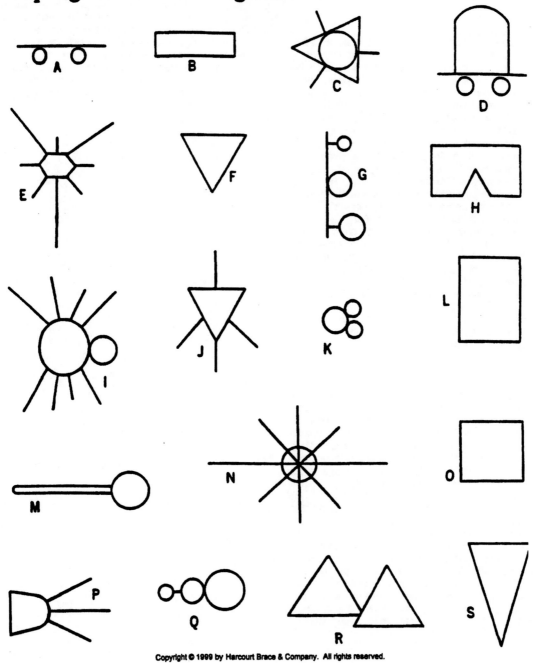

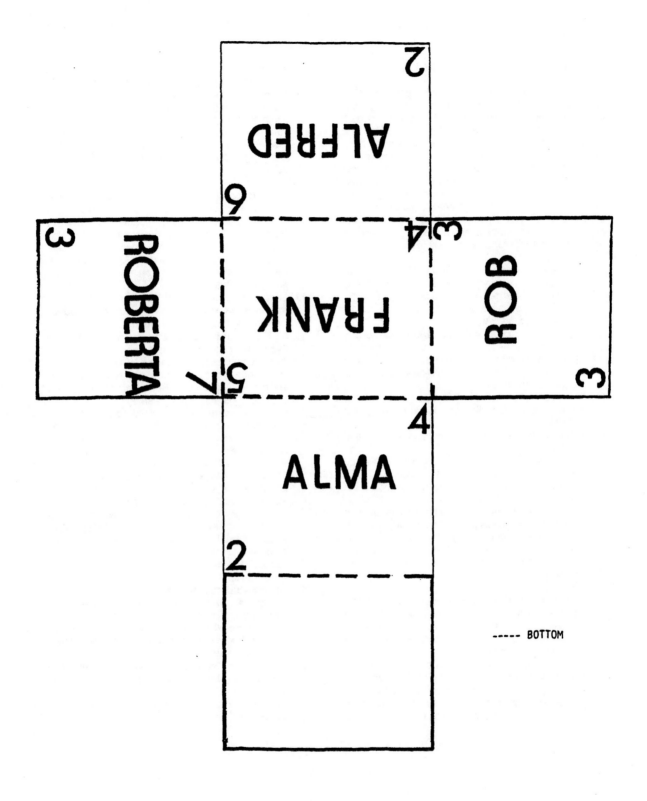

ALFRED

2

ROBERTA

3

FRANK

ROB

4 3

3

7 5

6

4

ALMA

2

----- BOTTOM

PREPARATION TIPS FOR THE FIRST DAY

From the start, you must establish your credibility and authority with the students while showing your enthusiasm for the subject matter of the course. Do not try to come across as "the tough guy," "the buddy," "the boss," "the understanding type," or whatever. You must be real, and you must try to meet the basic expectations of the students, for whom your course is a new experience. In the first class, you must be interesting and clearly explain the organization of the course. You must also establish your competence, while working to show respect for your students and creating a favorable climate for their work and communication. The following are ways to prepare for your first day of class.

1. **Visit the classroom before the first meeting.** Look at the seating patterns, location of the chalkboards, audio-visual equipment, and lighting. Make sure you have a key for the door, chalk, erasers, and a pointer.
2. **Organize all materials for the first class** meeting so that they flow smoothly as the class unfolds. Students will watch you closely at the first meeting to see if you are organized. A weak first impression will be hard to overcome.
3. **Prepare and rehearse the opening remarks,** maybe the first ten minutes. Avoid fumbling and searching for words.
4. **Arrive at the classroom a few minutes early** and greet students.
5. **Decide how to begin the class,** what name you want students to use when addressing you (not a minor consideration), how to take roll, and how to set the tone for the semester.
6. **Try a little selling.** Deal with the fundamental questions: Why is this course interesting? Why are you pleased to be teaching it? What will students know and be able to do at the end of the course? Give them the necessary guidelines, set pragmatic objectives, and be openly enthusiastic about the course.
7. **Don't be afraid of a little showmanship.** Show students the potential value and intrinsic interest of the course material. Remember: the effort spent preparing something special lets students know you care about the course.
8. **Share something about yourself.** Who are you? Why are you teaching this course? What knowledge and experience do you have with the content? Why do you teach college students? Personal information should not be highly revealing, but students sometimes can relate to the instructor if they see him or her as a human being, i.e., as something more than just an authority figure or subject-matter expert. Sharing personal stories and being able to laugh at yourself can help this process. Tell about your prior work experience, travel experience, or research and publications in this area. Having this knowledge can help students gain confidence that you know what you are talking about--but don't brag.

9. **Find out something about your students.** You need to know who's taking the course and what they might bring to it. Exchanging personal information "humanizes" the classroom environment and helps to establish a rapport with students. This might include finding out their hometown, academic profile, the state of their knowledge, and the motivation for taking the class.
10. **Encourage your students to meet each other.** Arrange short activities in which students introduce themselves to others around them.
11. **Actions speak louder than words.** As you go through your introduction, remember that, right from the start, your actions speak just as loudly as--if not louder than--your words. So, _say what you mean, and mean what you say_! Better yet, let students **do** something instead of just listening to you.
12. **Explain the organization of the course.** Present the organization of the course explaining the syllabus, in which you have included all of the important facts--objectives, content, assessment, specific requirements, and text.
13. **Create a favorable climate for positive interpersonal relations.** If there is a spirit of mutual respect, you can create a favorable climate for work and communication. Different instructors prefer different classroom climates--intense, relaxed, formal, personal, humorous, serious, etc. Whatever climate you want, you should try to establish this early and set the tone for the rest of the semester.
14. **Involve students quickly.** This can be done in a variety of ways: have students introduce themselves, allow them to think and write silently, have a whole-class or a small-group discussion, etc. But let students know right from the outset that they will be active participants.
15. **Introduce the subject, identifying its value and importance.** Not all students come to the class with a clear idea of why the subject is important. You should help them understand the significance of the course and the subject. The sooner this is done, the

sooner students will be ready to invest time and energy in learning the subject matter. Generally this introduction will be facilitated by starting with some kind of overview of the subject. What is it? What are the parts of the subject? How is it connected to other kinds of knowledge?

16. **Set high expectations.** This can involve such things as what you consider appropriate amounts of study time and homework for the class, the importance of turning homework in on time, expectations about in-class behavior, and how much interaction among students is desired. The first day also offers an opportunity to find out what expectations the students have of you and the class. (adapted from Weimer, 1989b; Davis, 1992; Fink, 1992; Heitz and Meyer, 1993; Pregent, 1994)

CHAPTER XIV. COMMON PROBLEMS OF TEACHING, AND DEALING WITH STUDENTS

The most frequently mentioned teaching problems of all new faculty are:

1. adapting to the appropriate pace and level of difficulty for students;
2. feeling professionally over-specialized, and not having a well-rounded knowledge of their own discipline; and
3. having trouble establishing an appropriate professional demeanor in their relationships with students. (adapted from Turner and Boice, 1989)

STUDENT EXPECTATIONS

Most students will respond in a positive way if you are open and honest with them and if you avoid preaching to them about what they should do or not do. It is best not to put them on the defensive with such questions as, "Why didn't you study more for the test?" Rather, ask "How did you study for the test?" which shows your concern while obtaining information that may help you help the student. Although all students are different from each other, there are certain reasonable expectations that most students have for their instructors. They include:

1. **being prepared**--students expect you to be knowledgeable in your professional discipline and prepared for the class;
2. **respect**--students expect to be treated with respect, even when you disagree with them. Don't talk to them like children;
3. **discipline**--students expect you to maintain discipline in the classroom;
4. **fairness**--students expect that you will be fair. You must say you treat all students the same (in public) but you might deal with individual students slightly differently depending on their particular problem. Also, being fair certainly doesn't mean that you are easy. Fairness means that you are consistent in your actions and that you don't over-penalize students. (adapted from Moore, 1991; Davis, 1992)

PERCEPTIONS OF STUDENTS' READINESS FOR COLLEGE-LEVEL WORK

Do not assume that all your students are at the same level of preparedness for college work. If students are poorly prepared and you do not address their problems, you create problems for yourself. For example, if you teach at too high a level, many students may fail the course. Students may not possess all the following characteristics at the beginning of your class.

1. Have an adequate academic foundation for college work. That is, students:
   a. have a working background knowledge,
   b. can read effectively, and
   c. can write effectively.
   (To address this, identify what misconceptions and level of understanding students possess. Also, for reading and writing problems, work with students individually or send them to your institution's student resource center.)
2. Readily accept their academic responsibilities, such as attending classes, doing assigned readings, handing in assignments on time, etc.
   (You might want to institute an attendance policy-- provide students with statistics to reinforce the importance of attending.)
3. Accept the importance of learning.
   (Focus on thinking and problem-solving skills--show students how the investigative processes that they learn in your class can be used all of their lives.)
4. Are motivated or eager to learn.
   (Use relevant examples, activities, and problems that help students see what they learn in class has application to the world outside of the classroom. This might help make students more eager to learn.)
5. Understand what they should learn in a class without being told.
   (You might review their class notes with them to point out problems and to help them focus on what is important.)
6. Are capable of abstract, formal thinking.
   (Provide students with continual practice in critical thinking skills.)
7. Can integrate what they learn in class into their personal and professional thinking.
   (You might use a problem-solving approach where students apply what they have learned in the classroom to the solution of "real-world" problems.)
   (adapted from Fink, 1984)

PROBLEM STUDENTS

Students May Become Obstructive for a Number of Reasons

As an instructor, you:

1. assign work or act as though your class is their only one, or at least the most important one;
2. lecture too fast, and fail to slow down when requested, or deliver the lecture in a monotone;
3. make students feel inferior when they ask a question or make a comment;
4. are not specific on what the test will cover, create "trick" questions, or give tests that don't correspond to lectures;
5. get behind and then cram a lot of information into the remaining time;
6. require a textbook or supplementary materials and then fail to use them;
7. assume students already have basic knowledge for the course; or
8. fail to communicate to students what is expected of them or make assignments beyond the ability, skills, or knowledge of your students;

Also, students may become obstructive because they:

9. have some underlying emotional problems;
10. are highly skilled at using manipulation to get their way;
11. do not perceive any incentives to cooperate;
12. act out transference feelings towards an authority figure;
13. receive secondary gains from the behavior (attention, feelings of power, etc.).
14. perceive you as being unreasonable, confusing, or difficult. (adapted from Kottler and Lanning, 1992)

KINDS OF PROBLEMS, AND SOLUTIONS

1. **Students talking in class, obviously not about the content.** Suggestions:
   (a) Look at the students directly so they know that you see them.
   (b) Direct a question to someone nearby the talking students. This focuses attention on that area, but doesn't put the talking students on the spot and make a scene.
   (c) Physically move toward that part of the room—perhaps not all the way, but close enough. From that vantage point, look directly at the students who are talking.
   (d) Speak to the students privately before or after class. Tell them their talking distracts you and other students and ask them to please refrain.

2. **Students sleeping in class, doing homework from another class, or in some way not paying attention.** Suggestions:
   (a) Address a question to a student right next to the one not paying attention. The attention to that part of the room may cause students to rejoin the class.
   (b) Direct lots of eye contact in that direction and move toward the student.
   (c) Break the class into mini-discussion groups or vary the method of presenting material.
   (d) Speak to the student privately.
   (e) Stop lecturing and quietly contemplate (for 30 seconds) the topic you are about to address.

3. **Students miss deadlines, come to class late, and are otherwise lax in matters of self-discipline.** Suggestions:
   (a) Design the class so that there are logical consequences resulting from these behaviors. If the policy is not to accept late papers, then don't accept them except under the most *extraordinary* circumstances, and then in private.
   (b) Meet your deadlines. Start and finish class on time. If you say tests will be graded and returned Friday, then get them back on Friday.

4. **Students challenge your authority, often by asking loaded questions (Why do you make the tests so hard? or Why do we have to know this?).** Suggestions:
   (a) Honestly answer the question, explaining (not defending) your instructional objective. If students continue to press, table the discussion until later and then continue it with them privately.

(b) Avoid responses such as: "Because I said so." Show students how this information fits into the grand scheme and how this information forms the basis for understanding other concepts. If you have a difficult time justifying your answer, you might consider if the information is truly that important to teach.

5. **Personality conflicts.** Some students will just not like you no matter what you do, and you won't like some students no matter how hard you try. The problem is often classified as a "personality conflict." This is obviously not a desirable relationship for teaching and learning, but it does exist, and it is manageable. Recognize this situation quickly and draw on your professionalism—take the lead in being sure that this student is still treated with respect and fairness. After all, learning to deal with this situation may be the most valuable lesson the student takes from the experience.

6. **Ethnic differences.** The college student population of the 21st Century will be diverse and multi-ethnic. The cultural differences can have a positive and enriching influence on the teaching-learning environment. They may also present problems due to negative experiences that students or you bring to the environment. Again, recognize such problems quickly and take the lead managing the situation. Even if the problem is between students, it is still your business! If the students respect the teacher, they will usually respond positively. If the problem is between you and one of your students, you might want to seek help from your peers or the appropriate administrator.

7. **Disruptive students.** A few students may become playfully or maliciously disruptive. They will ridicule, rebel, or refuse to accept the program in ways that frustrate most college instructors. This usually happens when students don't understand that there are orderly processes for addressing their problems. Don't attempt to crush such disruptions or the situation will escalate. Sometimes a little humor will settle down the rowdy students until you can determine the "real" problems and explain how they can be addressed. If this doesn't work, *discuss* the problem with these students after class—try not to yell at them or tell them they have to *change or else*.

8. **Personal problems.** As already mentioned, students come from different backgrounds. As a result, they often have problems that are personal in nature but affect that student's learning. If students have a good relationship with you and trust your judgment, they will often seek your advice on problems unrelated to the discipline. The problems may involve family, peer relationships, financial difficulty, dating, or disputes with other instructors. Sometimes the student will feel better simply by talking to someone or arrive at a solution through "talking it out." After listening carefully, you must decide if you are qualified to address the student's problem or should refer the student to "Student Services." Be very careful—try not to become involved in personal problems of students. Young, naive faculty can also be fooled by clever acting students who tell you "sob" stories about why they couldn't come to a test or hand in an assignment. Always show a professional level of sympathy to their stories of woe, however, if you have established rules, consider enforcing them.

9. **Teacher's pet.** There are times when a student comes along who meets all of your expectations. Such students are intelligent, well-prepared, and highly motivated. You may develop common interests inside and outside the classroom. You may want to assign this student additional or different work than other students, involve the student in classroom discussions too often, speak highly of the student in the presence of other students, and sometimes allow the student to act like the instructor. Other students may consider this person the "teacher's pet." It is often an unfair characterization of the relationship, but sometimes not. The student's relationship with other students can be negatively impacted by such behavior. Recognize such behavior and seek to manage it for the benefit of the class—cultivate interests but treat that student in the same manner as other students. And, of course, never become romantically involved with a student. (adapted from Weimer, 1988a and b, 1990; Davis, 1992)

DEALING WITH DISRUPTIVE BEHAVIOR

If a student behaves in a manner that annoys you, you have several options in how you deal with the situation. You may simply want to ignore the behavior--it, or the student, may go away. However, if the behavior continues and you find that it disrupts your class or your teaching, you need to **deal with the problem as soon as possible** rather than let it fester and build into a unsolvable situation.

Always try to deal with the situation in the least disruptive fashion. For instance, talk to the student outside of class and ask if there is a reason for him/her sleeping. If you berate or demean a student in the middle of class, you risk stifling discussion by him or her as well as other students. Try to turn the negative situation into a positive one--this sounds a bit like Pollyanna, but it can make a big difference. For instance, a student who hogs the computer might be asked to return after class hours to work on the computer while you're taking down the lab, instead of taking up lab time. In this way, the student can still work on the computer and you don't have to spend extra time to accommodate the student.

Tips for Dealing with Disruptive Students
1. Deal with disruptive students individually, not in groups.
2. Deal with disruptive students in person, not over the phone.
3. Deal with disruptive students outside of class, not during class where your credibility is on the line.
4. When talking to disruptive students, focus on how their behaviors affect you when you are teaching--not on the students.
5. Do not bluff when asked a challenging question.
6. Set policies and procedures at the beginning of the course--and stick with them throughout the class. Change policies and procedures that don't work, especially if the change makes everyone happy. In most cases, however, don't make the change until the next time you teach the course.
7. Do not foster a "me against you" attitude.
8. Do not deal with students when either you or they are emotional. (adapted from Weimer, 1990)

HOW TO PREVENT/DEAL WITH CHEATING

Depending on the study, it has been reported that between 40-90% of all college students cheat (The Teaching Professor, 1990). So, there is a high probability that you will have to deal with this problem at some time in your academic career. Most faculty members don't like to deal with such conflicts, and thus the best thing you can do is to reduce the number of problems by making your class less vulnerable to cheating. First of all, let students know that you will prosecute those who do cheat (if that is your wont) and what you consider cheating. Eliminate as many opportunities for students to cheat or to be tempted to cheat. If you believe that someone is cheating during an examination, first tell them to keep their eyes on their own exam. Then, if they repeat the behavior, ask them to move. Never accuse a student of cheating *during* an exam. If you suspect a student has cheated, make sure that you have sufficient evidence (physical evidence of an exam that has been tampered with, a crib sheet, or a corroborating witness). Then, carefully follow your institution's guidelines for dealing with student misconduct.

1. **State that cheating will not be tolerated in any way** on the cover sheet of the exam and that each student must do his or her own work. Warn them to keep their eyes on their own paper. This lets students know that you are aware of the possibility of cheating. Follow through on your "threat" to prosecute cheaters. Describe the penalties for cheating--for instance, some institutions stamp "academic misconduct" permanently on the students' transcript.
2. **Use multiple copies of exams** and alternate them from one seat to the next.
3. **Change the order of problems or questions** on the exam copies.
4. **Avoid true-false or multiple choice examinations** in an atmosphere where cheating is prevalent.
5. **Use open-ended questions** on problems where there are a variety of answers or solutions. (I recently polled my class about cheating at the University compared to cheating in my class. **Every** student stated that they believed that there was less cheating in my class than at the University as a whole because of the nature of the exams--mostly short answer and essay. Students frequently responded that there was no way that

they could cheat when they had to be able to explain the answers in their own words.)

6. **Consider including an honesty clause** on the cover sheet that each student must sign before the exam will be graded.

7. **Use oral examinations** when possible.

8. **Avoid using recycled problems or questions** directly from old examinations.

9. **Provide students with enough time** to do the problems on the exam. It is especially important that on essay exams the topics are clearly identified so that students don't feel the need to write a dissertation.

10. **Be vigilant during examinations.** Have at least one assistant to help you monitor test-taking activities. Watch for cheating—a warning sign is if a student looks up at you (checking to see if you are watching him/her). Also, cheating increases near the end of the examination period as students start to panic and when your attention is directed toward other students handing in completed exams. Ask students to remove their hats or to turn the bill around backwards (so they can't read anything written on the underside of the cap's bill and so you can watch their eyes during the exam). Check for writing on the hands or desks.

11. Photocopy a student's exam before handing it back if you suspect that person has changed an answer on previous exams. Then, if there is the same problem, you will have evidence that the exam's original answers have been changed. (adapted from Davis, 1992)

EVOLUTION/CREATIONISM DEBATE

Unfortunately, you may find yourself in a situation where you have to defend yourself for teaching about evolution. There are many resources to help you keep creationism out of and evolution in your classroom. One important organization, from which you can receive much information and support, is the National Center for Science Education (NCSE), P. O. Box 9477, Berkeley, CA 94709.

The following is a statement developed by the National Association of Biology Teachers (NABT), an organization made up of faculty at all levels, to help respond to questions students have raised about evolution. To receive more information about NABT, contact their web site at: www.nabt.org. or their national office at: 11250 Roger Bacon Dr., #19, Reston, VA 22090.

Statement on Teaching Evolution (NABT, 1995)

As stated in *The American Biology Teacher* by the eminent scientist Theodosius Dobzhansky (1973), "Nothing in biology makes sense except in the light of evolution." This often-quoted assertion accurately illuminates the central, unifying role of evolution in nature, and therefore in biology. Teaching biology in an effective and scientifically honest manner requires classroom discussions and laboratory experiences on evolution.

Modern biologists constantly study, ponder, and deliberate the patterns, mechanisms and pace of evolution, but they do not debate evolution's occurrence. The fossil record and the diversity of extant organisms, combined with modern techniques of molecular biology, taxonomy and geology, provide exhaustive examples and powerful evidence for genetic variation, natural selection, speciation, extinction and other well-established components of current evolutionary theory. Scientific deliberations and modifications of these components clearly demonstrate the vitality and scientific integrity of evolution and the theory that explains it.

This same examination, pondering and possible revision have firmly established evolution as an important natural process explained by valid scientific principles, and clearly differentiate and separate science from various kinds of nonscientific ways of knowing, including those with a supernatural basis such as creationism. Whether called "creation science," "scientific creationism," "intelligent-design theory," "young-earth theory" or some other synonym, creation beliefs have no place in the science classroom. Explanations employing non-naturalistic or supernatural events, whether or not explicit reference is made to a supernatural being, are outside the realm of science and not part of a valid science curriculum. Evolutionary theory, indeed all of science, is necessarily silent on religion and neither refutes or supports the existence of a deity or deities. Accordingly, the National Association of Biology Teachers endorses the following tenets of science, evolution, and biology education:

▸ The diversity of life on earth is the outcome of evolution: an unpredictable and natural process of temporal descent with genetic modification that is affected by natural selection, chance, historical contingencies and changing environments.

▸ Evolutionary theory is significant in biology, among other reasons, for its unifying properties and predictive features, the clear empirical testability of its integral models and the richness of new scientific research it fosters.

▸ The fossil record, which includes abundant transitional forms in diverse taxonomic groups, establishes extensive and comprehensive evidence for organic evolution.

▸ Natural selection, the primary mechanism for evolutionary changes, can be demonstrated with numerous, convincing examples, both extant and extinct.

▸ Natural selection--a differential, greater survival and reproduction of some genetic variants within a population under an existing environmental state--has no specific direction or goal, including survival of a species.

▸ Adaptations do not always provide an obvious selective advantage. Furthermore, there is no indication that adaptations--molecular to organismal--must be perfect; adaptations providing a selective advantage must simply be good enough for survival and increased reproductive fitness.

▸ The model of punctuated equilibrium provides another account of the tempo of speciation in the fossil record of many lineages: it does not refute or overturn evolutionary theory, but instead adds to its scientific richness.

▸ Evolution does not violate the second law of thermodynamics; producing order from disorder is possible with the addition of energy, such as from the sun.

▸ Although comprehending deep time is difficult, the earth is about 4.5 billion years old. *Homo sapiens* has occupied only a minuscule moment of that immense duration of time.

▸ When compared with earlier periods, the Cambrian explosion evident in the fossil record reflects at least three phenomena: the evolution of animals with readily fossilized, hard-body parts; a Cambrian environment (sedimentary rock) more conducive to preserving fossils; and the evolution from pre-Cambrian forms of an increased diversity of body patterns in animals.

▸ Radiometric and other dating techniques, when used properly, are highly accurate means of establishing dates in the history of the planet and in the history of life.

▸ In science, a theory is not a guess or an approximation but an extensive explanation developed from well-documented, reproducible sets of experimentally derived data and from repeated observations of natural processes.

▸ The models and the subsequent outcomes of a scientific theory are not decided in advance, but can be, and often are, modified and improved as new empirical evidence is uncovered. Thus science is a constantly self-correcting endeavor to understand nature and natural phenomena.

▸ Science is not teleological--the accepted processes do not start with a conclusion then refuse to change it, or acknowledge as valid only those data that support an unyielding conclusion. Science does not base theories on an untestable collection of dogmatic proposals. Instead, the processes of science are characterized by asking questions, proposing hypotheses and designing empirical models and conceptual frameworks for research about natural events.

▸ Providing a rational, coherent and scientific account of the taxonomic history and diversity of organisms requires inclusion of the mechanisms and principles of evolution.

▸ Similarly, effective teaching of cellular and molecular biology requires inclusion of evolution.

▸ Specific textbook chapters on evolution should be included in biology curricula, and evolution should be a recurrent theme throughout biology textbooks and courses.

▸ Students can maintain their religious beliefs and learn the scientific foundations of evolution.

▸ Teachers should respect diverse beliefs, but contrasting science with religion, such as belief in creationism, is not a role of science. Science teachers can, and often do, hold devout religious beliefs, accept evolution as a valid scientific theory and teach the theory's mechanisms and principles.

▸ Science and religion differ in significant ways that make it inappropriate to teach any of the different religious beliefs in the science classroom.

Opposition to teaching evolution reflects confusion about the nature and processes of science. Teachers can, and should, stand firm and teach good science with the acknowledged support of the courts. In Epperson v. Arkansas (1968), the U.S. Supreme Court struck down a 1928 Arkansas law prohibiting the teaching of evolution in state schools. In McLean v. Arkansas (1982), the federal district court invalidated a state statute requiring equal classroom time for evolution and creationism. Edwards v. Aguillard (1987) led to another Supreme Court ruling against so called "balanced treatment" of creation science and evolution in public schools. In this landmark case, the Court called the Louisiana equal-time statute "facially invalid as violative of the Establishment Clause of the First Amendment, because it lacks a clear secular purpose." This decision, "The Edwards restriction," is now the controlling legal position on attempts to mandate the teaching of creationism: the nation's highest court has said that such mandates are unconstitutional. Subsequent district court decisions in Illinois and California have applied the Edwards restriction to teachers who advocate creation science, and to the right of a district to prohibit an individual teacher from promoting creation science, in the classroom. Courts have thus restricted school districts from requiring creation science in the science curriculum and have restricted individual instructors from teaching it. All teachers and administrators should be mindful of these court cases, remembering the law, science and NABT support them as they appropriately include the teaching of evolution in the science curriculum.

Suggested Readings About Evolution

Clough, M. 1994. Diminish students resistance to biological evolution. The Am. Biol Teacher, 56, 409–415.

Futuyma, D. 1986. Evolutionary Biology, 2n ed., Sunderland, MA: Sinauer Assoc. Inc.

Gillis, A. 1994. Keeping creationism out o the classroom. BioScience, 44, 650–656.

Gould, S. 1977. Ever Since Darwin: Reflections in Natural History. NY: Norton & Co.

Gould, S. 1994. The evolution of life on earth. Scientific American, 271, 85–91.

Mayr, E. 1991. One Long Argument: Charle: Darwin and the genesis of modern evolutionar thought. Cambridge, MA: Harvard Univ. Press.

McComas, W., ed. 1994. Investigating Evolutionary Biology in the Laboratory. Reston, VA NABT.

Moore, J. 1993. Science as a Way o Knowing: The Foundations of Modern Biology Cambridge, MA: Harvard Univ. Press.

National Center for Science Education. Numerous publications such as Facts, Faith and Fairness Scientific Creationism Clouds Scientific Literacy by S. Walsh and T. Demere.

Numbers, R. 1992. The Creationism: The Evolution of Scientific Creationism. Berkeley, CA Univ of Calif. Press.

Weiner, J. 1994. Beak of the Finch-A Story o Evolution in Our Time. NY: Alfred A. Knopf.

FOSTERING CREATIVITY IN STUDENTS

Here are a few suggestions for motivating students to be creative and to perform well in your course.

Encourage individual thinking.

Help students challenge assumptions.

Provide recurring opportunities for development of observational skills.

Encourage the belief that nothing is ridiculous if you think it will work.

Use creativity exercises on a regular basis.

Provide alternative assignment possibilities.

Ask divergent questions daily; ask at least one "open-ended" question daily; include divergent and open-ended questions in tests.

Require hypothesis-making and predicting as part of the learning process.

Provide non-reading and non-writing learning opportunities.

See that students share results of their work.

Reward the unusual, the "far out"; share "far out" ideas with students.

Consistently demonstrate that you value creative ideas and behavior.

Explore with students the personal rewards that result from original thinking.

Avoid being predictable.

Use your sense of humor.

Share your creative thinking and work with your students. (adapted from Grambs and Carr, 1979)

WHAT STUDENTS CAN DO TO HELP THEMSELVES

There will be students in your class who you like and want to do well but who just won't be able to complete the course successfully, no matter how hard you or they try. If you have a large class, you won't be able to counsel each student as much as they or you might like. Thus, it is essential that you identify campus counseling/student support services, tutors (who can be seniors or graduate students in your department), and places undergraduates can get help. You can also help students help themselves.

How To Study Biology (Directed to Students)
I. Studying Is More Than Spending Time!
A.   Make a commitment to **understand** (*not* memorize)
　　1.   Knowing details at the expense of the "big picture" is not the goal.
　　2.   First build a foundation of understanding of the main concept.
　　3.   Then add details to complete the picture.
B.   No amount of memorization can help you understand such things as:
　　1.   **Concepts** (the ideas that connect the details).
　　2.   **New situations** (*applying* what you've learned to novel cases).
C.   Always ask yourself QUESTIONS (especially WHY and HOW)
　　1.   Never be satisfied with just knowing the example given in lecture. (How does this apply to other material?)
　　2.   Look for the underlying principles. (Why does this phenomenon work this way?)
　　3.   Make connections with previous material. (If true about "x", then is it true of "y"?)

II. What Can I Do to Improve My Study Habits?
A.   Be **responsible** for your own success
　　1.   *Attend class* on a daily basis.
　　2.   *Pay attention* during lecture.
　　3.   If you don't understand something, ASK QUESTIONS!
　　4.   Be sure to spend at least *2-3 different sessions per week* studying biology.
B.   Prepare for class *ahead of time*.
　　1.   Skim that day's assignment before class.
　　　　a.   Become familiar with figures, diagrams, and terminology.
　　　　b.   Ready your brain for that day's topic.

C. **Taking notes**
1. Your notes need only make sense to you, but they must make complete sense! Can you explain every figure and word in your notes? How does the information on one part of a page relate to other parts?
2. Develop a short-hand for common words, terms, definitions, e.g., b/c = because, w/n = within, ----> = leads to
3. Do _not_ attempt to write down every word the lecturer says--LISTEN FIRST, THEN WRITE! If necessary, use a tape recorder--but if you listen to the lecture again, make certain that you paraphrase what is being said. PUT THE NOTES INTO YOUR OWN WORDS! This is the most important aspect of notetaking. Can you explain your notes to someone else?
4. Use an outline format (this forces you to _organize_ the material).
5. Leave lots of room for later additions, ease of finding items, adding examples, etc.
6. Annotate your notes with things that remind you to:
   a. ask a question.
   b. clarify a point.
   c. refer to a diagram in the textbook.
7. Don't attempt to copy complex diagrams during lecture.
   a. Make a note in the margin to look up a figure in the textbook or to copy it later.
   b. _Listen_ to what is said about the figure (take **simple** notes).
8. Make sure you include drawings and examples. Both will help you remember the main point of the lecture.
D. **After class** (no later than the next day):
1. review your notes, filling blank spaces with information from class. Recopying your notes is a waste of time unless you actively work with them, adding examples and writing the notes in your own words. Spend time organizing your notes so they are easy to review and follow.
2. Add necessary figures from your textbook.
3. Carefully read text assignments and add information to your notes.
   a. Highlighting is OK, but it can lead to a false sense of security.
   b. Stop reading periodically, close the book and ask yourself questions such as:
      i. HOW and WHY does it work?
      ii. HOW does that relate to last lecture's material?

4. Mark all parts of the notes that you don' understand and get those questions answered immediately.
5. Link different sections of the notes to each other and make transitions between sections
E. Make use of objectives provided on handouts.
F. Use extracurricular help (Office hours, Tutors).

REMEMBER: 3-4 hours of serious study _per week_, for 4 weeks, is much more effective than 12-16 hours memorizing right before the exam!

III. **How to Prepare for and Take an Examination**
A. Take the exam **seriously** (your professors do!).
B. Plan ahead: begin preparing _3-4 days in advance_ of the exam.
1. This makes smaller bouts of more-intense work possible.
2. This provides time to have questions answered.
C. Take advantage of previous exams and practice exams (if available).
1. Treat them like real exams (test your understanding).
2. Make sure you know WHY the correct answers are correct.
D. Study with friends (but do it seriously!).
1. Ask each other the hardest questions you can think of.
2. Come up with your own exam questions.
3. Try to make connections among topics (look for the big picture).
4. Try to _draw_ pathways, relationships, etc. on paper or chalkboard.
5. Explain the major concepts in your own words
E. Exam taking strategies.
1. Get a good night's rest, RELAX! (This is easy if you've prepared.)
2. READ THE QUESTIONS CAREFULLY.
   a. What is being asked?
   b. What do I know about that topic? (write in the margin)
3. READ **ALL** THE ANSWERS.
   a. Systematically eliminate incorrect responses.
   b. Use logic to choose between remaining answers.
IV. **Some Methods for Effective Use of the Text**
1. Skim the chapter.
   a. Be able to explain in simple English what the chapter is about.

b. Get a general overview of the chapter. Don't get bogged down in facts.

2. Get a handle on the vocabulary. Make yourself flash cards--read it, write it, say it.

3. Look for statements you do not understand. Mark anything you don't understand and get your questions answered!

4. Consolidate your knowledge. Write a 2-3 page summary of the chapter from memory. Compare your summary to the chapter summary in the text.

5. Use the book to answer questions with someone else to determine what you understand and what you need to work on.

6. Be extremely selective in what you mark in the text. (adapted from Mager, 1988; Heppner, 1990)

THE P.E.E.L. METHOD (Directed to Students)

If you want to try to focus on what's important in your reading and to organize your lecture and laboratory notes and handouts, you might consider using the following method with each biological concept you are trying to understand. This idea is called the PEEL method, an acronym based on four simple steps that you should take when thinking about a concept, to help you "peel away" the layers of materials to get to the core information. In this method of analyzing a concept, you should ask:

P: What's the **Point**? What is the main idea and importance of the concept or topic?

E: What's the **Explanation** of the concept-- how does it work or what is its function?

E: What's an **Example** of the concept?

L: What's the **Link** between this concept and others? How does this concept relate to others you have read or heard about in your reading or lecture?

Use this method for every major topic discussed in class or laboratory to help understand the material, to identify what is important to know, and to know how to study for an examination.

CHECKING STUDENT NOTES

Check the notes your students take, discussing with them ways to improve their notetaking. Look for several specific landmarks of good (or poor) note-taking, including:

1. **Can students explain the notes in their own words?** This is the most important characteristic of well-prepared students. Many students learn information in a fragmented, disconnected way. They will memorize a list of items related to one subject, but be unable to explain the importance or relevance of this subject. Also, they may be unable to relate the subject to others.
2. **Are there ample illustrations?** A picture is worth a thousand words.
3. **Are there appropriate examples** for each major point? Examples illustrate the point and help students remember the major ideas.
4. **Are there clear headings and subheadings** identifying to what the written information is related? Also, are there links to what came before and after in the class, including lab?
5. **Are there errors in spelling, definitions, or information** that may confuse the student as she/he studies or takes the exam?
6. **Can they explain everything in their notes**--ask, "Why were we talking about this information?" "What does it have to do with the main concepts that we were discussing?"

CONCEPT MAPPING

The aim of concept mapping is to: (1) bring a structure of hierarchy and relatedness to what might seem to the student are disjointed topics, facts, and ideas; and (2) employ this structure as a guide in the synthesis of concepts associated with the topics being explored. The ability of students to organize and develop a "picture" from a list of nouns and verbs associated with a topic is a direct reflection of the student's understanding of the topic. Concept mapping is a tool that can help students learn by building on what they already know.

Concept maps demonstrate meaningful relationships between concepts through the use of propositions. A concept is a mental image, such as *plant*,

photosynthesis, or solar energy. A proposition is two o more concepts linked by words in a phrase or thought The linking words show how the concepts are related In developing a concept map, concepts and propositions are linked in a hierarchy, progressing from the more general and inclusive concepts at the top to the more specific at the bottom. The three concepts mentioned above could be linked in several ways. See the following page for an example. Links should be functional rather than descriptive (for example, "plants use energy" rathei than "plants such as trees"). Using these three concepts, it is possible to construct a useful concept map with the addition of a few related concepts, such as *leaves, chlorophyll, water, air, carbon dioxide, roots, soil,* and *veins.*

There is no single correct way to develop a concept map. Choice of concept words (usually nouns) and linking words depends on the information to be organized and the aim of the inquiry. Arrows, when used, indicate lateral or upward linkages. Once students have completed a map, as individuals, in small groups, or as a homework assignment, hold a follow-up class discussion to compare the completed maps. The variety should make it clear that there are many valid ways to structure a map. The follow-up also permits you to be sure that all maps show correct relationships and to discuss why some relationships are not correct. Make it clear that concept maps are meant to be rearranged and redrawn. As students work and learn, they will envisage new or different relationships. Explain that the first draft of a concept map almost certainly will have gaps or flaws and can be improved. If concept maps are a regular part of learning, students will become more skillful at the process.

As an introduction to a topic, a concept map helps students focus on the small number of key ideas required for specific learning tasks. It also shows them what they already know about the material to be studied. Used again at the end of the topic, concept maps demonstrate graphically how much the students have learned. Concept maps help both students and instructors recognize the importance of prior information, whether correct or incorrect, to the acquisition of new knowledge. (Adapted from BSCS, 1992)

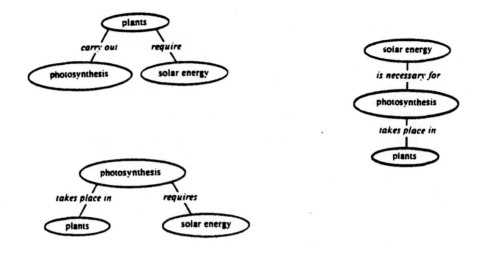

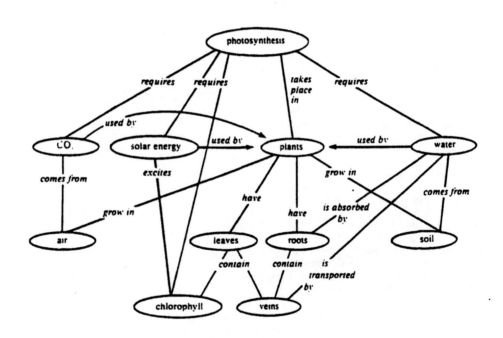

GETTING STUDENTS TO ASK THE RIGHT QUESTIONS

To investigate any natural phenomenon or problem, students need to ask the right questions. First-year journalism students learn to ask "Who, What, Where, When, Why, and How?" to investigate a news story. Similarly, the process of science is not a mystical experience that only a gifted few can undertake; there are several general questions that anyone can ask to learn more about any aspect of biology. Mastery of these questions can empower students to pursue investigations on their own and to develop higher levels of biological literacy throughout their lives.

By asking a combination of questions below, students may begin a study on their own. The first group of questions may be asked when a natural phenomenon or problem is first encountered. The second group of questions will help students explore the phenomenon or problem, and the third should help students think about future consequences. The last group of questions allows students to assess the validity of information used to explain the phenomenon or problem. By using these questions, anyone can conduct an investigation in a scientific manner.

Description Questions

What is it?
What does it do, or what is its function?
Is it typical?
Is it real or an artifact?
To what is the problem or phenomenon related?
What is its significance, importance, or advantage—if any?

Investigation Questions

Can it be investigated scientifically?
How can I find out about it?
How does it work or happen?
How does/did it begin?
What causes it to happen? (Is there a cause and effect relationship or just a correlation?)
What affects it, and what does it affect? (How does it fit into the whole picture?)

Prediction Questions

What are the expected results?
What would happen if...?
Has it changed or will it change through time?
What are its future risks, benefits, or consequences
Does it always happen like this?
Can knowledge about it be used to solve problem or be applied to other situations?

Evidence Questions

What is the evidence?
Is the evidence based on false assumptions?
Are the data or facts about it accurate?
How do I support my position about it?
What other questions do I need to ask about it?
Are there any other explanations? (adapted fror BSCS, 1994)

CHECKLIST OF COMMON SENSE ACTIVITIES

1. Make copies of your grade records and keep them in a place other than your office.
2. Make sure your syllabus is clear, and don't make major changes after you distribute it.
3. When grading exams, draw a red line through blank and incorrect parts on each student's test.
4. Have more activities and materials prepared than you think you can use on any given day.
5. Don't take evaluations personally, but look for common constructive criticisms that can be used to adjust your teaching methods, and ignore personal attacks (which is often very difficult to do).
6. Keep your office door open when talking to students.
7. Be vigilant in checking for cheating.
8. If your class depends on A-V, make sure you know where extra bulbs are and that all of the equipment is working.
9. Maintain an exercise and stress-reducing regimen. Make sure to devote time to an active health program. This is very important!
10. Don't post student grades with their social security numbers (you can use the last four digits of their social security number as an identifying code).
11. Come to class on time and keep your office hours.
12. Don't cancel class unless you are really sick or have an emergency. If you want students to come to class, so should you.
13. Try to learn the names of your students.
14. Try something new every year—new labs, new approaches to teaching—and keep what you like and what works well. Give new ideas a couple of tries before you scrap them, modifying them as you see fit.
15. Treat students with respect, and listen respectfully to their opinions. Never equate ignorance or lack of knowledge on the part of your students with stupidity.
16. Never laugh at your students, but laugh with them. Cultivate and use your sense of humor.
17. Don't get involved with students' personal problems. Be a sounding board if you want, but be very careful about any advice you might give.
18. Look at your students when you are teaching and be aware of their understanding.
19. Don't act like a know-it-all, and on the other hand, you don't have to know everything—it's okay to say you don't know—just don't say it all the time. Look up the information, and then report on it the next day.
20. Do not memorize your lecture--just understand your material. Be spontaneous, but don't wander aimlessly.
21. Never expect your students to learn or to understand anything that you cannot or did not learn or understand yourself.
22. Rethink your notes each time you teach--keep it fresh.
23. It's more important to determine how much to leave out than to jam everything in. It's always a temptation to teach everything you know, but it's better to select just the right content and program it in just the right way.
24. Don't take things--especially yourself--so damn seriously. It's OK to have a bad day occasionally.
25. Act out of the conviction that your teaching matters.
26. Keep a list of contacts who can help you in teaching and research. Meet as many people as you can at your University and at professional meetings who may be able to help.
27. Keep a teaching log for each course. Record special successes, problems, and insights as they occur. Use the logs to guide you the next time you teach the courses.
28. Illustrate your lectures with a lot of slides. Keep the slides for each topic in a separate carousel if you can for easier revision and use.
29. Be careful about loaning your books out to students--they don't have the sentimental attachment to them as you do. If you do, however, make sure you keep a written list of what is checked out and where you can reach the student. (adapted from Friedmann, 1991; Seller, 1992; Fisch, 1993; and my own painful experiences)

IN CLOSING

There are a lot of ideas presented in this handbook, but it is certainly not the intent for you to adopt all of them as you teach your course. However, it is hoped that you will incorporate new activities and try new methods each time you teach. Never become complacent in your teaching--always try to improve. Just remember that good teaching requires an effort on your part, but rewards return whenever you help students learn about biology, when you turn them on to science, or when you produce better-informed citizens.

LITERATURE CITED

AAAS. 1989. Project 2061: Science for All Americans. American Association for the Advancement of Science, Washington, D.C.

_____. 1990. The Liberal Art of Science: Agenda for Action. American Association for the Advancement of Science, Washington, D.C.

Albright, M.J. and D.L. Graf, eds. 1992. Teaching in the Information Age: The Role of Educational Technology. Jossey Bass Publishers, Inc., San Francisco.

Allen, R.D. and D.J. Stroup. 1993. Teaching Critical Thinking Skills in Biology. Lancaster Press, Inc., Lancaster, PA.

Altman, H.B. 1989. Syllabus shares "what the teacher wants." Teaching Professor 3(5): 1-2.

Altman, H.B. and W.E. Cashin. 1992. Idea paper no. 27: Writing a syllabus. Center for Faculty Evaluation and Development, Kansas State University, Manhattan, KS.

Alverno College. 1985. Behavioral criteria related to critical thinking components. Alverno College Productions, Milwaukee, WI.

_____. 1994a. Critical thinking: Alverno model. Alverno College Productions, Milwaukee, WI.

_____. 1994b. Planning a course to foster critical thinking. Alverno College Productions, Milwaukee, WI.

Arons, A.B. 1990. A Guide to Introductory Physics Teaching. John Wiley & Sons, New York, NY.

Auster, C.J. and M. MacRone. 1994. The classroom as a negotiated social setting: an empirical study of the effects of faculty members' behaviors on students' participation.. Teaching Sociology 22: 289-300.

Bates, G.R. 1978. The role of laboratory in secondary school science programs. In: M. B. Rowe (ed.), What Research Says to the Science Teacher. National Science Teachers Association, Washington, DC.

Biddle, A. and D. Bean. 1987. Writer's Guide: Life Sciences. D.C. Heath & Co., Lexington, MA.

Billingsley, R. 1993. Fostering diversity: teaching b discussion. Teaching Professor 7(2): 3-4.

Bloom, B.S. (ed.). 1975. Taxonomy of Objectives: Th Classification of Educational Goals. Handbook 1. Davi McKay Company, Inc., New York, NY.

Bonwell, C.C. 1991. The enhanced lecture. The Cente for Teaching and Learning, Southeast Missouri Stat University, Cape Girardeau, MO.

Bonwell, C.C. and J.A. Eison. 1991. Active learning Creative excitement in the classroom. ASHE-ERIC Higher Education Report No. 1. George Washingto University, Washington, DC.

Broadwell, M.M. 1989. It's so technical I have to lecture Training (March): 41-44.

Brufee, K. 1993. Collaborative Learning: Highe Education, Interdependence, and the Authority c Knowledge. The Johns Hopkins University Press Baltimore, MD.

BSCS (Biological Sciences Curriculum Study). 1992 Biological Science: An Ecological Approach Kendall/Hunt Publishing Co., Dubuque, IA.

_____. 1994. Developing Biological Literacy Kendall/Hunt Publishing Co., Dubuque, IA.

_____. 1997. Biology: A Human Approach Kendall/Hunt Publishing Co., Dubuque, IA.

Campbell, J.A. 1963. Kinetics--early and often. J. o Chemical Education 40(11): 578-583.

Candy, P.A. 1991. Self-Direction for Lifelong Learning Jossey-Bass Publishers, Inc., San Francisco, CA.

Cashin, W.E. 1987. Idea paper No. 17: Improvinç essay tests. Center for Faculty Evaluation { Development, Kansas State University, Manhattan, KS

Cashin, W.E. and P.C. McKnight. 1986. Idea paper No 15: Improving discussions. The Center for Faculty Evaluation and Development, Kansas State University Manhattan, KS.

CELS (Coalition for Education in the Life Sciences) 1993. Components of an exemplary biology program ASM News 59(5): 230.

Cherif, A.H. 1989. Inquiry: an easy approach in teaching science. Faculty of Education, Simon Fraser University.

Clegg, V.L. and W.E. Cashin. 1986. Idea paper No. 16: Improving multiple-choice tests. Center for Faculty Evaluation & Development, Kansas State University, Manhattan, KS.

D'Avanzo, C. and A. McNeal. 1996. Inquiry teaching in two freshman level courses: same core principles but different approaches. In: Student-Active Science: Models of Innovation in College Science Teaching. A. P. McNeal and C. D'Avanzo, eds. Saunders College Publishing, Philadelphia.

Davidson, C.I. and S.A. Ambrose. 1994. The New Professor's Handbook: A Guide to Teaching and Research in Engineering and Science. Anker Publishing Company, Inc., Bolton, MA.

Davis, C.A. 1992. Handbook for New College Teachers and Teaching Assistants. Davis and Associates, Kalamazoo, MI.

Dobzhansky, T. 1973. Nothing in biology makes sense except in the light of evolution. American Biology Teacher 35: 125-129.

Doyle, K. 1983. Evaluating Teaching. Lexington Books, Lexington, MA.

Eble, K.E. 1983. The Aims of College Teaching. Jossey-Bass Publishers, Inc., San Francisco, CA.

_____. 1988. The Craft of Teaching. Jossey-Bass Publishers, Inc., San Francisco, CA.

Fink, D. 1984. The First Year of College Teaching. Jossey-Bass Publishers, Inc., San Francisco, CA.

_____. (ed). 1992. What do we do on the first day of class? Spotlight on Teaching 14(1): 1, University of Oklahoma.

_____. 1994. Planning your course: a decision guide. Instructional Development Program, University of Oklahoma, Norman, OK.

Fisch, L. 1992. Using responsive questions to facilitate discussions. Teaching Professor 6(9): 5.

_____. 1993. Seven principles of teaching seldom taught in grad school. Teaching Professor 7(4):1-2.

Flaste, R. (ed.) 1991. Book of Science Literacy. Random House, New York. 385 pp.

Frederick, P.J. 1986. The lively lecture: 8 variations. College Teaching 34 (2): 43-50.

Friedler, Y. and P. Tamir. 1990. Life in science laboratory classrooms at the secondary level. In: E. Hegarty-Hazel (ed.), The Student Laboratory and the Curriculum. pp. 337-354. Rutledge, London.

Friedmann, H.C. 1991. Fifty-six laws of good teaching: a sampling. Teaching Professor 5(1): 3.

Gabel, D.L. (ed.). 1994. Handbook of Research on Science Teaching and Learning: A Project of the National Science Teachers Association. Macmillan Publishing Company, New York, NY.

Grambs, J.D. and J.C. Carr. 1979. Modern Methods in Secondary Education. Holt, Rinehart & Winston, New York, NY.

Grow, G. 1991. Teaching learners to be self-directed. Adult Education Quarterly, 41 (3): 125-149.

Gunstone, R.F. and A.B. Champagne. 1990. Promoting conceptual change in the laboratory. In: W. Hegarty-Hazel (ed.), The Student and the Curriculum, 159-182. Rutledge, London.

Haley, S.R. 1992. Advice for establishing an effective teaching attitude. Teaching Professor 6(2): 1.

Hazen, R.M. and J. Trefil (eds.). 1990. Science Matters: Achieving Scientific Literacy. Doubleday, New York. 294 pp.

Heitz, J. and M. Meyer. 1993. Teaching College Biology: A Resource Handbook. University of Wisconsin, Madison, WI.

Hemmings, B. and D. Battersby. 1989. Textbook selection: evaluative criteria. Higher Education Research and Development 8(1).

Heppner, F. 1990. Dr. Farnsworth's Explanations in Biology. McGraw Hill, Inc., New York.

Hirsch, E.D. 1987. Cultural Literacy: What Every American Should Know. Houghton Mifflin, Boston, MA.

Hofstein, A. 1988. Practical work and science education II. In: P. Fensham (ed.), Development and Dilemmas in Science Education, 189-216. Falmer, London.

Holcomb, D.F. 1988. Cornell undergraduate education in-house publication. Ithaca, NY.

Holden, C. 1989. Radical reform for science education. Science 243: 1133.

Holmes, S.K. 1988. New faculty mentoring: benefits to the mentor. J. of Staff, Program, and Organizational Development 6(1): 17-20.

Holt, D. and J. Eison. 1989. Preparing freshman to take essay examinations successfully. J. of the Freshman Year Experience 1(2): 108-119.

Igelsrud, D. and W.H. Leonard. 1988. Labs: what research says about biology laboratory instruction. American Biology Teacher 50: 303-306.

Jacobs, L.C. and C.I. Chase. 1992. Developing and Using Tests Effectively: A Guide for Faculty. Jossey-Bass Publishers, Inc., San Francisco, CA.

Jensen, E. 1994. Instructional rights and responsibilities. Oregon State University, Corvallis, OR.

Johnson, D.W. and R.T. Johnson. 1987. Learning Together and Alone: Cooperative, Competitive and Individualistic Learning. Prentice-Hall, Englewood Cliffs, NJ.

Johnson, D.W., R.T. Johnson, E. Johnson-Holubec, and P. Roy. 1986. Circles of learning: cooperation in the classroom (2nd ed.). Association for Supervision and Curriculum Development, Alexandria, VA.

Johnson, G.R. 1990. First Steps to Excellence in College Teaching. Magna Publications, Inc., Madison, WI.

Jungck, J.R. 1991. Constructivism, computer exploratoriums, and collaborative learning: constructing scientific knowledge. Teacher Education 3(2): 151-170.

Jungck, J.R. and J. Calley. 1985. Strategic simulations and post-socratic pedagogy: constructing computer

software to develop long-term inference throug experimental inquiry. American Biology Teacher, 4: 11-15.

Kottler, J. and W. Lanning. 1992. Dealing with difficu students. Teaching Professor 6(6): 5-7.

Lazarowitz, R. and P. Tamir. 1994. Research on usin laboratory instruction in science. In: D.L. Gabel (Ed. Handbook of Research on Science Teaching an Learning. Macmillan Publishing Company, New Yorl NY.

Ludewig, L.M. 1993. Student perceptions of instructc behaviors. Teaching Professor 7(4): 1.

Lumsden, A.S. 1994. Florida State Universi! Department of Biological Science teaching workshor Florida State University, Tallahassee, FL.

Mager, R.F. 1975. Preparing Instructional Objective: Fearon Publishers, Inc., Belmont, CA.

_____. 1984. Goal Analysis. David S. Lake Publisher: Belmont, CA.

_____. 1988. Making Instruction Work or Skillbloomers David S. Lake Publishers, Belmont, CA.

Magnan, B. 1990. 147 Practical Tips for Teachin Professors. Magna Publications, Inc., Madison, WI.

Maier, M.H. 1992. Teachers have fun; why can students? Teaching Professor 6(6): 3.

Martin, D.S. 1989. Restructuring teacher educatio programs for higher-order thinking skills. J. of Teache Education 40(3): 2-8.

Marzano, R.J. 1988. Dimensions of thinking: framework for curriculum and instruction. Association fo Supervision and Curriculum Development, Alexandria VA.

McIntosh, W.J. and M.W. Caprio. 1990. Survey result: on the quality of nonmajors science instruction. J College Science Teaching 20(1): 27-30.

Michaelsen, L.K. 1992. Team learning: i comprehensive approach for harnessing the power c small groups in higher education. To Improve the Academy 11: 107-122.

Moll, M.B. and R.D. Allen. 1982. Developing critical thinking skills in biology. J. of College Science Teaching 12(2): 95-98.

Moore, J.A. 1985. Science as a Way of Knowing: Genetics. American Society of Zoologists. 918 pp.

Moore, R. 1991. Preparing graduate teaching assistants to teach biology: ways to improve the teaching readiness of a critical educational influence. J. of College Science Teaching 20(6): 358-361.

NABT (National Association of Biology Teachers). 1995. Statement on teaching evolution. NABT, Reston, VA.

NCEE (National Commission on Excellence in Education). 1983. A nation at risk: the imperative for educational reform. U.S. Department of Education, Washington, D.C.

Neff, R.A. and M. Weimer (ed.). 1989. Classroom Communication: Collected Readings for Effective Discussion and Questioning. Magna Publications, Inc., Madison, WI.

Nelson, C.E. 1989. Skewered on the unicorn's horn: the illusion of tragic tradeoff between content and critical thinking in the teaching of science. In: L.W. Crow (Ed.), Enhancing Critical Thinking in the Sciences. Society for College Science Teachers, Washington, DC.

Novak, J.D. and D.B. Gowin. 1984. Learning How to Learn. Press Syndicate of the University of Cambridge, New York, NY.

NRC (National Research Council). 1990. Fulfilling the Promise: Biology Education in the Nation's Schools. National Academy Press, Washington, DC.

_____. 1995. National Science Education Standards. National Academy Press, Washington, D.C.

NSF. 1989. Report on the National Science Foundation disciplinary workshops on undergraduate education. National Science Foundation, Washington, DC.

O'Neil, J. 1992. Schools try problem-based approach. Wingspread: the journal 14(3): 1-3.

Ory, J.C. 1987. Improving your test questions. Measurement and Evaluation Division of the Office of Instructional Resources, University of Illinois, Champaign-Urbana, IL.

OSU. 1990. Teaching at the Ohio State University: a handbook. Ohio State University, Columbus, OH.

Pestel, B.C. 1990. Students "participate" with each other. Teaching Professor 4(5): 4.

Peterson, N. and J.R. Jungck. 1988. Problem-posing, problem-solving and persuasion in biology education. Academic Computing (March-April): 14-50.

Pregent, R. 1994. Charting You Course: How to Prepare to Teach More Effectively. Magna Publications, Inc., Madison, WI.

Project Kaleidoscope. 1991. What Works: Building Natural Science Communities. Volume One. Stamats Communications, Inc., Washington, DC.

Raloff, J. 1988. U.S. education: failing in science? Science News 133: 165-166.

Ramsey, G.A. and R.W. Howe. 1969. An analysis of research in instructional procedures in secondary school science, part II. Science Teacher 36: 72-81.

Roberts, D.A. 1982. Developing the concept of "curriculum emphases" in science education. Science Education 66(2): 243-260.

Rowe, M.B. 1974a. Wait time and rewards as instructional variables, their influence on language, logic, and fate control: Part I—Wait time. J. of Research in Science Teaching 11: 81-94.

_____1974b. Relation of wait-time and rewards to the development of language, logic, and fate control: Part II-- Rewards. J. of Research in Science Teaching 11: 291-308.

_____. 1978. Teaching Science as Continuous Inquiry: A Basic. McGraw-Hill Book Co., New York, NY.

_____. 1983. Getting chemistry off the killer course list. J. of Chemical Education 60: 954-956.

Sanders, N.M. 1966. Classroom Questions: What Kinds? Harper & Row Publishers, Inc., New York, NY.

156

Schlenker, R.M. and C.M. Perry. 1986. Planning lectures that start, go, and end somewhere. J. of College Science Teaching 15(5): 440–442.

Seller, S.C. 1992. Common sense for college teachers. Teaching Professor 6(5): 6.

Slavin, R. 1987. Cooperative learning and the cooperative school. Educational Leadership 45: 31-33.

Svinicki, M.D. 1994. Practical implications of cognitive theories. In: K.A. Feldman and M.B. Paulsen (eds.), Teaching and Learning in the College Classroom. Ginn Press, Needham Heights, MA.

The Teaching Professor, Jan 1990, 4(1).

Tobin, K., D.J. Tippins, and A.J. Gallard. 1994. Research on instructional strategies for teaching science. In: D.L. Gabel (ed.), Handbook of Research on Science Teaching and Learning. Macmillan Publishing Company, New York.

Tulloch, B., M.J. Bahret, A. Bertino, M. Colvard, S. Holt, and N. Ridenour. 1994. Regents biology program guide. New York State Biology Mentor Network.

Turner, J.L. and R. Boice. 1989. Experience of new faculty. J. of Staff, Program, and Organizational Development 7(2): 51-57.

Uno, G.E. 1988. Teaching college and college-bound biology students. American Biology Teacher 50(4): 213-216.

_____. 1990. Inquiry in the classroom. BioScience 40(11): 841-843.

Wandersee, J.H., J.J. Mintzes, and J.D. Novak. 1994. Research on alternative conceptions in science. In: Handbook of Research on Science Teaching and Learning. D.L. Gabel, ed. Macmillan Publishing Co., NY.

Weimer, M. (ed). 1987a. Course materials review. Teaching Professor 1(6): 3-4.

_____. 1987b. Fielding questions. Teaching Professor 1(7): 6.

_____. 1987c. Professors and the participation blues. Teaching Professor 1(7): 1.

_____. 1987d. Successful participation strategie: Teaching Professor 1(7): 5-6.

_____. 1988a. Dealing with disruptive behavior in th classroom. Teaching Professor 2(2): 4.

_____. 1988b. Ideas for managing your classroor better. Teaching Professor 2(2): 3.

_____. 1989a. Assessing those laboratory experience: Teaching Professor 3(3): 4-5.

_____. 1989b. The first day of class: Advice and idea: Teaching Professor 3(7): 1-2.

_____. 1990. Tips for productive classroom climates Teaching Professor 4(3): 4.

_____. 1991a. Group presentations in class. Teachin Professor 5(1): 4.

_____. 1991b. Teaching and techniques. Teachin Professor 5(6): 5.

Weimer, M., J.L. Parrett, and M. Kerns. 1992. How An I Teaching? Forms and Activities for Acquirin Instructional Input. Magna Publications, Inc., Madison WI.

White, R.T. 1988. Learning Science. Basil Blackwell Oxford.

OTHER USEFUL REFERENCES

ABLE (Association for Biology Laboratory Education). Annual Proceedings of Workshops/Conferences. (many ideas for labs.)

Allard, D.W. and C.R. Barman. 1994. The learning cycle as an alternative method for college science teaching. BioScience: 44(2): 99-101.

Alverno College. 1989. Advanced outcomes in the major discipline: biology. Alverno College Productions, Milwaukee, WI.

Armstrong, J.E. BIOLAB BBS FAQs: An internet repository for innovative, investigative laboratory exercises in biology. Illinois State University, Normal, IL. (biolab.bio.ilstu.edu)

Barnes, C.P. 1983. Questioning in the college classrooms. In: C.L. Ellner and C.P. Barnes (eds.), Studies of College Teaching. pp. 61-81. Lexington Books, Lexington, MA.

Barton, L.O. 1994. Ten advantages of a student-centered test design. Teaching Professor 8(1): 4.

Boice, R. 1992. The New Faculty Member. Jossey-Bass Publishers, Inc., San Francisco, CA.

Bort, M. and N.L. Buerkel-Rothfuss. 1991. A content analysis of TA training materials. In: J.D. Nyquist, R.D. Abbott, D.H. Wulff, and J. Sprague (Eds.) Preparing the Professoriate of Tomorrow to Teach: Selected Readings in TA Training. Kendall-Hunt Publishing Co., Dubuque, IA.

Brinko, K.T. 1991. Visioning your course: questions to ask as you design your course. Teaching Professor 5(2): 3-4.

Brown, G. and M. Atkins. 1993. Effective Teaching in Higher Education. Routledge, London, England.

Brown, G. and D. Tomlinson. 1980. How to improve handouts. Medical Teacher 2(5): 215-220.

Bybee, R.W. and G. DeBoer. 1993. Goals for the science curriculum. Handbook of research on science teaching and learning. National Science Teachers Association, Washington, DC.

Chiras, D.D. 1992. Teaching critical thinking skills in the biology and environmental science classrooms. American Biology Teacher 54(8): 464-468.

Clark, J.H. 1988. (Fall) Designing discussions as group inquiry. College Teaching. 36(4): 140-143.

Clearly, T. (ed.). Getting ready: A checklist of questions for the teacher. Learning and Teaching Centre, University of Victoria, Victoria, B. C. Canada.

Davis, B.G. 1993. Tools for Teaching. Jossey-Bass Publishers, Inc., San Francisco, CA.

Davis, J.R. 1976. Teaching Strategies for the College Classroom. Westview Press, Boulder, CO.

Dunlop, M. 1990 Fall. Promoting critical thinking in the classroom. B. C. Catylist: 14-17.

Ennis, R.H. 1985. A logical basis for measuring critical thinking skills. Educational Leadership 43(2): 44-48.

Ericksen, S.C. 1988. The Essence of Good Teaching. Jossey-Bass Publishers, Inc., San Francisco, CA.

Eve, R.A. and D. Dunn. 1990. Psychic powers, astrology and creationism in the classroom?: evidence of pseudoscientific beliefs among high school biology and life science teachers. American Biology Teacher 52(1): 10-21.

Feldman, K.A. 1987. Research productivity and scholarly accomplishment of college teachers as related to their instructional effectiveness: a review and exploration. Research in Higher Education; pp. 227-298.

Fink, D. 1989. Robert Griswold: Using discussion groups to encourage critical thinking. Notes on Teaching 11(1): 1-2, University of Oklahoma.

Fisch, L. 1992a. Lessons learned from life. Teaching Professor 6(5): 5.

Fleming, N.D. and C. Mills. 1992. Not another inventory, rather a catalyst for reflections. To Improve the Academy 11: 137-155.

Fraser, B., G. Giddings, and C. McRobbie. 1992. Science laboratory classroom environments at schools and universities: A cross-national study. Presented at the Annual Meeting of the National Association for Research in Science Teaching, Boston, MA.

Furlong, D. 1994. Using electronic mail to improve education. Teaching Professor 8(6): 7-8.

Gabennesch, H. 1992. Creating quality class discussion. Teaching Professor 6(9): 5-6.

Garcia, R. 1991. Twelve ways of looking at a blackboard. Teaching Professor 5(8): 5-6.

Germann, P.J. 1991. Developing science process skills through directed inquiry. American Biology Teacher 53(4): 243-247.

Goldstein, J. and E. Malone. 1984. Journal of interpersonal and group communication: Facilitating technical project groups. J. of Technical Writing and Communication 14(2): 113-131.

Grennan, K. 1989. The journal in the classroom: a tool for discovery. Equity and Excellence 24(3): 38-40.

Gullette, M.M. (ed.). 1994. The Art and Craft of Teaching. Harvard University Press, Cambridge, MA.

Hamilton, E.E. 1987-1988. A model for resolving classroom conflict and enhancing student commitment. Organizational Behavior Teaching Review 12(2): 40-50.

Hawthorne, E.M. 1991. Anticipating the new generation of community college faculty members: a window of opportunity to plan, scheme, and dream. J. of College Science Teaching 20(6): 365-368.

Heinich, R., M. Molenda, and J.D. Russell. 1989. Instructional Media and the New Technologies of Instruction. Macmillan, New York

Hunter, M. 1982. Mastery Teaching. TIP Publications, El Segundo, CA.

Jendrek, M.P. 1989. Faculty reactions to academic dishonesty. J. of College Student Development, September: 401-406.

Kibler, W.L., E.M. Nuss, B.G. Paterson, and G. Pavela. 1988. Academic integrity and student development: Legal issues and policy perspectives. The Higher Education Administration Series. College Administration Publications, Inc., Asheville, NC.

Kurfiss, J.G. 1988. Critical thinking: Theory, research, practice, and possibilities. Association for the Study of Higher Education, George Washington University, School of Education and Human Development.

Lambert, L.M. and S. L. Tice, (eds.). 1993. Preparing Graduate Students to Teach: A Guide to Programs That Improve Undergraduate Education and Develop Tomorrow's Faculty. American Association for Higher Education, Washington, DC.

Lawson, A.E., S.W. Rissing, and S.H. Faeth. 1990. An inquiry approach to nonmajors biology: A big picture, active approach for long-term learning. J. of College Science Teaching 19(6): 340-346.

Lowman, J. 1985. Mastering the Techniques of Teaching. Jossey-Bass Publishers, Inc., San Francisco, CA.

McKeachie, W.J. 1986. Teaching Tips: A Guidebook for the Beginning College Teacher. D. C. Heath and Company, Lexington, MA.

McLeish, J. 1976. The lecture method. In: The Psychology of Teaching Methods. Seventy-fifth Yearbook of the National Society for the Study of Education, Part I. University of Chicago Press, Chicago, IL.

Meyer, M., J. Croxdale, and J. Heitz. 1994. Teaching college biology. University of Wisconsin, Madison, WI.

Mills, G.C., M. Lancaster, and W.L. Bradley. 1993. Origin of life and evolution in biology textbooks--a critique. American Biology Teacher 55(2): 78-83.

Morholt, E. and P.F. Brandwein. 1986. A Sourcebook for the Biological Sciences. Harcourt, Brace, Jovanovich, New York, NY.

Morse, J.G. 1992. Designing a course--backward. Teaching Professor 6(5): 5.

NRC. 1995. Science Teaching Reconsidered: a Handbook. Committee on Undergraduate Science Education., National Research Council. Washington, D.C.

NSF. 1996. Shaping the future: new expectations for undergraduate education in science, mathematics, engineering, and technology. Directorate for Education and Human Resources. Arlington, VA.

Nuss, E.M. 1984. Academic integrity: comparing faculty and student attitudes. College Teaching: 140-144.

Nyquist, J.D., R.D. Abbot, H. Wulff, and J. Sprague (eds.). 1991. Preparing the Professoriate of Tomorrow to Teach: Selected Readings in TA Training. Kendall/Hunt Publishing Company, Dubuque, IA.

Prescott, S. 1994. Matching cooperative tasks to their instructional function. Teaching Professor 8(6): 5-6.

Riordan, T. 1993. Beyond the debate: the nature of teaching. Alverno College Institute, Milwaukee, WI.

Rogan, J. 1991. Testing accommodations for students with disabilities. Teaching Professor 5(3): 3-4.

Ryans, D.G. 1960. Characteristics of teachers: their description, comparison, and appraisal. George Banta Company, Inc., Menasha, WI.

Serey, T.T. 1987-1988. Interviewing the professor: an alternative to the drudgery of the first class. Organizational Behavior Teaching Review 12(2): 111-114.

Singhal, A. and P. Johnson. 1983. How to halt student dishonesty. College Student Journal Spring: 13-19.

Slavin, R.S., S. Sharan, S. Kagan, R. Hertz-Lazarowitz, C. Webb, and R. Schmuck (eds.). 1985. Learning to Cooperate, Cooperating to Learn. Plenum Press, New York, NY.

Strauss, M. and T. Fulwiler. 1990. Writing to learn in large lecture classes. J. of College Science Teaching 19(3): 158-163.

Truchan, L. 1994. Teaching and assessing for critical thinking in biology. Alverno College Institute, Milwaukee, WI.

Udovic, D. 1995. Workshop Biology Project Overview. University of Oregon.

Uno, G.E. 1984. A push-button electronic system to promote class discussion. American Biology Teacher 46(4): 229-232.

Wagenaar, T. 1984. Using student journals in sociology courses. Teaching Sociology 11(4): 419-437.

Weiss, C.A. 1992-1993. But how do we get them to think? Teaching Excellence 4(5): 1-2.

Weiss, I. 1987. Report of the 1985-86 national survey of science and mathematics education. Research Triangle Park, NC: Center for Educational Research and Evaluation.

Whitehill, S. 1987. Using the journal for discovery: Two devices. College Composition and Communication 38: 472-474.

Wright, D.L. 1987. Selecting the textbook. Teaching at UNL. University of Nebraska-Lincoln, Lincoln, NE.

Yeany, R.H. 1991. Teacher knowledge bases: What are they? How do we affect them? Keynote address. Southeastern Association for the Education of Teachers in Science.